Experimental Pragmatics

How does a listener understand a sarcastic "That was a wonderful speech" when the words point to a positive review? Why do students of introductory logic interpret "Some cabs are yellow" as "Not all cabs are yellow" when the meaning of "some" is compatible with "all"? Pragmatics aims to explain how listeners draw out a speaker's meaning from utterances, an astonishing feat when one considers that the words in a sentence hardly suffice for fully comprehending what the speaker intended. Given the nature of pragmatics, it is going to take the interdisciplinary firepower of many cognitive sciences – including philosophy, experimental psychology, linguistics, and neuroscience – to fully appreciate this uniquely human ability. In this book, Ira Noveck, a leading pioneer in experimental pragmatics, engagingly walks the reader through the phenomena, the theoretical debates, the experiments, as well as the historical development of this growing academic discipline.

IRA NOVECK is a research director at the Centre National de la Recherche Scientifique in France. He is based at the Institut des Sciences Cognitives – Marc Jeannerod in Lyon, France. He is coeditor of the first volume on *Experimental Pragmatics* (2004), is responsible for creating a European research network of experimental pragmatists (called EURO-XPRAG), and consults with regional networks, such as xprag.de and xprag.it.

Experimental Pragmatics

The Making of a Cognitive Science

Ira Noveck

Institut des Sciences Cognitives – Marc Jeannerod

CAMBRIDGE
UNIVERSITY PRESS

University Printing House, Cambridge CB2 8BS, United Kingdom

One Liberty Plaza, 20th Floor, New York, NY 10006, USA

477 Williamstown Road, Port Melbourne, VIC 3207, Australia

314–321, 3rd Floor, Plot 3, Splendor Forum, Jasola District Centre, New Delhi – 110025, India

79 Anson Road, #06-04/06, Singapore 079906

Cambridge University Press is part of the University of Cambridge.

It furthers the University's mission by disseminating knowledge in the pursuit of education, learning, and research at the highest international levels of excellence.

www.cambridge.org
Information on this title: www.cambridge.org/9781107084902
DOI: 10.1017/9781316027073

First published 2018

Printed and bound in Great Britain by Clays Ltd, Elcograf S.p.A.

A catalogue record for this publication is available from the British Library.

ISBN 978-1-107-08490-2 Hardback

In memory of my father, Simon Noveck (1921–2011)

Contents

Contents   ix

Figures

Tables

Preface

I begin the book by describing the contents of a genuine message-in-a-bottle in order to point out that there is a lot more to understanding a communicative act than just sentence decoding. Besides being amusing, analyzing the message's brief sentences is also a useful way to clarify the questions that motivate the research in the book, which can be summarized as follows: What are the cues that allow an interlocutor to gain a deeper (and more informative) understanding of an utterance, and where do such enrichments come from? I then plunge into a range of examples that reveals the extent to which language underdetermines a speaker's intended meaning. The discussion these examples engender leads to my introduction of the field of pragmatics, which includes a summary of the armchair theories that first inspired debate among philosophers as well as a detailed description of Paul Grice's (1967, 1989) seminal theory and the key post-Gricean approaches that followed (Chapters 1 and 2). I add here that I generally adhere to the convention found in linguistic-pragmatic texts in which speakers in illustrative exchanges are female and addressees are male (likewise, I describe experimenters as female and participants as male). To be consistent with my presentation of pragmatics, I provide a brief historical account of experimental psychology and an insider's view concerning the way experimentalists approach their work (Chapters 3–4). My intention behind this foundational presentation is to make the goal of experimental pragmatics rather obvious, which is to test theories of pragmatics as well as explanations of pragmatic phenomena through objective psychological experiments.

I then turn to the book's main task, which is to review key topics in experimental pragmatics. I start with "early" experimental work that began in the mid- to late-1970s in the wake of Grice's William James lectures (Chapter 5). I show how the work from this period employed Gricean principles largely to account for nonlogical responses in reasoning tasks or to investigate quintessential pragmatic phenomena, such as metaphor. I describe the lessons learned from these early attempts as well as why the field did not take off then. Later chapters show how hypotheses and data from this period often seeded more recent investigations.

There is no better way to begin a presentation of current experimental pragmatic work (Chapter 6) than through a review of studies on scalar implicature,
whose data have arguably been most responsible for driving the field forward
since the turn of the century. I describe how these investigations aim to experimentally isolate the emergence of pragmatically enriched readings of relatively
weak terms (e.g., cases in which *some* is clearly understood in an utterance as
some but not all) by comparing them to situations that apparently prompt minimal – logical or semantic – readings (e.g., cases in which *some* is understood
as *some and perhaps all*). I then review the data inspired by "conventional"
approaches, which aim to account for scalar implicature outcomes while down-
playing the apparatus of Gricean reasoning (Chapter 7). To follow up, I turn to
two other pragmatic phenomena that appear to be, or are said to be, similar to
scalar implicatures. One concerns the invited inferences linked to conditionals (Chapter 8) and especially *affirmation of the consequent* (this refers to the
tendency of participants to accept *p* as true from the premises *if p then q; q,*
even though that conclusion is not logically valid). The other (presented in the
first third of Chapter 9) concerns the way we refer to objects through adjectival
modifications (consider the expression *pass me the tall glass*), which can be
a means to simply describe something or a way to pragmatically enrich the
situation (i.e., one can use the adjective to imply that there is at least one other
glass that is not tall).

The rest of Chapter 9 is devoted to completing a review of experimental
work on reference. In the second section of this chapter, I summarize the findings from the clever experiments on infant *pointing* that reveal the extent to
which very young humans are communicative beings, despite their lack of
verbal skills. In the chapter's last section, I describe the debates and the data
that have arisen around the way adults refer to objects in context. This line
of research aims to determine whether or not adults instinctively consider a
speaker's perspective when processing a referential utterance.

I then turn to topics that have been traditionally categorized under "figurative language." This portion of the book begins by reviewing post-Gricean
accounts of metaphor (Chapter 10). The research aims to determine whether
the literal meaning of a metaphoric expression plays a role in its processing. To
put it another way, do features of heavy machinery figure into *John is a bulldozer* or can these be bypassed altogether? I then turn to irony (Chapter 11) and
the rich set of theories that have long been poised to inspire experimental pragmatic research. I point out that ongoing debates in the psychological literature
about the speed of irony comprehension (*is the ironic reading of a sentence as
fast as its literal reading?*) overshadow another important issue, i.e., the way
that Theory of Mind (ToM) (intention-reading) figures into irony comprehension. That said, I aim to address both concerns. Given that figurative language
was operationalized in seminal investigations concerning the communicative

difficulties found among those with autism, it made sense that I review the work on autism and pragmatics at this point of the book (Chapter 12). The aim of this research is to determine the extent to which communicative difficulties among those with autism are due to Theory of Mind deficits.

To complete my panorama of experimental pragmatic research (Chapter 13), I describe work concerning five other topics: logical metonymy, metonymy, negation, presupposition, and prosody. Like the book's other more notorious pragmatic phenomena, these topics expose differences between a spoken sentence's literal and extra-literal readings. As always, I discuss how experiments aim to capture the pragmatic import in each.

At the end of the book (Chapter 14), I shed my heretofore objective stance in order to present my own "opinionated conclusions." Along the way, I make reference to an investigative technique used in archeological research – what can be called the wide excavation approach – which enjoins teams of collaborators to progressively and systematically descend at several, critical areas of the same site in order to appreciate the human interactions that took place there. In a similar vein, my own aim as an experimental pragmatist – and as author – has been to dig at several pragmatic sub-sites and increasingly deeper. This way, one can better understand the nature of individual pragmatic phenomena while also comparing them. More generally, one gets to see just how critical intentions are to understanding utterances. I hope to have shown that this approach is indispensable for developing pragmatic theories.

Acknowledgments

The archetypal end product in our line of work is the scientific article. We teach students how to write articles, we come to master making arguments in the limited space these provide, and we aim to place them in the most impactful journals. For over three years, I kept telling myself (and those who would ask) that a scientific article is to a short story what this book is to a novel. While I have become accustomed to writing the short stories of science, I have never written a book-length account. Writing this book has forced me to tap into new resources.

Fortunately, the scientific enterprise behind this book has been underway for over twenty years now, so there has been much to draw on. I am also privileged to have been involved in experimental pragmatics from the beginning and to have had collaborators, colleagues, role models, and students, as well as supportive friends and family, who have given me encouragement throughout. Allow me to describe, from my egocentric perspective and in a roughly historical order, who these people are (while keeping in mind that some characters in this story are recurring), starting with some prehistory.

When I first came to Paris as a gap-year graduate student of reasoning (starting in September 1988) with no plan (other than to support myself as I learned French), I came with one professional address in my pocket – Guy Politzer's. While I had admired pragmatics from a distance, it was Guy who would properly introduce me to the topic and who would show me how it can impact on reasoning; we even put together a research project on Kahneman and Tversky's Linda problem while I was there (see Chapter 5, "Early Experimental Pragmatics"). At the end of my stay that year, just after I had given my first talk in French, I met Dan Sperber, who had developed relevance theory with Deirdre Wilson and who was (and remains) fascinated with human reasoning. Dan – as the current book makes obvious – would end up providing some central insights with respect to my own work as well as to experimental pragmatics generally (not to mention the name for the field). Knowing that there was a crew of pragmatists in Paris encouraged me to pursue my own pragmatics-in-reasoning research even when I was not based in France. When I moved permanently to Paris in 1995, we would form a group that Dan dubbed "Le Groupe de la Recherche sur l'Inférence et la Compréhension Elémentaire" (Le GRICE). Beside Dan and Guy, Le GRICE included Daniel Andler, Jean Baratgin, and Jean-Baptiste van der Henst, with guest appearances from people such as François Recanati and Pierre Jacob (who were both down the hall), Luca Bonatti (who was across town), and others from abroad, such as Sue Carey and Deirdre Wilson (who would spend time in Paris on visits and sabbaticals). Le GRICE ended up being a launching pad for experimental pragmatics (and many other endeavors) and clearly would not have existed if it weren't for Dan.

When I was lucky enough to put together my own lab five years later at the Institut des Sciences Cognitives in Lyon and thanks to the Centre National de la Recherche Scientifique, aka the CNRS, I found myself in a position to do experimental pragmatics full time and to talk to others who were interested in pursuing this line of study. With a grant from the European Science Foundation (ESF), I organized an experimental pragmatics workshop with Dan in Lyon, which allowed us to invite those who supported bringing experimental methods to pragmatics as well as those who had actually put this into practice. This included the late Josie Bernicot, Anne Bezuidenhout, Robyn Carston, Gennaro Chierchia, Billy Clark, Herb Clark, Seana Coulson, Aidan Feeney, Ray Gibbs, Rachel Giora, the late Vittorio Girotto, Sam Glucksberg, Teresa Guasti, Simon Handley, Guy Politzer, Anne Reboul, Tony Sanford, Deirdre Wilson, and Jean-Baptiste van der Henst. This led to a volume that Dan and I edited (Noveck & Sperber, 2004), which would become a modest reference for this fledgling field.

My lab at the Institute also became a real home for a host of students and post-docs on experimental pragmatics. Nausicaa Pouscoulous earned (at least part of) her PhD with me there; and Lewis Bott (another reasoner-cum-pragmatist) carried out his first Post-doctoral research at the Institute (thanks to my first French grant). Over the next fifteen years, experimental pragmatics played an important role in bringing in other PhD students such as Jerome Prado, Coralie Chevallier, Nicola Spotorno, and Tiffany Morisseau, as well as other post-docs such as Edmundo Kronmüller and Diana Mazzarella.

From where I was perched at the Institute, I could see how experimental pragmatics was catching on, especially because the topic of *scalar implicature* (described in Chapters 6 and 7) was capturing the attention of folks across disciplines. Evidence for this was most obvious through the increasing number of workshops and conferences. For example, Gennaro Chierchia, a semanticist, organized a workshop in Milan in 2003 that concerned scalar implicatures. Richard Breheny and Napoleon Katsos – who were writing one of their influential papers on scalars – would go on to organize what I (and many others) consider to be the first proper experimental pragmatics conference (in Cambridge) in 2005. In fact, their format has become the model for what has become a regular biennial conference known as XPrag (since held in Berlin, Lyon, Barcelona, Chicago, and Cologne), with the next one planned for Edinburgh in 2019. This series of conferences brought to the fore a quartet of XPrag organizers that included Uli Sauerland, Bart Geurts, Richard Breheny, and me. My favorite sentence from the "Guidance Notes for Conference Organisers" (a document that we recently began circulating for each biennial organizer) is: "Ideally, invited speakers are those who have been doing experimental pragmatics (or considering theoretical issues generated by experimentation) without realizing it." This is the kind of attitude that keeps our doors open.

This quartet expanded somewhat when my proposal for a Research Networking Program (also sponsored by the ESF) was accepted and ran from 2009 to 2013. This project involved finding researchers who shared our vision for experimental pragmatics, along with financial sponsorship from individual European countries. Beside the four of us, who represented Germany, the Netherlands, the United Kingdom, and France, respectively, we succeeded in finding partners in eight other European countries (Bergljot Behrens in Norway, Katarzyna Bromberek-Dyzman in Poland, Anne-Marie Bülow in Denmark, Louise McNally in Spain, Jacques Moeschler in Switzerland, Peter Pagin in Sweden, Josef Perner in Austria, and Walter Schaeken in Belgium). While the program was designed to encourage collaborations across countries, I had also insisted that proposals should include *adversarial collaborations* (see Chapter 7) so that experiments would be sharp and decisive between competing theoretical positions, and this worked out to some extent. The best example of such a partnership – discussed in Chapter 10 – arose between Petra Schumacher and Valentina Bambini. In order to increase the number of proposals, though, we had to drop this condition. Looking back on it now, the best part of the EURO-XPRAG program was that it fostered work from young rising researchers such as Emmanuel Chemla, Chris Cummins, Cat Davies, Judith Degen, Heather Ferguson, Francesca Foppolo, Suzanne Grossman, Napoleon Katsos, Danielle Matthews, Paula Rubio, Ye Tian, Jack Tomlinson, Bob van Tiel, and many others. This was a very satisfying adventure and one that clarified for me how semanticists and pragmatists had much to offer each other.

It was while I was stationed at the CNRS's center in Jerusalem (Le Centre de Recherche Français à Jérusalem [CRFJ]) for three years (2011–14) that I had the idea of writing this book. I am thankful to my friend Olivier Tourny, who recruited me and convinced me (and my wife, Monica) to leave Lyon to join the CRFJ. Olivier also waited until I had finished my turn as lab director in Lyon before making room for me.

Many of the chapters have profited from notes and slides for classes that I have given on experimental pragmatics over the last six years. The most notable of these were a Utrecht (Netherlands) summer school on the Neuroscience of Communicated Meaning (organized by Jos van Berkum in 2011), a series of classes on experimental pragmatics at the Institute for Advanced Study in Pavia (Italy) (organized by Valentina Bambini in 2012), and a week-long class in Manizales (Colombia) (organized by María Mercedes Suárez de la Torre) that allowed me to present some of the chapters for the first time (in 2016).

I am also grateful to Uli Sauerland and Petra Schumacher for designating me a Mercator scholar for their own Germany-wide networking program on experimental pragmatics, called XPrag.de, from 2014 to 2017. This has kept me abreast of the extensive (mostly formal) work going on in Germany and allowed me to routinely give talks there. Classes, talks, and discussions have found their way into this book or have at least made me think more carefully about many of the issues raised therein. For example, one class in Berlin concerned the history of psychology and its role in experimental pragmatics, which helped form Chapter 3, while a talk for a workshop devoted to trends in experimental pragmatics informed parts of Chapter 14. The feedback from these exchanges has been extremely useful.

In preparing actual chapters, I have taken advantage of the now worldwide network of experimental pragmatists. Nearly twenty people read a chapter or two. That is, each chapter was vetted by at least two experts, and no expert read more than two. These reviewers were Valentina Bambini, Lewis Bott, Coralie Chevallier, Pierre Jacob, Napoleon Katsos, Mikhail Kissine, Edmundo Kronmüller, Diana Mazzarella, Tiffany Morisseau, Guy Politzer, Nausicaa Pouscoulous, Petra Schumacher, Nicola Sportono, Ye Tian, Ingrid Lossius Falkum, Jean-Baptiste van der Henst, and Bob van Tiel. I am indebted to each of them. While this procedure might have slowed down the process for the publisher, it certainly made the book sharper and reduced its number of potential gaffes. Any remaining errors are of course my own. I am also grateful to Csaba Pléh, a historian of psychology from Budapest, who spent the 2016–17 academic year in Lyon (and who also happened to be the ESF's liaison for the EURO-XPRAG network) – he was the first to read and critique the entire manuscript as a gestalt. The same appreciation goes to an anonymous reviewer.

I have a number of friends and colleagues who have written books (including several who had *just finished* writing one), and their words of advice were much appreciated. This group includes Billy Clark, Ann Demarais, Pierre Jacob, Mikhail Kissine, Monica Martinat, Hugo Mercier, Julien Musolino, Anne Reboul, Emmanuel Sander, Dan Sperber, and Thom Scott-Phillips. I also wish to thank Helen Barton, the coordinating editor from Cambridge University Press, who always addressed my concerns with *politesse*, Emmanuel Niollet, a colleague in Lyon who periodically provided me with some sage advice, and two people, Ruth Brody and Nicolas Petit, who helped with several editorial undertakings in preparing the book. I would also like to acknowledge and thank the many people who unhesitatingly shared their own figures and photographs for the sake of the book: Cat Davies, Kathleen Eberhard, Yi Ting Huang, Boaz Keysar, Tiffany Morisseau, Jack Tomlinson, and Matea Razec.

As many expats know, living in a foreign country (or two) can be disorienting even after twenty-five years. For the last twenty of those, Monica Martinat has been my home. While pragmatics often breaks down in our daily Italo-Anglo-Franco communication, our shared passions – including professional ones – are never misunderstood. Aside from reading parts of the manuscript, Monica has been unceasingly encouraging. I am also grateful that two of our other shared passions, Noemi and Isaac, put great effort into their own writing and could share in this adventure without teasing me too much.

Abbreviations

AC	Affirmation of the Consequent
AQ	Autism quotient
ASD	Autism spectrum disorder
BA	Brodmann area
DA	Denial of the Antecedent
EEG	Electroencephalography
ERP	Evoked response potential
fMRI	Functional magnetic resonance imaging
GCI	Generalized conversational implicature
HFA	High-functioning adults with autism
IFG	Inferior frontal gyrus
lTPJ	Left temporal parietal junction
MEG	Magnetoencephalography
MP	Modus ponens
MPFC	Medial prefrontal cortex
MT	Modus tollens
MTurk	Amazon Mechanical Turk
N200	Negative-going ERP component that peaks around 200 milliseconds post-stimulus
N400	Negative-going ERP component that peaks around 400 milliseconds post-stimulus
PC	Precuneus
P300	Positive-going ERP component that peaks around 300 milliseconds post-stimulus
P600	Positive-going ERP component that peaks around 600 milliseconds post-stimulus
rTPJ	Right temporal parietal junction
RLPFC	Rostro-lateral prefrontal cortex
RT	Relevance theory

SPM	Standard Pragmatic Model
TD	Typically developing
TFA	Time–frequency analysis
ToM	Theory of mindUBCUpper-bounded construal
UBC	Upper-bounded construal

1 Defining Pragmatics

The What, *the* How, *and Areas of Disagreement*

Mind the gap.

Ubiquitous warning on the London Tube[1]

Imagine walking along a beach and coming across a genuine message in a bottle, one that was dropped in the ocean decades earlier. It reads:

> Mary, you really are a great person. I hope we can keep in correspondence. I said I would write.
>
> Your friend always, Jonathon, Nova Scotia 1985

A note with these very words was indeed found in a bottle on a beach in Croatia in 2013 (McKeon, 2014).[2] How should its sentences be understood? At first blush, the note seems straightforward because it provides enough critical information to allow for the interpretation of not only each of its sentences but also of a speaker's deeper intended message. With little effort I have come up with three possible explanations for this message. Let's consider what these might be.

One is that the message is an uncomplicated expression of Jonathon's desire to stay in touch with Mary after they have known each other for hours, weeks, months, or years as friends. It is similar to the kind of note one would find in a high-school yearbook or in a scrapbook commemorating summer camp. The sentences suggest that they have met and talked and that Jonathon was left impressed. The second possibility, which is more intense, is that the note is part of an awkward post-breakup "let's stay friends" scenario. The key sentence for this hypothesis is "I said I would write." Given that the dropped-in-the-ocean note was a ham-fisted way for Jonathon to keep his word, he arguably did not want to face her. He could not have expected her to ever get the note, or at least he knew the probability was extremely remote. The third reading is a bit darker and sadder for it is entirely possible that Mary does not even know Jonathon. Perhaps Jonathon observed her from a distance, admired her, and convinced himself that he would write; in this case, the message in the bottle was his shy, and useless, way of keeping a promise, to *himself.* These are the three *hypotheses* that I came up with. I am sure there are others that I have not considered.

1

Notice that the note's details are rather sparse and that none of these intended readings can be assumed with confidence. So, on second thought, what the message leaves out also leaves doubt about any of the interpretations I tried to draw. Let me underline five features that make the note *gappy*. First, it is difficult to know what "great" means. Is Mary a great person because she is a good friend, because she is wise, or because she is a leader of a club or civic organization? Is she great compared to others who are not? Perhaps she is just above average (as my online dictionary for "great" indicates). Second, Jonathon goes on to write about his "hope" that the two of them will correspond, before adding "I said I would write." This is the part that leaves much to the imagination. One can invent quite a few scenarios (as I did above) to make sense of this sentence. Third, one can get more detailed still and ask what does "can" refer to? Does it refer to the physical ability to write or the know-how to do so? (Consider the frequent request heard over meals, "Can you pass the salt?" A jokester could answer "yes" and continue eating.) We can see that it is hard to draw firm conclusions from the letter writer's words alone. Fourth, even the handwriting (a photo of the note is available on the Internet, see Figure 1.1) does not help us narrow the possibilities from the many scenarios I described; as best as I can tell, the letter writer is at least a teenager. Note that my inference about the letter writer's age goes beyond the words and sentences written. Finally, and most importantly, the letter writer hardly guaranteed that his message would be comprehended by his receiver. Normally, a listener can signal that a message has been received; that is obviously not the speaker's intention here.

These gaps exemplify the sort of issues that *pragmatics* aims to address, which is to determine what the speaker intended to mean through the provided words. One way to view pragmatics then is as a subfield of linguistics concerned with determining the intended meaning of an utterance. While a syntactician might analyze what makes a sentence such as "Mary, you really are a great person" grammatical (e.g., what links "you" with "are" and, ultimately, with "person"), and while a semanticist would be concerned with the logical entailments one can draw (how "you really are a great person" entails "you are a person"), a pragmatist would be concerned with working out the speaker's meaning when that sentence is *communicated* to a listener and in the specific context in which it is presented. As the above analyses indicate, questions pragmatists ask are: What did Jonathon *mean* by using the word "great"? Is he speaking sincerely (or perhaps cynically)? One could go further and ask: Why did he use the rather vague word "person" rather than "woman," "lover," "athlete," or "stand-up comedian"? When one draws out more refined readings from a given word or, more broadly, from a sentence, and when one detects attitudes through the words uttered in context, this enriched understanding is not coming from the sentence itself, that is, it is not part of the sentence's *linguistically encoded* meaning.

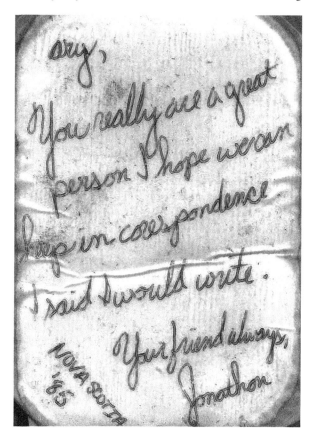

Figure 1.1. Photo of a real message in a bottle found in Croatia (shared here by the finder and photographer of the message, Matea Medak Rezić)

For many scholars, resolving these pragmatic aspects of a sentence is a reducible part of a linguistic system that can be determined by, say, features of the context. According to this approach, to get a clear sense of "great" all one needs is more context (which is absent in the message-in-a-bottle example). Other researchers would go further and argue that pragmatics is not so easily reducible. Linguistic pragmatics, for many theoretical pragmatists, concerns the way a sentence is incorporated as part of a *communication* between interlocutors. Thus, pragmatics for these researchers is not a matter of figuring out a few missing details but is concerned with representing the speaker's intention, which contributes to figuring out the propositional content of an utterance. In the process of doing this, one can enjoin the linguistically encoded meaning carried by the words in the sentence. Note that the aim is similar for both sorts of scholars – to draw out a richer interpretation from a sentence's linguistically encoded reading. This takes us beyond linguistics and, given our concerns about features such as intentions, into the cognitive sciences more generally. Nevertheless, this tension between the two approaches provides the backdrop for much of the research covered in this book. But it does not change what are considered to be the phenomena, for there is general agreement about where the gaps are. Let us turn to these in greater detail.

Sources of Gappiness: A Nonexhaustive List

To elucidate the gap which separates the words in a sentence from the interpretation(s) they are intended to generate, let us consider in greater detail six cases that are discussed by those who are interested in pragmatics. One of my aims is to present some well-thought-out, well-constructed examples that are typically described when talking of gaps. Another one is to show the extent to which these pragmatic phenomena have been investigated so far, and by whom, in the cognitive sciences.

Indexicals

Utterances have lexical features that refer to people, objects, moments in time, and places. While words, such as "I," "you," "now," and "here," remain constant and clear, to whom or what they refer to will change as a function of speaker, time, or location. These are indexicals. If I were to say, "It is raining here now," it is only true if I am referring to the specific time when, and place where, the sentence was uttered (Lyon, on March 8, 2016). While my interlocutor, who could be in another country, would understand that I am referring to my area and my current time, it might no longer be true if the same sentence were said at another time or in another place. We can see, then, how readily a speaker's meaning changes as a function of context. The identical sentence spoken in rainy Seattle could be true when uttered by one speaker, and false when uttered by another speaker in sunny Miami Beach.

It is probably due to the relative ease with which an addressee can attribute indexicals to their intended targets that there have not been many experimental investigations on the way, say, indexical processing changes as the context does. Debates about indexicals have largely remained the province of philosophers of language who ask to what extent indexicals are automatic or *discretionary* (see Dokic, 2012). For example, whereas "I" does not require much intention reading ("I" = the speaker) and is considered pure, "he" requires a bit more work to understand since it only goes as far as picking out a male; on the other hand, "That paper is impressive" calls for more effort than "I" and "he" because it is not clear what paper the speaker is referring to (e.g., is it an article, a newspaper, or wallpaper?). Context is arguably more important in resolving the reference for "that paper" than the reference for "I."

Background Knowledge

It is often not clear what the background of an utterance is, which is why an out-of-the-blue sentence can often lead to bizarre interpretations, as is often evident in newspaper headlines. Jay Leno, a now-retired late-night talk show host in the United States, used to have a segment of his program devoted to unintentionally funny headlines or advertisements. While many were funny due to malapropisms or typos (where "cul-de-sac" was written as "cold-a-sack" or "trailblazer" became "trailbalzer"), others were due to unintended meanings. The headline (in 1.1a) undoubtedly described a get-together for owners and trainers of guide dogs and not a culinary retreat featuring those dogs on a grill. The headline in (1.1b), which I found on the web, can leave the impression that one should fill one's own stomach with gas. Background knowledge (e.g., that associations have annual social gatherings and that gas stations often have attached convenience stores) helps us to make proper sense of these sentences and to reject the unintended, bizarre readings. Often, headlines assume familiarity with a topic that, in turn, license phrases that make no sense or are unintentionally funny to those who are not in the know. Without that specific knowledge, the headline in (1.1c), about a baseball player who plays for a team called the Angels, can seem funny:

(1.1) a. 10th Annual Southeastern Guide Dog BBQ
     b. Empty stomach? Try filling up at a gas station.
     c. Royals to get a taste of Angels' Colon

Experimental psychologists have long investigated issues of background knowledge and arguably consider it key to completing a sentence's meaning. For example, a classic study from Bransford and Johnson (1972) showed how participants recall a long, generic-sounding paragraph (that described how "items" need to be "arranged" and procedures "completed") better when provided with an appropriate title ("Washing Clothes") as opposed to no title. Pragmatists, as far as I can tell, have not considered long-term memory or background knowledge to nearly the same extent as experimental psychologists who study text comprehension (e.g., see Kintsch & Van Dijk, 1978).

Unarticulated Constituents

Utterances are often incomplete while saying something that is, otherwise, trivially true (as in 1.2a) or obviously false (as in 1.2b). In (1.2a), the speaker must have eaten at one point in her life, but she is probably indicating that she has eaten recently. In (1.2b), an example that comes from Kent Bach (1994), the speaker is not falsely asserting that the listener is immortal, but that perhaps a bruise is not fatal.

(1.2) a. I already ate.
      b. You are not going to die.

In other words, speakers are intending to say something more specific (such as 1.3a and 1.3b):

(1.3) a. I already ate (*today*, *this morning*, or *lunch*).
      b. You are not going to die (*from that bruise*).

These particular phenomena are very common in everyday language, but while discussed by philosophers of language, they have not been investigated directly as such by experimentalists.

   If we loosen this category somewhat (from unarticulated constituents) to the many cases in which a speaker makes a reference to some feature of an object or of an act that is left unarticulated, one begins to see experimental pragmatics emerge. For example, *metonymy* involves making reference to an object or concept by referring to something that is associated with it. In the best-known example (from Nunberg, 1978), "The ham sandwich left without paying," the "ham sandwich" is referring to a customer who ordered a sandwich; likewise, when Mary says that she "drank the bottle," she is referring to the liquid contents and not the solid respectacle (Schumacher, 2014). Likewise, when I say, "I began the book," a deeper meaning can be drawn out (Pylkkänen, 2008). For example, it could mean I began *reading* the book, *writing* it, *editing* it, or many other things one does with books. These topics are also fair game (see Chapter 13).

Multiple Meanings

Words can have several meanings or different shades of meaning. For example, the word "bank" could refer to a financial institution or the side of a river, while the word "bat" could refer to the flying mammal or the club used in baseball to hit a ball. These are homonyms and the intended meaning will usually be clarified by context. Other cases of multiple meanings arise from a word that prompts a range of overlapping – polysemous – meanings. As Searle (1980) pointed out, meanings related to the word "cut" intersect with one another, but one meaning cannot easily replace the other:

(1.4) a. The surgeon cut open the patient.
      b. The gardener cut the grass.
      c. The mother cut the cake.
      d. Macy's cut their prices in half.

As Searle (1980: 222–3) wrote:

If someone tells me to cut the grass and I rush out and stab it with a knife, or if I am ordered to cut the cake and I run over it with a lawnmower, in each case I will have failed to obey the order. That is not what the speaker meant by his literal and serious utterance of the sentence.

Polysemous meanings have been investigated experimentally (e.g., Klein & Murphy, 2001) but not specifically to test linguistic-pragmatic concerns.

When one loosens this category further, one can add metaphors ("John is a dolphin") which call for *ad hoc* changes in meaning (so that the listener is obliged to figure out which feature of dolphins is intended to describe the presumably human John). One can also include approximations ("France is hexagonal"). Metaphors have long been investigated experimentally from a pragmatic point of view and will be addressed in Chapters 2 and 7.

Underspecificity

Utterances can be seen to be underinformative and in need of enrichment and adjustment:

(1.5) a. I got to the party and everybody was there.
   b. Some of their identity documents are forgeries.

In (1.5a), there are two features that call for enrichments. One concerns the conjunction "and." Its meaning simply conveys that two events (getting to the party and observing who was there) occurred. Yet, the utterance appears to convey that either there is an order to the two events (getting to the party and *then* making the observation) or that the two events occurred conjointly, in that the speaker got to the party and *at that point* realized who was there. Second, the "everybody" (who was there) obviously does not refer to everybody in the universe, but to the persons that the speaker and listener considered to be relevant.

In (1.5b), borrowed from Levinson (2000), the quantifier "some," which is the single most investigated term in experimental pragmatics, has a minimal reading that could refer to, say, two identity documents. Left unsaid is whether all of the documents are forgeries. Semantically speaking, the utterance remains true if the speaker goes on to discover that all of the documents are forgeries. On the other hand, the use of the existential quantifier, "some," can be a source of an enrichment, one that allows a reading of the kind "Not all of their identity documents are forgeries." While often considered intuitive and automatic, this enriched reading is not in evidence as much as one might think. As will be seen, this question has taken a very large place in the experimental pragmatic literature (see Chapters 6 and 7).

Attitudes

There are also gaps with respect to attitude. How could one gather the attitude behind an ironic "That was a great meeting" if one were left with only the words? Attitudes are usually understood by listeners (even if it takes a bit of effort when compared to the same utterance spoken sincerely). Note, though, that if one were to consider only the words (i.e., the semantics), one would only get so far and not get the intended meaning of the speaker. Prosody is a way to help signal the intended attitude, and this merits discussion too (see Chapter 13). But even prosodic cues do not guarantee that a speaker's attitude will be processed.

As this partial list makes clear, pragmatic phenomena have been investigated by a variety of cognitive fields. It is also fair to point out that some of this volume's topics are covered in neighboring literatures that would not employ our moniker. The topics that have become emblematic of experimental pragmatics – underinformative expressions (such as the one in 1.5b), reference, metaphor, and irony, to name a few – represent only a handful of phenomena that point to the gap between what is minimally said (in a sentence) and what is ultimately understood (as intended by the speaker). While each of these topics has received an experimental pragmatic treatment, the moment when experiments were first employed on these topics varies. The investigation of utterances with relatively weak scalar terms, such as "some," has been a hot topic in the experimental pragmatic literature for nearly twenty years, whereas metaphor has fascinated experimental researchers for a much longer time.

Labeling the gaps between an utterance and the speaker's intended meaning can leave the impression that specific features are numerable and perhaps relatively rare. This is not the case. Each of these sources of *gappiness* is an example that scratches the surface of pragmatic processing (note the idiom, another pragmatic phenomenon that has been studied experimentally). Resolving gaps becomes important to understanding the speaker's intended meaning. For the sake of putting my cards on the table, I will assume – like many radical pragmatists – that there is *always* a gap between the words in a sentence and what they are intended to mean when used in an utterance in a given situation. In this I am using a key concept from the professional pragmatist's toolbox, which is the *underdeterminacy* hypothesis (Carston, 2002). This says that the sentences in ALL utterances fall short of being explicit enough for determining the speaker's intention.

The gappiness I keep alluding to is ubiquitous and screams out for investigation. Identifying these gaps is a critical step, but we also want a satisfying approach for dealing with them generally. So, before addressing this issue further, it is important to better understand how theorists have moved the gap-question forward so that it would eventually be ripe for an experimental turn. As we will see, the way and the extent to which one considers gaps surmountable is revealing of one's approach to the study of pragmatics.

How to Conceive of Gaps and the Ways to Bridge Them

Before we get to actual proposals about the way gaps can be addressed, let me present a little background as to how philosophers initially approached the sentence/meaning gap. One issue is what sort of meaning are we aiming to attain? For one school, it concerns what the words properly mean when put together in a sentence. Going back about a century, one can see the development of this school of thought whose approach still remains influential. It was not necessarily interested in communication or linguistics, the way pragmatics is today. Rather the *Ideal Language* approach was concerned about what a sentence meant if it was transformed into a logical formula. This was important for the agenda at the time because sentences were viewed as tools, as a means to present facts, premises, parts of arguments, and deductions that scientifically describe the world. Proponents of this school, such as Bertrand Russell and Gottlob Frege, noticed that the way a sentence is presented often obscures the proposition, the *ideal*, that it was intended to represent. When a sentence is obscure, it is difficult to properly assign a truth value to the full-fledged proposition. One can see how this school keeps the idea that sentences come up short in fully expressing a speaker's meaning, but note too that it is more concerned with coming up with a way to transform a sentence into a logical form that can then be determined true or false. Moreover, this school deals with sentences that *can* express truth-evaluable propositions. This leaves out questions, commands, wishes, and a whole host of other types of speech acts.

Proponents of this school largely assumed that a sentence has within it the means to be transformed into a clearer, full-fledged proposition. All one needs to do is decompose a sentence (even an obscure one) so that it can expose the logical representation that it was meant to represent. In taking this step, one can remove ambiguities and other obscurities. Natural language descriptions need to be saved from themselves, so to speak, and the best way to do that is to build up a sentence from its elements so that it can be turned into a proper logical proposition. From this perspective, the semantics of the sentence should be very largely determinative in resolving the speaker's meaning.

To give a flavor of this approach, consider Bertrand Russell's well-known example in (1.6), which seems, at face value, to be paradoxical and perplexing. With careful decomposition, he argued, one can determine its truth value, thus eliminating any ambiguity.

(1.6) The present King of France is bald.

The first reaction could very well be that this sentence cannot be judged true or false because it presupposes that there is currently a person who is the King of France and we know that there are presently no official kings of France, so it is impossible to conceive of such a person being bald. In order to come up with a truth value, one can, according to Russell, reduce it to its parts as a series of conjunctions (1.7).

(1.7) There is one, and only one, object X such that X is the present King of France (and) X is bald.

Given that one of the conjuncts in (1.7), *there is an X that is at present the King of France*, is false, so too is the sentence. Since Russell, there have been other suggestions for understanding this sentence (see Carston, 2002 for a summary) that can turn it into a logical proposition that (a) captures all the relevant features and (b) determines whether or not it is true. But that is not our concern here. The goal for now is to see how the Ideal Language approach operates, which goes as follows:

One needs to take a sentence – even if it is ambiguous, obscure, under-informative, or complicated – and determine what it represents logically so that one can then determine whether it is true or false. When this can be done, one has an important method for determining the speaker's meaning of a sentence. In the case of the message in a bottle, the listener (or, rather, the correspondent) can determine whether the message is true. Let us assume that Mary got the note. She can then determine whether she is indeed great in some way in order to determine that this statement is minimally true, and she could confirm whether or not Jonathon had promised to write.

That said, the above approach – worrying only about the truth conditions of the sentence – is unsatisfying because it hardly makes a dent into the list that I compiled earlier. For example, the unarticulated constituents that I mentioned in (1.3) are features that go beyond what is actually in the sentence. In the message in a bottle, the question is not so much about whether or not it is true that Mary is great (that would be difficult for anyone outside their conversation to ascertain, partly because it is vague), but to know what he *meant* precisely when he said that (in what way is Mary great or how great is she?). It would not even be relevant to turn any of the sentences in the message into a proper logical proposition. These sorts of facts lead to a second school of thought, which developed in reaction to the first.

The *Ordinary Language school* refers to philosophers – such as Austin, Grice, and Searle – who "emphasized the pragmatic nature of natural language as opposed to say, the language of *Principia Mathematica*" (Recanati, 2004,

p. 1). Ordinary Language philosophy is keen on describing the link between a spoken sentence and its *uses*.[3] One tack that these philosophers took to argue against the Ideal position was to point to utterances that have a straightforward logical interpretation but that remain interpretatively unsatisfying. Consider the cases in the left part of (1.8a–c). While their logical interpretations (as expressed on the right for each case) appear crystal-clear, these do not necessarily capture what the speaker has in mind:

(1.8) a. I am not unhappy ≠ I am happy.
　　　 b. You can have soup or salad ≠ You can have soup or salad or both.
　　　 c. Monica had a baby and got married ≠ Monica had a baby, got married, or vice versa.

While *not not A* is equivalent to *A* in standard logic, the speaker's use of the double negation in (1.8a) can be taken to deny unhappiness (without asserting happiness). Whereas disjunctions are inclusive in standard logic, the disjunction in (1.8b), at least in certain contexts, can be taken to be exclusive. Whereas the conjunction *A & B* is equivalent to *B & A* in standard logic (that is, order does not matter when one conjoins two propositions), the presentation of the conjuncts in (1.8c) can be understood implicitly as expressing order. Turning sentences into logical formalisms clearly has its limits.

Meaning for Ordinary Language philosophy is concerned with what the speaker meant when she said it. While determining what an idealized form of a sentence conveys and discerning whether that sentence is true is going to be relevant, it is still not going to provide the listener with everything he needs in order to understand the speaker's intended meaning when she said it. The underdeterminacy hypothesis mentioned earlier emerges from a basic tenet of the Ordinary Language school, which is that sentences do *not* provide enough explicit information for a listener to fully gather all the communicated information and to understand the speaker's intention. Gaps always remain and these need to be filled, not by idealizing away components of the sentence that are problematic, but through some form of reasoning. As Korta and Perry (2015) write:

Pragmatics involves perception augmented by some species of "ampliative" inference – induction, inference to the best explanation, Bayesian reasoning, or perhaps some special application of general principles special to communication...a sort of reasoning that goes beyond the application of rules, and makes inferences beyond what is established by the basic facts about what expressions are used and their meanings.

The speaker's words, according to the Ordinary Language school, are just part of the communication picture. In fact, as will be underlined later, there are all kinds of communication that can take place, even without words. The words in the sentence cannot be idealized away in order to simply determine whether its meaning is true or false. According to the Ordinary Language school, the words are a starting point to understand the speaker's intended meaning.

Where Do We Go from Here?

This brief introduction depicts pragmatics as a discipline that is concerned with the interpretation of everyday utterances. While it could be, and is often, considered a subdiscipline of linguistics, it is unlike its fellow subdisciplines in that it is necessarily interdisciplinary in at least three ways. First, its emergence as a field is owed, at least in part, to a *philosophical* cleavage that initiated discussions between those who aimed to account for meaning through a logical analysis of the speaker's words (the Ideal Language school) and those who say that a speaker's words are only part of a listener's effort to get at the speaker's intended meaning (the Ordinary Language school). According to the latter, the gap can only be bridged through nonlinguistic abilities (through some form of inference); the words uttered are but evidence that can help the listener come up with a hypothesis about the speaker's intention. As becomes clear in the following chapters, pragmatics is largely focused on determining the *speaker's* intended meaning, much like the Ordinary Language school proposed. However, logical analyses of spoken sentences still have a role to play (by fully appreciating the extent to which semantics matters), so insights from the Ideal Language school continue to have an impact. Second, accounting for pragmatic enrichments inevitably leads to theories that include psychological processes. After all, one of the central terms used in pragmatics – *intention* – concerns mental states, making pragmatics a concern for psychologists as much as linguists. Third, and this is what made experimental pragmatics unique, starting fifteen to twenty years ago, many pragmatic theories compete for our attention and none of them can be substantiated through linguistic introspection alone. Experimentation, in its most classic form, is especially called for in pragmatics because it can help (a) discover empirical facts that lie beyond linguistic intuition and (b) test between contemporary accounts of pragmatics in order to determine which can best account for generated data. An experimental mindset is critical in order to rigorously test theories and partly to put limits on armchair explorations.

All of the above considerations put us in a position to treat experimental pragmatics as a more general, cognitive science. This is how the book will consider experimental pragmatics. This is not a novel notion. John Austin (1956b, 1979) from early on endeavored to transform ordinary language, viewed as a philosophical object, into a (cognitive) science of language:

In the history of human inquiry, philosophy has the place of the initial central sun, seminal and tumultuous; from time to time it throws off some portion of itself to take station as a science, a planet, cool and well regulated, progressing steadily towards a distant final state ... Is it not possible that the next century may see the birth, through the joint efforts of philosophers, grammarians, and numerous other students of language, of a true and comprehensive science of language? Then we shall have rid ourselves of one more part of philosophy (there will still be plenty left) in the only way we ever can get rid of philosophy, by kicking it upstairs.

Austin (1956b/1979, p. 232)

This quote, written at the dawn of the cognitive revolution, prophesied that it will take a combination of efforts – from a wide range of investigators – to create an inclusive science of language, one that addresses concerns that are central to *utterance understanding*. The work in this book can be viewed as a way to make that vision real, for it provides a prominent place for armchair theorists (philosophers and theoretical linguists), while also emphasizing the importance of data collected from all kinds of language researchers, including linguists (most obviously), experimental psychologists (including psycholinguists of course), neuroscientists, anthropologists, and anyone else interested in communication.

Central to this effort is the quest to better understand the sentence/utterance meaning gap. Through philosophical approaches, on the one hand, and the reliability of experimental data on the other, one can (to adopt a slightly different metaphor) begin to climb the intellectual chimney so that we – collectively – can see the structure below us as we rise. At its start, one cannot know what this structure will look like. We can only advance by considering theories and by carrying out experiments to test them. In the next chapter we consider Paul Grice's seminal account, which is generally recognized for having moved pragmatics forward in one giant step.

Notes

1. Also see Horn (2006), who ended his article with "Mind the GAPP [Golden Age of Pure Pragmatics]."
2. The original story can be found here: www.digitaljournal.com/article/348150. A picture of the note can also be found here: http://imgur.com/riZMikH.
3. This is why Austin's (1975) book is entitled *How to Do Things with Words*, in which he proposed a classification that made distinctions among utterances, not along the lines of truth-functionality but, in terms of what a speech act does. While this approach makes for useful distinctions among classes of utterances, it does not necessarily help us describe a given utterance, which continually provides all sorts of gaps, such as the six types of cases above. For example, *illocutionary* acts are speech acts that are for specific instances, such as promising (*I promise to x*), christening (*I hereby name this ship the y*), and ordering (*Go get the forks*), and cannot be reduced to truth conditions. Instead of considering truth conditions, he described "speech acts in terms of felicity conditions, interpreted as conditions for appropriate usage" (Levinson, 1980).

2 Grice's Monumental Proposal and Reactions to It

Exactly what this [general] principle [governing the use of language] is I am uncertain but a first shot would be the following: "One should not make a weaker statement rather than a stronger one unless there is a good reason for so doing."

Paul Grice (1961: 132)

When I first moved to Paris, with a serviceable but weak command of French, one of my favorite activities (nearly every afternoon) was to visit a patisserie for a *gouté* (an afternoon snack). One day, I went into a rather ritzy shop to order a strawberry tart. When my turn came, I pointed to the tarts and made my request. Surprisingly, rather than follow through on my order (e.g., by moving toward the tarts in the showcase and packaging one up), the *serveuse* (shop assistant) stood still and said something that I just did not understand. This prompted me to say to myself something like: "She didn't package up my tart, nor did she do anything else for that matter (it must be my French); she must intend for me to understand that she didn't comprehend my request ... so I suppose I should repeat it." In other words, I figured that in order to convey my intention (*please sell me a strawberry tart*), I needed to repeat my request, which I did. In fact, I ended up making the same gesture and putting together slightly different versions of the same sentence three times ("*Est-ce que je peux ...*," "*Puis-je ...*," "*S'il vous plaît, donnez moi ...*" ["Can I ... ," "May I ... ," "Please give me ... "]) as we comically went through the same routine over and over again. Even after my third attempt, she continued to stand still and mutter something. Between each try, however, I realized that perhaps my earlier hypothesis was wrong. My first hypothesis was that my French was wanting, and my second was that the delicious-looking strawberry tarts were reserved for someone else or perhaps they were fake, so she was actually saying that there were none available. After my third iteration I thus paid even closer attention to *her* third take (what seemed like the same utterance). The mystery quickly unraveled – partly because, this time, she also made a gesture (she pointed her finger downward). It was then that I finally understood that my earlier hypotheses (about her intention) were wrong. She hadn't misunderstood me, nor was she telling me that the tarts were unavailable. She was actually telling me: "Don't touch the window display!" Her intention became clear (along with the meaning of her words) when she added that finger-pointing gesture which captured my attention.

With a slight flush of embarrassment (though strangely satisfied that she thought my French was good enough to understand her admonishment), I sheepishly pulled back my own still-pointing finger from the glass case. She then made her way to the tarts and packaged one up for me. Interestingly, she could have ignored my failure to understand her request, placed the tart in a box, and put paid to the exchange. I would have been none the wiser and I would have made fewer fingerprints. However, it was important for her that I should understand her intended meaning, i.e., it was crucial for her that I should appreciate that she was fully communicating with me.

I tell this (true) story because it lays bare important features of a conversational exchange that are often ignored. From the speaker's side – the *serveuse* in this case – it demonstrates that she has two sorts of intention when communicating. One intention is the content of her utterance, which in this example was (to paraphrase) "Get your fingers off my glass showcase." The other subtler intention is crucial too; this one can be loosely described as "I want you to recognize my intention that I want you to take your fingers off my glass showcase." It is this second sort of intention that ultimately made her communication successful, because she waited until I fully understood both intentions.[1] Again, she could have served me quickly to get me out of the shop – meaning she would have been spared further fingerprints – but she wanted me to understand that she wished to communicate something. It also helped that she added the pointing gesture, because it provided a further ostensive cue concerning the information in her utterance.

The story is also illustrative of what goes on from the addressee's side: As a listener, I was making inductive inferences in order to better decipher her words. I had linguistic limits, for sure, but I ultimately managed to do it – partly thanks to her hand signal. She would not move until she got me to produce the response she intended me to produce *and* she got me to recognize her intention.

The elements highlighted here – the recognition of a speaker's intention, the way a listener forms a hypothesis about the speaker's intention, and how these activities interact with an action or an utterance – are at the very heart of a proposal made by Paul Grice, a philosopher from the Ordinary Language school who sought synthesis with the Ideal Language camp. Grice ultimately wanted to address the way a spoken sentence comes to mean what it was intended to mean. This chapter will describe his proposal as well as influential post-Gricean theories that followed. As will become obvious, there is much theoretical brushwood to be cleared before getting to a point where the gap between a sentence's meaning and its intended meaning can be usefully described; and much of the brushwood-clearing will be done by making definitions and fine distinctions. Ultimately, these fine distinctions will put us in a position to explore Grice's account regarding how sentence meanings interact with inference making in order to arrive at an approximation of a speaker's intended meaning.

Natural versus Nonnatural Meaning

What does "to mean" something mean? The first of Grice's distinctions concerns the difference between what he called *natural* and *nonnatural* meanings. This essentially distinguishes between the natural interpretation of events or observations (those that arise through natural laws) and those that require communication. To use Grice's own example of a natural meaning, consider the case where spots "mean" measles. In such a case, *meaning* (or the verb "to mean") occurs through the existence of a direct causal relationship in the environment to the observer and it cannot be falsified. If someone were to pronounce, "These spots mean measles, but he doesn't have measles," that would not make sense. Grice presents these kinds of natural meaning in order to set up his main concept, *nonnatural meanings*, which arise through communication. (The nomenclature is not intended to indicate that the way people communicate is nonnatural; *nonnatural* refers to conversational sorts of "meaning" which are unlike law-like *natural* meanings.) As Grice (1989) put it, nonnatural meanings are those cases in which one says that "in such contexts ... 'His remark meant so-and-so'" (Grice, 1989: 291). It is this kind that needs further explanation if we are to understand the way utterances communicate meaning.

According to Grice, to mean something nonnaturally involves three types of intention. The first is the speaker's intention for the listener to form a belief. We can call this the *what* intention, because it is what the speaker wants the listener to know. Grice went on to argue that this intention is not enough to *mean nonnaturally*, because one can imagine a case where someone anonymously provides evidence that would make her addressee believe something (imagine a murderer who leaves behind someone else's identification papers so that a detective would think that that person is responsible for the crime). To have *nonnatural meaning*, the speaker needs to intend the addressee to recognize that the speaker has the *what* intention that the speaker wants the listener to know. We can call this second intention the *that* intention because the speaker also has an intention that the listener should recognize *that* the speaker has a proposition (information) to communicate. One might think these two intentions are collectively good enough to communicate a proposition (i.e., to *mean nonnaturally*). However, Grice did not think so. Grice argued that there is a third intention, which completes what the previous two started; that is, nonnatural meaning is completed when the hearer fulfills the first (*what*) intention based on recognizing the speaker's second (*that*) intention. As Scott-Phillips recently (2014) wrote, this third (final) intention is crucial:

> it is the heart of Grice's account of meaning: to mean something, I should intend that my audience believes it, *and they should believe it at least in part because they recognize that this was my very intention*. This is the meaning of (Gricean, non-natural) meaning.

In current parlance, any Gricean proposal is *ostensive-inferential*, because a communication is successful when the speaker gets the addressee to recognize the speaker's intention to the addressee *that* there is a *what* intention to capture. When the hearer recognizes the speaker's *that* intention, it allows the hearer to form inferentially an approximation of the speaker's *what* intention.

Grice's proposal to distinguish *natural* from *nonnatural* meaning and to explicate what is involved in the latter was immediately impactful, and for two reasons. First, his proposal underlined how a listener's attention is focused, not only on appreciating the contents of the speaker's message, but also on recognizing that the speaker has an intention to communicate it. Grice's nonnatural meaning introduced a novel view on human communication. Prior to Grice, the working model of communication – for researchers and non-researchers alike – assumed that human communication is based on a code model.

Technically known as the Shannon–Weaver model or informally as the conduit metaphor (see Figure 2.1), a code model views an utterance as a message that needs to be transferred to another person's head, if you will, and then decoded. The only source of error in the code model comes from the medium

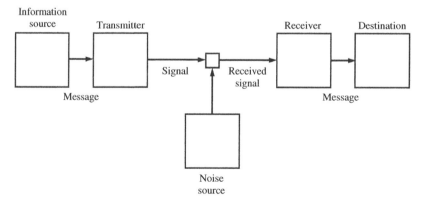

Figure 2.1. An illustration of Shannon–Weaver's model of communication (freely available from https://commons.wikimedia.org/wiki/File:Shannon_communication_system.svg)

in which the message passes. If the message is deformed in some way, then it will not be properly transferred. Implicit in this view is the notion that the message contains everything that the listener needs in order to understand the speaker's transmission. All a listener needs to do is capture the utterance, decode it, and unpack it. There is not much else. Grice's proposal, which is based on a listener making an approximation of a speaker's intention based on presented evidence, represents a radical shift from this vision and points in a new direction for theories of communication.

Second, and relatedly, Grice's ostensive-inferential account explains what makes human communication unique. In fact, Grice's account was quickly recognized as a way to distinguish human communication from "the multitude of patterns of communicative interchange between living creatures" (Denkel, 1985). In other words, it is a basis for distinguishing human communication from nonhuman communication, the latter of which relies almost exclusively on codes (Scott-Philips, 2014).[2] Nonhuman communicators generally do not rely on making the addressee infer the "speaker's proposition" and they generally do not require that the addressee recognize that the speaker has an intention to communicate information, i.e., nonhuman communicators do not capture a conspecific's attention in order to indicate something particular. While there are some exceptions to this human specificity (e.g., my own dog has on occasion ostensively dropped her bone loudly enough so that I will turn my attention away from the computer, look at her, and guess what she wants, which is to play or go out), humans have this ability in spades and this is what makes us unique with respect to other species.

Let's review Grice's notion of nonnatural meaning by considering a new scenario, one in which I would like to tell my colleague, whose office is facing mine and whose door is wide open, that I would like him at this moment to keep his voice down while on the phone; and, along the way, let's see how Grice's three intentions become integral to my efforts to mean something nonnaturally, even without communicating verbally. A first step, according to Grice, consists of the *speaker intending to change something in the addressee's mental state*. This much is easy. I am the agent in this scenario and I intend to change something in my neighbor's mental state. This gives rise to the *what* intention (*neighbor, keep your voice down, please*), but as speaker I have yet not done anything to affect a change. Grice's second intention consists of *the addressee recognizing that the speaker has an intention to change his (the listener's) mental states*. This means that my colleague needs to recognize that I have the intention to let him know that I would like him to keep his voice down. Now, this is the tricky part. How can I go about that? One option would be to close my door (loudly and forcefully), with the intention *that* my neighbor detect my *what* intention, which is again that I am disturbed by his loud talking and would like him to keep his voice down. However, even if his conversation suddenly ended or quieted down after I loudly closed my door, it would still not be the case that he fully detected that I wanted him to recognize my intention. It could have been coincidental that he quieted down or he might have thought it was someone else beside me who slammed a door loudly. I did not make it clear to my neighbor that I expressly wanted him to gather my intentions. The nonnatural meaning of my gesture was not guaranteed. It is going to take something more for him to properly form a hypothesis about what I have in mind. This leads to Grice's third intention, which consists of the addressee forming the belief (the *what* intention) that the speaker intended the addressee to form in virtue of the recognition of the speaker's *that* intention. More technically, *by recognizing the speaker's intention (the second "that" intention above), the addressee fulfills the "what" intention (i.e., the addressee now believes what the speaker intended him to believe).* I would guarantee that my addressee recognizes my intention through some form of action, such as a conspicuous shrug and grimace directed at my colleague or perhaps a "shush" with my finger to my mouth. By carrying out these three steps, my addressee is in a position to believe what I, the speaker, intended him to believe.

What Is Said versus What Is Meant

Now, let's turn our attention to a second distinction that Grice aimed to explain: the much more intuitive one between a sentence's meaning, which can be analyzed for its grammatical and phonological properties, and the intended meaning of that sentence when it is used as an utterance. While a *sentence's* features will need to respect syntactic and semantic principles, the meaning of an *utterance* will change as a function of what is considered to be the nonnatural meaning. This will depend on the hypothesis that the addressee considers and on who is speaking, when it is spoken, what the intended consequences are that the speaker had in mind, what the addressee's expectations and skills are, and so on. Ultimately, both the sentence itself and the efforts to get at the nonnatural meaning will play a role in discerning the utterance's meaning. As in Chapter 1, when I talk about the sentence's contributions to utterance understanding, I will refer to *linguistically encoded* contributions (or, on occasion, the *semantic* contributions) made by the utterance. When I consider extra-sentential concerns, I will refer to these as *pragmatic* contributions to utterance understanding.

In his William James lectures, Grice (1967) proposed that conversation rested on a principle of cooperation, requiring interlocutors to "make [their] conversational contribution such as is required, at the stage at which it occurs, by the accepted purpose or direction of the talk exchange in which [they] are engaged." This principle was explicated through a number of maxims of conversation, which speakers are supposed to follow. Most notable are the *Maxim of Quality*, which refer to speaking truthfully and the *Maxim of*

Quantity, which refer to giving amounts of information that are appropriate for a given situation and not more so. For the sake of completeness, I spell them out as Grice did below:

Maxim of Quality

1. Do not say what you believe to be false.
2. Do not say that for which you lack adequate evidence.

Maxim of Quantity

1. Make your contribution as informative as is required (for the current purposes of the exchange).
2. Do not make your contribution more informative than is required.

Maxim of Relation

1. Be relevant.

Maxim of Manner

1. Avoid obscurity of expression.
2. Avoid ambiguity.
3. Be brief (avoid unnecessary prolixity).
4. Be orderly.

The passage to the speaker's meaning can then be described by an inferential process that is guided by an interaction between the linguistically encoded meaning of an utterance and the maxims. I say "interaction" because an addressee could use the maxims to extract more information from an utterance that was literally true but underinformative or from one that was literally false. Let's consider some examples.

The utterance in (2.1a) is one of Grice's well-known examples in which an utterance can be made richer through inference. According to Grice, (2.1a) violates the Quantity Maxim (and more specifically its first submaxim) because it appears unnecessarily underinformative and allows the addressee to extract further information of the sort specified in (2.1b):

(2.1) a. X is meeting a woman this evening.
       b. X is meeting a woman who is not his sister, mother, or wife.

Given that the speaker was not very informative and that it would have been very easy to say one of the alternatives in (2.1b) instead of the word *woman*, a listener is entitled to narrow (2.1a) to mean that *X is meeting a woman who is someone other than his sister, mother, or wife*. Grice's approach can also explain the underspecific cases such as those described in (1.5) in Chapter 1, "Some of their identity documents are forgeries," which can be said to be underinformative with respect to the Maxim of Quantity's first submaxim. Such underinformativeness prompts a listener to interpret the utterance further.

To give a flavor of the way a false literal reading can prompt inference making, consider a metaphoric statement (as will be covered in greater detail in Chapters 3 and 10). According to Grice, metaphor (as well as meiosis, irony, and hyperbole) works by "flouting" the Maxim of Quality so that the speaker's intended meaning can be accessed. For example, a speaker uttering (2.2) presents a "categorial falsity" (Grice, 1989, p. 34):

(2.2) You are the cream in my coffee.

As the word "flouting" implies, the speaker is *purposely* saying something false, with the net result being that the listener is compelled to find an alternative intended meaning. On first blush, this can explain cases of figurative language generally. The metonymy in *the ham sandwich* example, described in Chapter 1 as an indeterminacy linked to unarticulated constituents, can be considered a case which violates the first submaxim of Quality and prompts the listener to come up with another interpretation.

Grice's distinction between *sentence meaning* (the properties of a sentence assigned to it by the grammar) and *speaker's meaning* (what the speaker actually intended to communicate by uttering a sentence) is arguably the basis for all the work in pragmatics, whether or not it involves experiments. This explains why his general approach has remained seminal to nearly everything that has followed since. Critically, he viewed the retrieval of sentence meaning from an actual utterance as a matter of decoding (discovering the semantic properties that the grammar pairs to its acoustic form) and he viewed the retrieval of the speaker's meaning as a special kind of intention reading that provides the *nonnatural meaning*. Importantly, he showed that, although linguistic communication is partly code-based, it cannot be reduced to a mere encoding–decoding process; it involves the attribution of mental states to the speaker too. The centrality of the inferential process to understanding utterances is the critical insight that distinguishes modern accounts of pragmatics from its predecessors and that distinguishes pragma*tists* from nearly every other professional linguist.

Along the way, Grice introduced a new vocabulary that was quickly taken up by philosophers and linguists alike. For example, *conversational implicature* has become known as a kind of inference that emerges from a speech act but not directly through the meaning of the speaker's words (Grice, 1989). In order to appreciate this, let's consider some (now famous) examples. First up, suppose Professor Requestor asks Professor Provider for a recommendation about Student Smith, and Professor Provider writes:

(2.3) Mr. Smith has excellent handwriting and is always very punctual.

While fulfilling the request from Professor Requestor, the letter is obviously very underinformative. Aside from the fact that letters of recommendation are usually chock-full of relevant (as well as laudatory) information, the abject lack of such information in Professor Provider's letter indicates that Professor Requestor can now conclude that there is not much to recommend about Student Smith.[3] The paucity (and the irrelevance) of (2.3) reveals that Professor Provider does not have a high opinion of Student Smith. There are expectations in discourse, and when these are not met it allows the addressee to draw conclusions in the form of implicatures.

By now, it is probably not surprising to find out that other distinctions emerge. Another one from Grice is between *conversational implicatures* and *conventional implicatures*. While the first arises indirectly through a speech act (as in 2.3), the latter refers to pragmatic information that is encoded in language. For instance, the conjunction "but" in "George Clooney is famous but he is nice" has the same meaning as "and"; however, the word "but" pragmatically (and additionally) contrasts the two conjuncts conventionally through language. He further divided *conversational implicatures* into two sorts: *generalized conversational implicatures* and *particularized conversational implicatures*.

Generalized conversational implicatures arise when "the use of a certain form of words in an utterance would normally (in the ABSENCE of special circumstances) carry such-and-such an implicature or type of implicature" (Grice, 1975: 56). One Gricean example is (2.1a) above, but he presented others, such as (2.4):

(2.4) He took off his trousers and he got into bed.

From the Maxim of Manner one could draw the conclusion that the subject first took off his trousers and then got into bed.

Grice's generalized implicatures were assumed to occur systematically, although the context may be such that they do not occur and were contrasted with particularized implicatures, which were assumed to be less systematic and always clearly context-dependent. For example, in the following exchange, there is no single form or word that can account for the extra-linguistic inferences.

(2.5) Sasha: "Is Dad home?"
        Malia: "Well, I saw his basketball in the hallway."

Malia's response does not answer the yes/no question directly. However, one can work out the Gricean implicature (*yes*). Note that there is no general rule like one for temporal order in (2.4) that follows from a specific term. His reasons for making the distinction had to do with his debates with fellow philosophers on the meaning of logical connectives and quantifiers, and there is some vagueness in his view of the exact role of the context in the case of generalized implicatures (see Carston, 2002: 107–16). In summary, one can see how he inspired work on implicatures by providing a framework and a vocabulary.

As can be seen, Grice ultimately highlighted a distinction between core linguistic and pragmatically derived parts of meaning and thus broke new ground in philosophy and linguistics (these ideas will be unpacked further in Chapter 5). In the meantime, it should be clear that Grice's proposal sets the stage for a view of communication that is much different from the Shannon–Weaver model. A communicator's act is part of a scenario that allows an addressee to draw inferences. While a communicator's act can range from eyebrow raises to eye-rolling, and from pointing to grunting, the act that interests pragmatists most is an utterance. But even an utterance leaves a lot of room for inference making, so that an addressee can ultimately gain access to an approximation of the speaker's *what* intention.

Reactions

While Grice's proposal was generally well received and prompted debate among philosophers, it also led to three reactions (alternatives) that would become integral to launching the experimental pragmatic enterprise – Default accounts, Relevance Theory, and what I will call a Convention-and-common-ground account – which are introduced here. While each recognized the impact of Grice's monumental proposal, each latched on to different features of it in an effort to make generalizations from it, or improve it, or criticize it, or even minimize it. Let us see how this played out.

Default Accounts: Making Utterances More Informational

Neo-Gricean Views
One of the early reactions to Grice's proposal was to make it fit more snugly into linguistic theory (Gazdar, 1979; Horn, 1973, 1984, 1989, 1992; Levinson, 1983, 2000). *Neo-Griceans* stayed relatively close to Grice's formulation of the maxims by aiming to integrate pragmatic inferences alongside syntactic operations. Larry Horn, for example, focused on the derivation of generalized implicatures and argued that these rely on preexisting linguistic scales consisting of elements ranked by order of informativeness. A scale is typically represented with less-than and greater-than symbols on each of its ends along with elements that are ordered. In the scale <some, most, all>, an element on the right entails those (or the one) to its left. When "all the children have teddy bears" is the case, it follows that "most of the children have teddy bears" and that "some of the children do." Interestingly, when a speaker uses a term (e.g., "some") that is low in order of informativeness; the speaker can be taken to implicate that the proposition that would have been expressed by

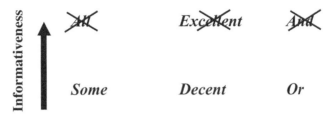

Figure 2.2. A depiction of "scalar implicature" derivation

the stronger term in the scale ("all") is false. Hearing the statement "Some children have teddy bears" can implicate that *not all children do*. This can be generalized to a host of scales. Consider one that ranges from "decent" to "excellent" upon hearing, e.g., "This meal was decent"; or consider the logical terms "or" and "and" (where the former is less informative than the latter). If a speaker says that her suitor brought "flowers or champagne," it can implicate that *it is false that he brought both*, because the speaker would have been more appropriately informative by saying "flowers *and* champagne." It is the ubiquity of scales that prompted many to dub this kind of narrowing a *scalar implicature*. See Figure 2.2 for an illustration, which aims to show how a weak-sounding term – when it is uttered – prompts a stronger associate on the same scale, which is then rejected, prompting an inference of the form, not-the-STRONGER TERM.

In a similar vein, Levinson (2000) argued that information processing is slowed considerably by human speech articulation and that speedups can be attained through what are essentially heuristics. According to his Generalized Conversational Implicature (GCI) theory, enriched readings in many cases – e.g., scalar implicatures – go through by *default*. While keeping Grice's application of maxims as well as the conversational principle, Levinson was much less concerned about intentions (Levinson, 2000: 13). Instead, Levinson defined three basic principles linked to three of Grice's maxims (here in abridged form):

Q-Principle: *What you do not say is not the case*

Speaker's maxim: Do not provide a statement that is informationally weaker than your knowledge of the world allows.

I-Principle: *What is expressed simply is stereotypically exemplified*

Speaker's maxim: Produce the minimal linguistic information sufficient to achieve your communicational ends.

M-Principle: *What's said in an abnormal way isn't normal*

Speaker's maxim: Indicate an abnormal, nonstereotypical situation by using marked expressions that contrast with those you would use to describe the corresponding normal, stereotypical situations.

These principles, unlike Grice's, are meant to be *inferential heuristics* that save time and effort in interpreting certain classes of statements. For the Q-Principle, which is based on the first submaxim of Grice's Maxim of Quantity, the idea is to provide a quick and dirty way to make what will be referred to later as *scalar inferences*. These are cases like those in (2.6) below:

(2.6) a. "Some of the boys are coming."

+> not all

b. "Three boys came in."

+> not four

c. "Possibly, there is life on Mars."

+> not certainly

The I-Principle adopts the second submaxim from Grice's Maxim of Quantity. These cover cases that have "a tendency to select the best interpretation to the most stereotypical, most explanatory exemplification." So rather than leaving cases unspecified, listeners will adopt a stereotypical interpretation as in (2.7) below:

(2.7) a. "John's book is good."

+> the one he read, wrote, borrowed, as appropriate

b. "A secretary."

+> a female one

c. "John turned the switch and the motor started."

+> p then q, p caused q, John intended p to cause q

The M-Principle refers to cases of manner and is contrasted with the I-Principle. Whereas the I-Principle stereotypes banal structures, the M-Principle takes note of unusual ones. While "Bill stopped the car" is stereotypical and is likely to conjure up a standard slowing down by pressing on the brakes, the statement in (2.8a) is likely to draw exceptional readings. Likewise, a statement such as "John left the party" might conjure up an image of a man ending an activity; the statement in (2.8b) provides an alternative portrayal. Similarly, a description of hitting a baseball in (2.8c) leaves the distinct impression that the batter was not purposeful in his gestures.

(2.8) a. "Bill caused the car to stop."

+> he stopped a rolling a car by stepping in front of it or he used his left foot from his seat

b. "John walked out of the party, putting one foot in front of another."

+> he had a difficult time walking or he left indignantly.

    c. "He maneuvered his body so that the ball (he hit) ended up in right field."

        +> he (improbably) managed to hit the ball

As one can see, for Griceans and neo-Griceans, expectations derive from principles and maxims, i.e., *rules* of behavior that speakers are expected to obey but which they may, on occasion, violate. For Grice, a violation of a maxim or a clash among maxims may be committed on purpose in order to indicate to the hearer some implicit meaning. Indeed, in the Gricean scheme, the implicit content of an utterance is typically inferred by the hearer in his effort to find an interpretation which preserves the assumption that the speaker is obeying, if not all the maxims, at least the Cooperative Principle. For a neo-Gricean such eccentricities (underinformativeness, unusual formulations, or gaps in language) are rendered as sources of greater informativeness through heuristics.

Grammatical Approaches

As we will see in Chapter 7, there is a nearly direct line from default explanations to another class of accounts that rely on features attributed to grammar (Chierchia, 2001; see also, Chierchia et al., 2008). While focused almost exclusively on scalar inference, these accounts do not draw on speakers' intentions at all but on compositional semantics. According to such an approach, certain grammatical environments encourage semantic readings while others permit pragmatic ones. So, to take (2.6a), a pragmatic reading (that enriches "some" to "not all") is said to disappear when put in a downward-entailing context. As will be described later, an entailment relationship is *downward* when a universal covers the particular. (So when my friend Diana says, "I do not eat meat," it downward entails *I do not eat beef, chicken or pork*). One finds these kinds of grammatical environments are generated by negation (as Diana's remark shows), question forms, antecedents of conditionals, and other situations. So (2.6a)'s statement in the form of a question – "Are some of the boys coming?" – should only allow for semantic readings (i.e., it should not produce a *not all* enrichment). This is a *non*-Gricean way of viewing scalar inferences and it is the source of much discussion – mostly in the semantics literature. However, it has also led to cross-border discussions that concern the way Gricean concepts are introduced into sentence processing (as we will see in Chapters 7 and 14).

Relevance Theory: A Cognitive Account of Communication

Default accounts were largely built on Grice's edifice in order to turn pragmatic steps into linguistic ones. Meanwhile, they largely ignored or did away with key parts of Grice's proposal, such as a role for Grice's second and third intentions (the nonnatural meaning aspect in which the speaker wants her intention to be recognized by the addressee so as to change some aspect of the latter's perceptions or understanding). In contrast, *relevance theory* (or RT for short) (Sperber & Wilson, 1986) largely preserves fundamental Gricean concepts while providing a cognitive architecture. The upshot is that RT revamps Grice's approach with the goal of, among other things, developing a processing account that describes the goals of communicators who produce utterances or signals and those of addressees who need to process them. Ultimately, RT makes fundamental claims and characterizations about communication that are unique, making this another post-Gricean account.

Its starting point is to describe a person's natural cognitive abilities in a way that views people as *information* processors (Sperber and Wilson considered it important to characterize the way cognitive systems do such processing). This led to the notion of *relevance*, which is a property of the inputs to information processing. Whether information comes in through external stimuli or mental representations, input will be *relevant* when it combines with a processor's mental states or background knowledge in order to produce new effects. Relevance underlines what makes information worth attending to. Its processing claim is that there are two features that can capture the relevance of incoming input. One is how much *effort* it takes to process the input and the other is the cognitive *effects* that this input produces (e.g., in terms of new conclusions produced). The word "relevance" in RT is a technical term that describes how processing is determined by the interplay of effort and effects.

Before appreciating the two features in tandem, let's first view each separately. *Effort* refers to the ease with which the information can be integrated by the processor. If two stimuli provide the same effect, but one requires more effort to process than the other, the easier-to-process one will be higher in relevance. When reading an instruction on the back of a packet that is presented bilingually, the reduced effort in reading the instruction in your preferred language increases its relevance with respect to the other. *Effects* refers to the cognitive impact that a stimulus can have on the human processor. Conclusions drawn from an utterance or even a single scene could be different depending on who you are or what you know. Consider a Japanese garden whose thoughtful layout is designed to prompt cognitive effects among its visitors. While the stimulus is the same for every observer, the effects it will produce on its visitors will vary. A viewer with greater familiarity with Japanese gardens and its traditions will be provided with more cognitive effects than a first-time visitor, whose appreciation will be limited to its general aesthetic appeal and little else. Someone who has specific memories of a given garden will process more effects than someone who does not know that garden. Input will always depend on the specifics of the person and the situation: Who the addressee is and what the specific stimulus is each play a vital role in the effects produced. In this way, *every* situation is particularized.

We will see in a moment how relevance is determined by the interplay of effort and effects, but let's first turn to the general structure of RT, which lays out its general claims or "principles" about the role of relevance in cognition and in communication. The first is the *Cognitive Principle of Relevance*, which is as follows:

Human cognition tends to be geared to the maximization of relevance.

Cognition here refers to how one's attention is grabbed by something in the environment. It is a claim more than a prescription, and basically says that we are designed as human beings to interpret the stimuli that impinge upon us. Viewed evolutionarily, it does not assume that everyone does so in the same manner or that there is a right or wrong way to do it. It is a highly individual affair, but something that we all must do to survive.

One might say, cynically, that this seems like a harmless general account about making observations in gardens, but what does it have to say about communication and linguistics? Here, we turn to the second general claim, the *Communicative Principle of Relevance*:

Every act of communication conveys a presumption of its own optimal relevance.

This says that interlocutors or communicators make signals that call for the addressee to do the same kind of cognitive processing described above and that guarantee that the outcome of this processing will achieve a certain level of relevance.[4] This puts utterance processing in a privileged position with respect to other competing attention-seeking features of the environment. According to RT, a signaled communication prompts the cognitive processing described above; in other words, an utterance (or an ostensive act) generated by a speaker's intended meaning, is worth processing. Consider Thom Scott-Phillips's (2014: 86) description of a well-circulated example, about an ostensively empty glass (originally Sperber & Wilson, 1986, but also see Csibra, 2010; Tomasello, 2008; Tomasello et al., 2007):

Suppose that we are in a bar. My glass, which is visible to both of us, is empty. It is possible that I would like another drink, but unless I say or do something to indicate as much, you would not have any grounds to conclude that I do want a drink. If, however, I pick up my glass and wave it in front of you, then, by the Communicative Principle, I effectively announce that the emptiness of my glass has an interpretation that is relevant for you. Knowing this, you now have grounds to conclude that I do indeed want a further drink.

This is a nonverbal form of communicating. But it is a valid description of every utterance because, according to RT, *speaking* to an addressee is, in itself, a way to provide evidence that the utterance is worth the addressee's time and that it pays to begin processing it.

So, one central idea is that a listener needs to recognize that the speaker has a *communicative* intention, that is, that the speaker intends the listener to become aware of something that the speaker wants to communicate. This is comparable to what I have been calling the *that* intention with respect to Grice's account. Making my addressee aware of my intention to communicate is akin to my making an ostensive signal that will prompt my addressee to stand up and notice, so to speak, that there is a communication that I, the speaker, would like to complete. The fact that we, as humans, have figured out how to get people's attention through a noise, a grunt, or more generally a signal that tells the addressee "Look, I have something that I want to tell you" is a central part of intention gathering and is generally referred to technically as an *ostension*. The communicator is making it mutually manifest that she wants the addressee to notice something, along with the promise that it is worth processing. Just as ostensive acts were central to Grice's proposal,[5] so are they to RT's.

This is just part of the story. Once the communicative intention is made "manifest," there is still the interpretation process. The addressee needs to figure out *what* it is that the speaker or communicator wants to impress upon him. The *what* (as we saw with Grice) is referred to in RT as the speaker's *informative* intention, which is the speaker's desired state of affairs that wants to be impressed upon the addressee and that the addressee is going to try to figure out. An utterance or a nonverbal communicative act (e.g., waving a glass to indicate "more to drink") will help do that, but these get the listener only part of the way. Given that linguistic pragmatics is mostly concerned with utterances, let us focus on these.

How does processing work? According to RT, the presumption of optimal relevance conveyed by every utterance is precise enough to ground a specific comprehension heuristic that basically tells one to take the utterance and use inference making to insert premises or conclusions that provide the most reasonable interpretation. Moreover, one should do so in the most economical way possible, so one should stop when relevance has been satisfied. Much like with any thirst, one knows intrinsically when one has had enough. This is how RT puts it:

Presumption of optimal relevance:

(a) The utterance is relevant enough to be worth processing;
(b) It is the most relevant one compatible with communicator's abilities and preferences.

Relevance-guided comprehension heuristic:

(a) Follow a path of least effort in constructing an interpretation of the utterance (and in particular in resolving ambiguities and referential indeterminacies, in going beyond linguistic meaning, in computing implicatures, etc.).
(b) Stop when your expectations of relevance are satisfied.

Sperber and Wilson (1986/1995)

Relevance theory begins by assuming that listeners are aware of their surroundings and that they can pick out when something gets their attention.

To appreciate RT's approach with a single set of similar verbal statements, imagine that I have spoken to my son, Isaac, twice today about a ping-pong tournament in which he is competing. During the first call, he informed me that he had made it to the semifinals. The second call was to tell me he won his last two matches, meaning that he had won the tournament. Now consider three ways – in (2.9a–c) – in which he could have shared the second bit of news.

(2.9) a. "I won my last two matches."
      b. "I won my last two matches, against Johan and Sylvain."
      c. "I won my last two matches, against Johan and then Sylvain."

If all I cared about was my son's performance, the cognitive *effect* of the three sentences would be the same, because all three versions lead to the conclusion that he won the tournament. On the other hand, the added information in versions (2.9b) and (2.9c) would only be adding extra information, reducing their relevance in terms of costs. That is, in wearing my egocentric-papa hat, (2.9a) would be more relevant than both (2.9b) and (2.9c), because knowing the names of those he defeated adds unnecessary processing costs.

Now imagine that I know the two boys he mentioned (in fact, Johan and Sylvain are Isaac's good friends and they all practice at the same club; moreover, I am the club's treasurer so I know that the three often dominate competitions). For the sake of clarity, I will add that I do not know the fourth semifinalist. In this scenario, the information in (2.9a) would not achieve optimal relevance because I would not know against whom exactly Isaac played from the semifinal onward. While wearing my informed-club-treasurer hat, (2.9a) is less relevant than (2.9b) in terms of effects, for (2.9a) does not indicate that Isaac played against both of his fellow club-members. Nevertheless, (2.9b) would still appear as slightly underwhelming. If Isaac first beat Johan and then Sylvain, that would mean that Sylvain came in second (because he lost the final) and that Johan could have come in, at best, third (assuming the two losers of each semifinal play against one another). If Isaac first beat Sylvain, that would mean Johan came in second. The sentence in (2.9b) provides fewer effects than (2.9c), which adds sequence. Both the number of propositions and the precision in them increase by stating (2.9c). Below, in (2.10a–c), there is a summary of the effects from each of the possibilities in (2.9a–c):

(2.10) a. Isaac won the tournament (full stop).
       b. Isaac won the tournament. While Johan and Sylvain did not win the tournament, one of them is runner-up.
       c. Isaac won the tournament. While Johan and Sylvain did not win the tournament, Sylvain is runner-up.

While there is a minimal processing cost for having an extra word "then" in (2.9c), with respect to (2.9b), this extra effort in processing is compensated by generating further cognitive effects. The number and precision of the conclusions drawn (the cognitive effects) grow as we move from (2.9a) to (2.9c).

Let's briefly highlight key features of Grice's theory again and describe how it is expressed (either similarly or not) in RT terminology. Grice presented his principles as a way to provide a rational reconstruction of a speaker's behavior. Relevance theory's principles are employed as part of a descriptive theory, used to explain how utterances are decoded so that pragmatic inferences are made. While Grice's maxims are designed to describe how listeners are destined to come up with interpretations that maintain the conversational principle through, for example, flouting or the detection of under- or overinformativity, RT is designed to explain how a listener arrives at a set of assumptions (or propositions) based on a speaker's utterance. While speakers engage with Gricean maxims (either they respect them at the level of what is said or they respect them at the level of what is meant), in the RT approach there are no maxims that set in motion new interpretations. Rather, there are interpretations made with greater or lesser accuracy or with greater or lesser confidence. For RT, the very act of communicating raises in the intended audience precise and predictable expectations of *relevance*, which are enough on their own to guide the hearer toward the speaker's meaning. Speakers may fail to be relevant, but they may not, if they are communicating at all, produce utterances that do not convey a presumption of their own relevance.

Convention and Common Ground:
The Adventures of Lewis and Clark

One way to look at the contributions from the neo-Gricean and post-Gricean accounts is to note that, while Levinson and Horn were concerned chiefly with Grice's Maxims of Conversation (1989) and how people derive enrichments from sentences in a quasi-automatic away, RT was inspired by Grice's thesis on nonnatural meaning (1957) and how communication is based on making intentions manifest by ostensive behavior. Another philosopher who was influenced by Grice's early writings was David Lewis, who viewed mutually manifest intentions as primary to communication and eventually addressed the way conventions play a role in language and behavior.

While Grice described how intentions are shared when a speaker induces a belief in her audience, Lewis argued that meaning is the result of a natural coordination of intentions between speakers and addressees. This kind of coordination is not limited to language but applies to any behavior that calls for simple solutions that will maximize results at a low cost. Take, for example, the side of the road one drives on. Groups of people could decide to drive either on the right side of the road (e.g., in the United States and Continental Europe) or on the left side of the road (e.g. in the United Kingdom and Japan); but once it has been decided, it is going to be the maximal choice because it limits traffic jams and accidents. Another example Lewis gave was calling someone back after getting cut off on the phone. He argued that, through convention, the caller would call back – partly because it was easier. If this sounds like game theory, that is not surprising because Lewis was influenced by Schelling (1960), who went on to win the Nobel Prize in Economics for his work on game theory and developed a notion of a *coordination device* in order to describe how coordination problems are resolved.

As far as language and communication go, Lewis – like Grice – proposed that meaning emerges from the *coordination* between a speaker and a hearer. The speaker has communicative intentions to impose and the addressee has expectations to fulfill, and the two interlocutors succeed because they maintain a convention of truthfulness. Rather than work out a speaker's intention through ostensive signals at each encounter, shared intentions are presumed to be there from the start by virtue of shared common knowledge. When a speaker asks the hearer, "Do you have the key?," the addressee needs to know which key is the intended one, and the answer can depend on any one of many factors:

Most situations – perhaps every situation for people who are practiced at this kind of game – provide some clue for coordination behavior, some focal point for each person's expectation of what the other expects him to expect to be expected to do. Finding the key, or rather *a* key – any key that is mutually recognized as the key becomes *the* key – may depend on imagination more than on logic; it may depend on analogy, precedent, accidental arrangement, symmetry, aesthetic or geometric configuration, casuistic reasoning, and who the parties are and what they know about each other. (Schelling, 1960: 57)

Herb Clark developed a Lewis-inspired theory underscoring the importance of joint activity. Rather than view communication in a "listener-free" way, which nearly every other Gricean and post-Gricean theory assumes, Clark (1996) views utterance interpretation as a joint act akin to many others, from driving on the road, to dancing and playing duets, sharing gossip, and much else. Critical to Clark's thesis is that interlocutors seek "common ground" that comprises shared assumptions or shared knowledge along with newly constructed knowledge through joint actions. When two physicians meet, they share quite a bit already – e.g., medical training and a technical language – and they can go on to share much more in conversation. Utterance is a joint act that no longer works if one of the partners is absent.

Clark's vision considers the speaker and listener as equally active in constructing utterance interpretation (which explains why listeners cash out their participation with "ah-hums," "yeahs," and head shakes) and represents a different approach entirely. I underline the differences partly because Clark's claims have come with some diminishing comments about Grice-inspired notions; for example, Clark writes that the effort to reduce the number of Grice's maxims is, as is done by the neo-Griceans and RT, "misdirected," since "Grice's rules of thumb can never be more than that – rules of thumb" (1996: 146). One might wonder how this approach has found a place in an area – experimental pragmatics – that considers Grice so central. The fact is that Clark's approach, while starting out from a different set of assumptions about coordination, has been very productive and innovative with respect to key pragmatic phenomena and particularly with respect to reference and irony.

Where Do We Go from Here?

Now that we have described (critical parts of) the theoretical playing field, we are in a better position to evaluate these theories through experimentation. The goal will be to investigate individual claims or, better still, to set up experiments that can compare competing theories. But, our pre-experimental preparations are still not complete. We need to think about what it is that we want to accomplish when we carry out an experiment. It pays to appreciate the scientific attitude needed when preparing an experiment. We need to understand how experimentation can be applied to psychological – and now psycholinguistic – settings. Just as I did for pragmatics, it pays to provide a little background on experimental psychology so that we can better appreciate why it became useful generally to run psychological experiments and for our current concerns specifically.

Notes

1. The source for this distinction comes from Grice's definition of meaning. In order to mean something by an utterance, the utterer must intend the addressee:

   (1) to produce a particular response r
   (2) to think (recognise) that the utterer intends (1).
   (3) to fulfill (1) on the basis of his fulfillment of (2).

   This third clause (3) is understood as stipulating that the addressee's recognition of the utterer's intention in (1) must be "at least part of his reason for producing r, and not merely the cause of his producing r" (Grice, 1989: 92). As Sperber and Wilson (2015) write, "Despite some debate in the literature about whether this third clause was needed (Bach, 1987; Neale, 1992; Recanati, 1986; Schiffer, 1972; Vlach,

1981; Wharton, 2009), it remained central to Grice's later discussions of meaning and his distinction between natural and nonnatural meaning" (Grice, 1989: 290–7, 349–59).

2. For example, bees code direction through dance, and vervet monkeys code three different alarms (one for snakes, one for leopards, and one for eagles) without expressly (presumably) paying notice to, or confirming the recognition of, the interlocutor.

3. There are of course exceptions, such as a short letter of recommendation written for John Nash, proclaiming him a mathematical genius.

4. As will be seen later, the level of expected relevance is defined as (i) relevant enough to be worth processing and (ii) the most relevant modulo the speaker's abilities and preferences.

5. Through his second and third intentions.

3 The Experimentalist's Mindset

> Everyone, left to his own devices, forms an idea about what goes on in language which is very far from the truth.
>
> *Ferdinand de Saussure (1910)*

Scholars of linguistic pragmatics often present "pragmatic anomalies" (typically denoted with a # in linguistics papers) to make theoretical claims. These are sentences that are considered odd or surprising, and whose strangeness begs for a principled explanation. They are essentially exceptions that justify a theorist's rule. To make this concrete, consider these four examples:

(3.1) I went inside a house today and found a tortoise inside the front door.

(3.2) He is rich nor (is he) handsome.

(3.3) If Paul or Bill and not both come, Monica will be upset.

(3.4) John lives in Paris or France.

The first can be found in Paul Grice's (1989) original work and the second in Larry Horn's (1989) classic text on negation and pragmatics, while the third comes from a talk I heard by Gennaro Chierchia, and the fourth is a well-known constraint about disjunctions that linguists like to discuss, known as the Hurford constraint.

When I was more of an outsider to linguistic pragmatics, I found these kinds of anomalies surprising for two reasons. First, I was amazed at how language scholars seemed to agree that certain utterances were anomalous, whereas I would (easily) come up with interpretations for them (typically by imagining contexts for each). To make my case, let me return to the above examples. The statement in (3.1) is supposed to be surprising, if one later learns that the mentioned house was the speaker's own house (which should signal a possessive or definite article, as in "I went inside *my* house" or "I went inside *the* house"). However, if one knows that the speaker has several homes (imagine he is a landlord), there is no surprise at all. The statement in (3.2) is supposed to contrast poorly (from a pragmatic point of view) with an acceptable version, i.e., "He is rather poor, nor is he exactly handsome." However, if one considers the possession of wealth as a negative quality, then (3.2) is perfectly interpretable (whether meant sincerely or in jest), and the attitude need not be so difficult to see. As far as (3.3) is concerned, Gennaro wanted to point out that exclusive disjunctions in the antecedents of conditionals are difficult to parse. We will take up the theory later (see Chapter 7), but when I first heard the example (and saw it coupled with a #), I did not see what was wrong with it. I was able to conjure up a scenario that would make sense. For example, imagine a situation in which Paul and Bill are fighting and Monica wants the two to make up. If only one of the two comes (to a party perhaps), it would be evidence that there had been no peace process. The fourth case (3.4) is supposed to be difficult because the constraint says a speaker will not include a set and its subset. While (3.4) might reflect a rare turn of phrase, it is not nonexistent. Potts et al. (2016) have found attested examples of "violations" of the constraint on the Internet from taxi companies that service areas such as San Francisco or Northern California. So, as far as making general rules about pragmatic inferences goes, I think it behooves us to be careful when relying on intuition, even (or perhaps especially) expert ones. In the case of these so-called infelicitous sentences, it is often not too difficult to discern something meaningful from a speaker's utterance. My own intuitions are able to counter another's.

Whenever I realized that I was not in league with other audience members or with the author's intended readers, I initially assumed that – as an experimental psychologist (i.e., an outsider) – I just did not have the level of expertise necessary to notice what was pragmatically odd about such cases. Looking back on it now, I do not think there was anything wrong with me. My current view is that language researchers rely on their intuitions to create what appears to be a pattern; once established, the pattern (which is sometimes considered a *constraint*) makes exceptions apparent. These exceptions are the anomalies. But this does not mean that the out-of-the-blue examples themselves are through-and-through nonsensical. The so-called anomalies could be entirely sensible and meaningful in other contexts (and without requiring a twisted worldview). The critical theoretical step appears to occur when armchair categorizations (of pragmatic phenomena) arise through intuitive judgments or introspection. As Dan Sperber and I (Noveck & Sperber, 2007) wrote, this kind of approach is dodgy:

Genuine pragmatic intuitions are those that addressees have about the intended meaning of an utterance addressed to them ... it is important to keep in mind that these are not about how an utterance is interpreted, but about how an utterance would be interpreted if it were produced in a specific situation by a speaker addressing a listener, with referring expressions having actual referents, and so on. These intuitions are educated guesses – and, no doubt, generally good ones – about hypothetical pragmatic facts, but are not themselves pragmatic facts and they may well be in error. That is, we may be wrong about how, in fact, we would interpret a given utterance in a given context.

Given that an utterance occurs in a given place and at a given time, which can have enormous effects on the way it is interpreted, it is difficult to make general claims about the intended meaning of an utterance from its structure. Relying on intuitions to create categories and to make pragmatic judgments can lead to incorrect conclusions.

Would one want to put a blanket ban on intuition-based linguistic data? Actually, no, because there are cases where it is helpful to use intuitions for data-collecting. In some linguistic areas, such as for syntactic judgments, it is arguably useful to employ one's own intuition (i.e., a native speaker's intuition) to determine whether a sentence is grammatically correct or not. The same holds for making observations about semantic entailments. For example, one arguably does not need to carry out experiments to point out that the meaning of "John is smart and handsome" entails (logically includes) that "John is handsome," or to note that when it is true that "all of the students are playing football, it guarantees (monotonically) that "all of the students are playing a sport" (see Katsos et al., 2016).[1] These are semantic facts that can be recovered by logical intuition.[2]

To get back to my early encounters with (scholarly approaches to) so-called pragmatic anomalies, the second reason why I found them surprising (again, as an experimental psychologist) is that the analysis of anomalies (along with the underlying patterns that the anomalies break) strongly relies on introspection. As any experimentalist will argue, the history of experimental psychology should make one doubtful about the scientific value of introspective techniques. In fact, introspection as a source of data is anathema to experimental psychologists. This is why, in the rest of this chapter, I want to provide some historical background to experimental and cognitive psychology. We will see that the earliest attempts at psychological data gathering relied on introspection and that these attempts failed. This led to an anti-introspectionist crusade in the early part of the twentieth century, which then led to the advent of objective measure-taking of observable behavior. We will then see that the inclusion of higher-level cognition in the mid- to late-1950s led to the onset of modern cognitive science. My ultimate aim is (a) to show how experimentalists address psychological questions, and (b) to underline how contributions are made by cognitive psychology. Such a summary can serve as a guide for understanding an experimental psychologist's approach to empirical investigation, which extends to experimental pragmatics.

Experimental Psychology: A Very Condensed History

Wilhelm Wundt established the world's first psychology laboratory in Leipzig in 1879. His main focus concerned conscious experience. Wundt's method consisted of putting a trained observer (typically one of his students) in front of a scene and having him (they were typically men) describe a particular perceptual experience. This was done while a second lab assistant recorded the first's description. For example, in what was called the *flying colors* experiment, the observer was requested to look toward a window as a curtain behind it was rolled up. This would occur during the day, so that the curtain's removal would flood the room – and the participant's eyes – with light. Because Wundt and his school were determined to get at pure observations, the student-experts were requested to separate their internal perceptions from the experience (in a way analogous to a chemist who aims to break down salt into its component parts). After twenty seconds of staring toward a vertical bar in the window, the participant closed his eyes and reported what he saw. This would last several minutes. When carried out with several subjects, these expert introspections were expected to lead to a certain "uniformity of the phenomenon [that] soon becomes apparent" (this and the following are quotes from Titchener, a student of Wundt's, Schwitzgebel, 2004); in other words, the expectation was that "observers who at first gave radically different accounts of the after-image will reach agreement upon all essential points." This approach, based on the idea that perception – and psychology in general – was made of components, came to be known as *Structuralism*.

Structuralism turned out to be neither as productive nor as reliable as expected. In fact, the data proved to be so unreliable that Structuralism was largely abandoned. The hope that trained experts could isolate perceptual features (what would probably be called *qualia* today) and provide consistent descriptions of them in identical conditions proved to be elusive.[3] This sort of failure contributed to a radical break from the Structuralist school – one that opened up psychology to an entirely new approach.

In 1913, John Watson wrote what was essentially a manifesto against this existing order and declared that progress in psychology could be gained only through *behaviorist psychology* (see Schultz, 1975). The manifesto attacked the study of consciousness and the experimental reliance on introspectionism. This is Watson's (1913) opening paragraph from the *Psychological Review*:

Psychology as the behaviorist views it is a purely objective experimental branch of natural science. Its theoretical goal is the prediction and control of behavior. Introspection forms no essential part of its methods, nor is the scientific value of its data dependent upon the readiness with which they lend themselves to interpretation in terms of consciousness.

This influential approach put the focus on observables, specifically with respect to animal behavior. It thus concentrated its efforts on classical conditioning, operant conditioning, and learning, and gave birth to the laboratory rat, which would be placed in a chamber for the psychologist to observe under varying conditions. For example, one could determine whether a rat learned that the presence of a sound indicates that a "reinforcement" (e.g., a pellet of food) is available, or whether the rat learned that pressing a bar a minimal number of times prompts the appearance of a reward (again, pellets of food). Theory-making was limited to observable outcomes in constrained situations and solid data-collecting reigned supreme. This transformation from introspection to observable data-collecting augured an approach and nomenclature that has since become commonplace among psychologists. It is safe to say that specialists and nonspecialists understand what it means when an experimenter introduces an *independent variable* and what it means when she measures the outcome, which is the *dependent variable*.

This effort paid off. Non-introspective experiments provided reliable results and replicable experiments. To give an example of a Wundtian topic (attention) that was transformed into an elegant objective study, consider the classic, eponymously named Stroop task (Stroop, 1935), which got its start in 1931 (apparently there was a similar and less-known attempt slightly earlier; see MacLeod, 1992) and holds the record for the most replicated study in psychology. In this task, participants are presented with a word or a colored geometric shape as a stimulus, and are then required to name the color of the word's or shape's ink (or, these days, pixels). The celebrated finding, the one that made this task so reliable and intriguing (even and especially decades later), is that participants experienced interference (and are thus slowed down) when the printed word and the ink color are in conflict with one another. For example, imagine a correct response is to say "black" when the stimulus is the word "RED" (which refers to the color of the letters in this word). To make such a claim, one needs to compare these experimental cases to control items, which would be: (a) trials in which color-names and ink-colors are consistent, or (b) trials whose stimuli are colored shapes instead of words. The most prominent explanation for this effect is that the automatic processing of reading the word interferes with, or even precedes, the ability to detect and name the color of the ink (or pixels). This classic task does not score many theoretical points (it points to interference when two processes compete) and it does not rely on reinforcement (as behaviorist studies famously do), but it does reveal how psychological processes can be consistently measured through third-person measurements, and without gauging one's own internal (automatic) perceptions.

As part of this very concise history, it is important to underline the Gestalt school's impact on experimental psychology. Gestalt psychology, which dates back to the early twentieth century and was centered in Berlin, is concerned not with breaking down a stimulus into its component parts but with the way observers form a whole from what they perceive. This explains why one of the credos of Gestalt psychology is that "the whole is other than the sum of its parts."[4] As the fine writer Michael Lewis (2016) put it, Gestalt psychologists

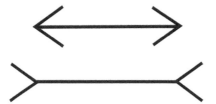

Figure 3.1. A depiction of the Müller-Lyer illusion

posed "the question that the behaviorists had elected to ignore: 'How does the brain create meaning?'" This is why Gestalt psychologists would ask what the principles are behind the way we group units together (whether they concern proximity, common movement, color, size, etc.), as opposed to viewing units as a rag-tag ensemble. They would analyze phenomena in which we infer motion when all we are seeing is a sequence of lights being turned off and on in quick succession (as another example of inferred motion, consider the movement we see when a flip-book animates a stick figure when all we actually see is a stack of pictures). We as observers impose our interpretations onto phenomena that do not exist as such in nature. Gestalt psychology has provided the framework for investigating many illusions that now populate all fields of psychology (but especially perception). Let me mention two, the Müller-Lyer illusion and the McGurk effect. The Müller-Lyer illusion (Figure 3.1) shows two lines whose outward and inward tails provide the illusion that the shafts of the arrows are of different lengths, even if we *know* that the two lines are of equal lengths.

An illusion from speech perception is the McGurk effect (McGurk & MacDonald, 1976). This effect, which was discovered by accident when the two authors were preparing some materials for an experiment, refers to the way we hear sounds differently when watching lips. If I were to play a recording of my voice making the sound "ba-ba," but I formed my lips so as to simulate making the sound "fa-fa," it is the latter sound one would hear (one can find examples on YouTube). In other instances, we can perceive a third sound that neither the lips are forming, nor the (previous) recording is making. The way an utterance can express a speaker's meaning in a way that goes beyond the contributions made by its linguistic components can easily be viewed as a Gestaltian undertaking.

To return to our condensed history, behaviorism's focus on observable behavior (such as key presses or reaction times) was largely responsible for generating methodological advances in psychology. The drawback, however, was that it forced certain high-level and less visible behaviors, such as thinking, language, and communication, to take a back seat to learning, conditioning, and other areas. After all, the argument would go, thinking and language comprehension are not readily quantifiable or observable (nor would it be ethical to create controlled laboratory conditions that reinforce certain forms of thinking or that interrupt language learning). Eventually, B. F. Skinner, one of the leading lights of the Behaviorist school, did provide an account of language in *Verbal Behavior* (Skinner, 1957), a book based on his 1948 William James Lectures (for a more cogent defense, see Skinner, 1986). Skinner described how a sound could eventually be viewed as reinforcement for an act. For example, babbling among infants can be viewed as "essentially random sounds that, when picked up by reinforcers" help determine which sounds to keep[5] as part of one's native language (Skinner, 1986). A "tact," as Skinner described it, is a nonreferential feature of language that can nevertheless serve as a prompt. For example, if a traveling salesman sees a fish on his client's wall, its presence could raise the probability that the salesman will use the word "fishing" while searching for an item in his suitcase.

It was Noam Chomsky who, through his devastating review of B. F. Skinner's book (Chomsky, 1959), played a pivotal role in ushering the next movement in psychology, the Cognitive Revolution. On the one hand, he pointed out how behaviorist concepts such as *stimulus* and *response* are ill-equipped to deal with language phenomena and how the notion of reinforcement is overused to the point that it has little meaning.[6] On the other hand, he underlined how a behaviorist approach fails to account for "the remarkable capacity of the child to generalize, hypothesize, and 'process information' in a variety of very special and apparently highly complex ways which we cannot yet describe or begin to understand, and which may be largely innate," and furthermore, it fails to account for a child's syntactic competence, even though the input – from which a language is learned – is imperfect. For the Cognitive Revolution, this review, along with a focus on internal representations, brought on interactions among linguists, philosophers, anthropologists, psychologists, and others interested in human and nonhuman comprehension. One of the first experimental topics to emerge in this era was psycholinguistics (Rieber, 1980). By combining theories of internal mechanisms (such as language) along with rigorous methodology, the field of psychology put itself in a position to study higher-level cognitive processing.

By the time the cognitive turn prompted psychologists to look carefully at higher-order mental events, experimental psychology had inherited the tough-minded methodology that made behaviorist studies so forceful. The net result is that today's cognitive psychology investigates people's hidden mental processes, e.g., reasoning, memory, or language, by using observable data that usually come from participants who are not even aware of an experiment's objectives. Third-person investigations collect data from unsuspecting participants who are asked to hear utterances or to read sentences or lines of text.[7] Based on their reactions (e.g., truth judgments, self-paced reading times, or noninvasive neurological measures), an experimenter can isolate the proposed factors that affect outcomes.

To provide a notable example, consider a question that has long preoccupied philosophers and psychologists, which is, "How do we cognitively represent images?" Are images manipulated cognitively as such, or do we represent them propositionally? Cooper and Shepard (1973) cleverly addressed this question by asking participants to determine whether a letter that was presented at different angles (tilted to some degree or other) would be in its standard or else inverted position if it were put upright. For example, imagine a case where the letter "R" is presented lying on its spine, so to speak, with its rounded head above on the right and its tail emerging upward and leftward; if this letter were to be put upright, it would appear inverted. Cooper and Shepard had such stimuli presented at different angles and found that the length of time to answer corresponded with the amount of mental rotation necessary to respond on the task (plus, inverted images caused a categorical slowdown compared to letters in a standard position). This indicated, rather decisively, that people represent objects and manipulate them internally as if they existed in the outside world.

Cognitive Psychology Itself Investigates Intuitive Judgments

Given the history of experimental psychology and its learned avoidance of introspection, it is perhaps not surprising to see that experimental psychologists would actually investigate the way participants *make* intuitive judgments. Consider one of the first reasoning tasks that I got to know, Wason's (1960) 2-4-6 task, which is famous for exposing our biases when making hypotheses. In this task, participants are asked to find a rule that accounts for the sequence 2-4-6. Before they declare their rule, participants can test their hypothesis by proposing their own "triples" (to which participants get feedback). Whereas the task's official rule is a very general, "any ascending set of three numbers," most participants come up with hypotheses that are much more specific, such as "even numbers ascending by 2," and to test their rule they present triples such as 4-6-8 and then 8-10-12. Wason (1968) stressed how participants do not aim to falsify their immediate hypotheses but rather confirm them, which is why he considered the typical strategy an expression of *confirmation bias*. If participants would only seek to falsify their intuitions (i.e., if they provided triples – such as 11-13-15 or 2-5-6 – which would fit the rule while rejecting their own overly specific ones), they would make more progress. The point is, that we have a tendency as human beings to seek confirmation of our hypotheses (also known as the *myside bias*) and this is also true in scientific endeavors.

Warnings about introspective judgments do not end there. Psychologists have periodically shown how intuitions or self-reports can lead investigators astray in both the linguistic and psychological literatures (Levelt, 1972; Nisbett and Ross, 1980). Basically, these warnings tell us that we are prone to unconscious biases that could make our intuitions unreliable. As Tversky and Kahneman (1973) made abundantly clear years ago, the explanations we give ourselves are often influenced by features of a task that we are not even aware of.

For example, Tversky and Kahneman (1974) cataloged the multiple biases that manifest themselves in judgment tasks and reasoning.[8] *Availability* is the name they gave to one sort of bias, which describes how people judge the frequency of an event "by the ease with which instances or associations come to mind." For example, in one of Tversky and Kahneman's (1973, Experiment 3) well-known studies, a large majority of participants were asked whether there are more words that start with the letter "R" or more words that have the letter "R" as its third character. By a 3:1 margin, typical undergraduate participants said that there are more words that start with the letter "R," even though databases show a clear preference in the opposite direction. Tversky and Kahneman's account for the effect is that we organize words in terms of their first letter and thus the ease with which we can recall these words is facilitated, which biases us when making judgments. Based on this kind of evidence, Nisbett and Wilson (1977) argued that self-reports are not reliable sources of experimental evidence.

This worry about self-reports becomes clearer still through findings from neuropsychology. Split-brain patients are people whose corpus callosum (fibers that provide a means of communication across the left and right halves of the brain) has been severed. Roger Sperry and Michael Gazzaniga, who spearheaded investigations of such patients, found clever ways to determine the division of labor between the two hemispheres. Through one, now well-known, experimental technique, Gazzaniga discovered how spontaneous verbal explanations appear to be lateralized to (and produced by) the left hemisphere. Remarkably, due to the lack of communication between hemispheres, these researchers showed how a split-brain patient could be thoroughly unaware of sources of information emanating from the right hemisphere. Let me spell this out through one, slightly involved, example.

Consider a study in which the experimenter presents an image of a scene, e.g., a snowed-in house, to the left visual field (which is processed by the right cerebral hemisphere) and then asks the split-brain participant – through options available to his left hand (also controlled by the right hemisphere) – to choose an appropriate photo from an array of otherwise-irrelevant possibilities. The participant would appropriately choose the relevant picture, i.e., a shovel, with his left hand, with the idea being that the right hemisphere is able to make the thematic connection between the snowed-in house and a shovel. So far so good. At this point, the participant is shown an image of another object, e.g., a chicken claw, to the right visual field (controlled by the left hemisphere) and asked (figuratively speaking) to pick an appropriate photo (again from an array of inappropriate options) with the right hand (still the left hemisphere). The patient would then pick out the best option – a picture of a chicken.

Critically, when asked why he chose the shovel and the chicken (which were now available to both hemispheres), a split-brain participant would say, "Oh that's simple, the chicken goes with the claw and the shovel is to *clean out the chicken shed*" (from Cooney and Gazzaniga, 2003, my italics; see their article for a nice depiction of the experimental scene). The patient seemed oblivious to the root cause of his response. Gazzaniga's (2003) explanation is that the left hemisphere answers because it controls the ability to talk – "because it could not know why the right hemisphere was doing what it was doing [rather, why it had done what it did], it made up a story about what it could see" (Gazzaniga, 2003, p. 29). The link between the two chosen pictures was essentially invented on the spot. As Cooney and Gazzaniga (2003, p. 162) write:

Studies of split-brain patients reveal that the left hemisphere of the human brain has a unique capacity to reflexively formulate causal theories about why events occur ... Strikingly, studies of both split-brain and neurologically normal individuals indicate that the interpretive process continues to function when the range of available information is incomplete.

These kinds of studies are revealing about the ease and certainty with which one can come up with causal accounts of actions already taken.[9] They also show that "reflexive causal theories" can hardly be counted on, especially when working with partial information or with inferences that are not consciously available.[10]

These observations about psychological processes carry over to intuitive judgments about infelicity. The linguistic structure of a spoken sentence comes with implicit features that can provide meanings that are beyond the theorist's immediate awareness and many examples consider contexts that are not as limited as an introspective theorist imagines. Inducing generalized rules from utterances cannot be determined confidently through introspection. We are not only prone to bias (often favoring our own preferred theoretical orientations) in making judgments, but also to introspection, which is influenced by processes that we are not even aware of. Recognizing our limitations in this regard is probably the best first step that one can make as an experimentalist. In order to do proper science (and experimental pragmatics), it pays to take an approach that will avoid introspection and that will go beyond confirming our preferred hypotheses.

How Does One Test a Theory?

Our human tendency to produce confirmatory explanations of behavioral phenomena was not lost on philosophers of science. Karl Popper (1963) recalled how he was fascinated, as a student, by the way theorists and their advocates would cling to and apply theories in his hometown of Vienna. As he put it:

> I found that those of my friends who were admirers of Marx, Freud, and Adler were impressed by a number of points common to these theories and especially by their apparent explanatory power ... The most characteristic element in this situation seemed to me the incessant stream of confirmations, of observations which "verified" the theories in question; and this point was constantly emphasized by their adherents. A Marxist could not open a newspaper without finding on every page confirming evidence for his interpretation of history ... The Freudian analysts emphasized that their theories were constantly verified by their "clinical observations."

Based on the above considerations, Popper argued that it is important to set up a system that allows for the testing and falsification of theories because when one seeks to support a theory it is easy to find corroborating evidence.[11] He argued that testing has a logic. It is more fruitful to set up paradigms that consider a prediction (deduced from a theory) that is testable (meaning *falsifiable*), rather than merely verifiable. When an experimental result turns out to *verify* a theory, it has, for the time being, passed its test (there is no reason to discard the theory). But if the decision is negative (the conclusions have been falsified), then the theory from which the conclusions were logically deduced needs to be reconsidered, i.e., rejected or reworked. Popper argued that verification gets us only so far because we are never in the position to undermine what are essentially inductively derived rules. This is not to say that verifications are useless; when they are investigated, they should be "risky" in that they provide an opportunity for the prediction to be wrong. All this explains why experimental psychologists typically adopt an attitude in which a theory to be tested is viewed skeptically rather than sacredly. It also explains what inspired Wason to later come up with his 2-4-6 task.

As we will see, experimental pragmatics is carried out with Popper's experimental approach in tow. Participants are put through their paces in a task and their results serve as an objective means to test a claim or a theory's prediction. Advances are made by (a) testing theories or hypotheses, or (b) presenting a novel or "risky" result. Then, findings ought to be confirmed in follow-ups, so that one can be sure that a result is robust.

Relevant Positive Achievements from the Cognitive Sciences

All of these warnings can leave the impression that, other than a clever experiment or two, nothing substantial will ever get done. This is far from the case. Below I present two major conceptual developments that owe their success mostly to cognitive science – Theory of Mind (often referred to as *mindreading*) and proposals about modularity. (I chose these two because they are relevant to the purposes of this book.) Mindreading is central to Grice's description of nonnatural meaning and discussions about modularity are important for understanding theoretical approaches to sentence-processing. Let us look at each of these in turn.

Theory of Mind

For nearly 40 years now, the most consistently investigated phenomenon in cognitive psychology has focused on *Theory of Mind*. Theory of Mind (ToM) refers to one's capacity to attribute beliefs and desires to others and to use those attributions to make hypotheses about another's behavior. When I see a man stop in front of a store's display, I readily suppose that something caught his attention, and when I see a boy on his hands and knees in front of a car after chasing a rolling tennis ball, I can transform his belief by telling him that I saw the ball continue rolling to the other side. Our ability to attribute intentions to observed events is so central that Daniel Dennett (1989) gave it a name, the *intentional stance*.

Initiated by the work of Premack and Woodruff (1978), who investigated whether chimpanzees have an ability to infer the mental states of human actors, investigations into this topic would soon come to dominate the cognitive sciences. Theory of Mind studies have had a huge impact on developmental psychology, especially when the question turned to: "At what age do children show mastery of Theory of Mind?" For a long while, it was practically biblical to assume that children are not competent at Theory of Mind inference-making before the age of four. Much of this evidence came from variations of the Maxi task (Wimmer & Perner, 1983), in which child-participants were shown a scene in which a boy, Maxi, had seen a chocolate cake placed in a (blue) cabinet before leaving the room. The task goes on to show (to the child-participants) that the chocolate cake is moved from the blue cabinet to another (green) cabinet. The question for the child-participant is essentially: Where will Maxi look for the cake when he rejoins the scene? The question for the experimenter is: Will a young participant be able to separate her own recently acquired knowledge about the cake's location from what Maxi last knew? The data – which are highly replicable – show that three-year-olds are practically unable to attribute "false beliefs" to the character, meaning that three-year-olds would say that Maxi would look for the cake in its current position (in the green cabinet), as opposed to Maxi's latest understanding of where it is (in the blue cabinet). The argument goes that four-year-olds, in contrast, become more competent and recognize Maxi's state of mind.

A variant on Wimmer and Perner's task, the Sally-Anne task, which would later become instrumental in investigations of autism (see Chapter 12), asks a child-participant to follow a scene in which a character (Sally) places a marble in one of two places (e.g., a basket), and is out of the room when a second character (Anne) shows up and places the marble in a different receptacle (e.g., a box). Baron-Cohen et al. (1985) reported that autistic participants (who successfully answered control questions) are much like the three-year-olds above, proposing that autistic people are lacking in a Theory of Mind. Both of these articles – Wimmer and Perner and Baron-Cohen et al. – are among the top three most-cited articles of all time in the venerable journal *Cognition* because the issues raised about Theory of Mind have generated such a vast amount of scientific inquiry, especially in developmental psychology, social neuroscience, and animal cognition.

Issues of Theory of Mind are central to experimental pragmatics because understanding a speaker's utterance depends on the listener making inferences about the speaker's intention. The utterance is critical information for accessing the speaker's meaning in the context. Consider the metaphor, "You are a tadpole," when it is made by a swim instructor to a child in her class. If this utterance were an out-of-the-blue observation to a child who a week earlier was afraid to jump in the pool, the remark could indicate encouragement and that the instructor thinks that, this week, the child seems quite comfortable. In contrast, if the same metaphoric remark were made in response to a question, such as "Can I swim across the whole pool?" one could draw a different set of assumptions. In this case, the metaphor could be taken to mean: "No, you're too young" or "What's the rush?" Here, we see the same remark in two slightly different contexts, each drawing the listener's attention to different aspects of the speaker's intentional state. Inferences about the speaker's intentions are called on in each case in order to understand the remarks. Abilities in Theory of Mind (reasoning to infer the speaker's intentions) are then needed in order to fully appreciate the speaker's meaning.

Modularity

A second important concept that emerged through the collective efforts of the cognitive sciences and that is relevant to pragmatics is modularity, which is – as the name suggests – a way to view the mind's architecture as being made up of modules dedicated to certain kinds of tasks. There are actually two well-known theoretical approaches that invoke the notion of modularity. One comes from Jerry Fodor, who proposed that specific parts of perception and cognition are handled by modules. That is, certain inputs – for example, visual and linguistic information – are considered basic to the cognitive system and are dealt with as autonomous modules. More technically, Fodor describes these modules as domain specific, innately specified, informationally encapsulated, hardwired, autonomous, and not assembled (see Coltheart, 1999). Modules are contrasted with higher level activities, such as analogical reasoning, which are carried out by a central system. One of Fodor's preferred examples for describing modules comes from the Müller-Lyer illusion. As we saw earlier, a human observer cannot help but see one of two identical lines as longer when its ends are joined to two more lines radiating outward, instead of inward. This illusion persists even when we know that the lengths of the compared lines are equal.

Another kind of account of modularity has been championed by evolutionary psychologists, such as Leda Cosmides and John Tooby, who view the human mind as a set of adaptations that have survived evolutionary pressures. They advocate for a modularity that runs throughout cognitive processing and that needs to be viewed through the prism of what helped our ancestors survive. Examples of modules include face recognition, tool-use, fear, social-exchange, kin-oriented motivation, childcare, social-inference, sexual attraction, friendship, grammar acquisition, and Theory of Mind (Tooby and Cosmides, 1992, p. 113; see Grossi, 2014, for a review). The two forms of modularity have often been confused by researchers to the point that evolutionary psychologists have had to point out that encapsulation is not a requirement of their system.[12]

It is Fodor's proposal that had an immediate impact on the sentence-processing literature, whose findings concern syntactic processing and whose techniques have had an influence on experimental pragmatics. When syntactic information is considered a module, it follows that syntax has an encapsulating role to play in the processing of language. Lyn Frazier (1979), for example, argued that syntactic structures are automatically engaged and that other contextual factors should not come into play immediately. This could explain how readers or listeners go about disambiguating sentences. Consider (3.5), which has two readings:

(3.5) Michael opened the safe with the dynamite.

One reading has the safe getting blown up *by* dynamite and the other has Michael opening the safe *containing* dynamite. Both are feasible (to appreciate the second one more readily, change the word *safe* to *cabinet* and the word *dynamite* to *chocolate*). Modularists argued that syntax is processed automatically by a cognitive subsystem and that its results are as automatic as those found with respect to perception in the Müller-Lyer illusion (for a summary, see Altmann, 1998). With this viewpoint in mind, Frazier suggested that the preferred reading is the first one I described *because* it is less complicated syntactically and is thus more readily accessible.[13]

An alternative point of view is that syntax does not determine how people interpret sentences, but that context interacting with sentences does. According to the *constraint satisfaction* approach (Trueswell & Tanenhaus, 1994), alternative interpretations arise during sentence processing and are graded as a function of background features, i.e., preferred readings are not based solely on syntax, but rather on several features that include frequencies of occurrence (of one kind of syntactic structure) and plausibility. For example, if I were to provide supporting context for (3.5) indicating that there were two safes, one with jewels and another with dynamite, it would seem highly plausible to understand that the dynamite was not an instrument for blowing up the safe, but rather its contents (despite the fact that this second scenario seems improbable). That contextual factors influence interpretations resonates with pragmatic sorts of phenomena, and will be introduced later.

Much like in the sentence-comprehension literature, experimental pragmatics sets up paradigms in which sentences have two potential interpretations. An important difference is that in experimental pragmatics one meaningful reading typically leads to a true evaluation, while another leads to a false evaluation. Another key difference is that paradigms in experimental pragmatic literature usually test a Post-Gricean theory or, preferably, compare two theories. The following are some of the questions asked:

- To what extent is the linguistically encoded stimulus alone responsible for an interpretive reading?
- To what extent does context resolve a choice between two different readings?
- To what extent is a true reading relevant to an interpretation?
- When there are two or more possible readings, which requires more effort?
- To what extent does a listener's capacities and tendencies determine a preferred reading?

Where Do We Go from Here?

We began the chapter by trying to appreciate how a theorist of language goes about developing and evaluating pragmatic hypotheses, which inevitably leads to the forming of categories and the pointing out of exceptions. I argued that using (only) introspection about pragmatic phenomena can lead to incorrect conclusions because, in pragmatics, every individual utterance is intricately connected to the context in which it was made and, besides, introspection is a flawed process. This is not to say that the theories themselves are intrinsically questionable, but that introspective methods are not reliable. This contrasts with an experimentalist approach, which entails severely testing theories and not merely confirming them. Along the way we considered some historical findings and two developments – Theory of Mind and Modularity – that were advanced by experimental investigations. This approach has been used profitably for nearly a century and is ideal for experimental pragmatics. In the next chapter, we will consider some of the better-known techniques that have been used to gather data and we will then be in a position to start reviewing experimental pragmatic phenomena in Chapter 5.

Notes

1. Quantifiers that guarantee inferences from sets to supersets in this way are known as *monotone increasing*, and quantifiers, such as "none," that guarantee supersets to sets are known as *monotone decreasing* (e.g., "None of the students are playing football" entails that "None of the students are playing football in the rain").

2. That said, it would pay to determine how and whether participants perform when one utterance entails another. For example, Braine et al. (1995) showed that the *A&B therefore A* inference is exploited but is often not explicitly articulated in a reasoning task that required participants to write down every logical step.

3. A more modern approach to the study of unconscious processes emerged in the 1980s, but this hardly resembles Wundt's approach. For example, Dehaene et al. (2001) showed how *masked words*, which are strings presented for a brief moment (29 milliseconds), but that are bookended by scribbles, which prevent participants from saying that they even see a word, nevertheless prompt cerebral activity in a subset of the regions that are activated when words are unmasked and correctly read out.

4. As my colleague (and historian of psychology) Csaba Pleh put it to me, the idea behind Gestaltism is that "Wholes are primary; parts are secondary."

5. This is not too far from Eimas et al. (1971), who showed that even 1-month-olds the world over can discriminate between syllables, such as /ba/ and /pa/, even if some of them lose that ability as adults (if their language community does not exploit the distinction).

6. Here's the tail end of Chomsky's (1959, p. 59) very long list of cited uses of reinforcement: "An individual may also find it reinforcing to injure someone by criticism or by bringing bad news, or to publish an experimental result which upsets the theory of a rival (p. 154), to describe circumstances which would be reinforcing if they were to occur (p. 165), to avoid repetition (p. 222), to 'hear' his own name though in fact it was not mentioned or to hear nonexistent words in his child's babbling (p. 259), to clarify or otherwise intensify the effect of a stimulus which serves an important discriminative function (p. 416), and so on."

7. There are some seminal findings that could be mistaken for introspection. For example, Ebbinghaus famously used himself as a subject to capture the rate of forgetting "nonsense" words (non-meaningful three letter words such as "DAX"), but this was more of an attempt to objectify himself (other "participants" were expected to provide similar outcomes and they did).

8. Kahneman and Tversky's prodigious research program led to a very influential view that separates reasoning into two systems. One that is intuitive and a second that is more reflective (see Kahneman, 2011).

9. Also see the literature on Choice blindness (Johansson et al., 2009), which reveals how people justify their explanations for a choice (with respect to, say, face preference), even when their original choice was furtively replaced by the option declined.

10. Mercier and Sperber (2011, 2017) have proposed Argumentation Theory to explain reasoning from an evolutionary perspective; it is built upon the insight that we, as humans, instinctively come up with reasons to explain things and many of these reasons are wrong. The theory proposes that reasoning is based on representing

other's representations, which allows groups of people to, among other things, correct others' false conclusions. In fact, we are better at correcting our own false conclusions when we think that they come from someone else (Trouche et al., 2016).

11. This led Wason (1960) to carry out his seminal experiment showing how participants, when given the opportunity, aim to confirm hypotheses as opposed to falsify them.

12. From a video interview with Robert Wright (see Wright, 2014).

13. See Altmann (1998).

4   A Consideration of Experimental Techniques

And we'll call it experimental pragmatics.

Dan Sperber (to author, circa 1997)

Nearly all the pieces are in place for doing experimental pragmatics. We have described the phenomena that call for a pragmatic account, we have provided the philosophical context that brought about Gricean theory, and we have briefly accounted for the way experimentalists approach their scientific vocation. Missing are descriptions of specific methodologies, which are largely inherited from experimental psychology. These are the last introductory steps to complete our panorama before taking on issues of experimental pragmatics. Globally, data collection concerns how a listener reacts. Production studies are generally rarer, even if they are equally important. We will start with a fundamental form of pragmatic data – developmental investigations – before turning to methods that measure reactions at the millisecond level. We will then examine neuroscientific methods and conclude with the latest innovation, crowdsourcing.

Developmental Data

I remember being stuck in a traffic jam when my daughter, who was seven at the time and sitting behind me in her booster chair, said, "When there is a lot of traffic, there is a lot of pollution." Pleased by her astute observation, I responded straightaway and idiomatically by saying, "You can say that again!" There was a very brief pause before she came back with the following: "When there is a lot of traffic, there is a lot of pollution." I giggled when I heard her reply, and became slightly ashamed when I realized that she was serious. She did not understand why her response was the source of laughter (after all, she was making a serious statement and I even asked her to repeat it!). Communicational confusion aside, her reaction resonated with two oft-reported findings in the developmental pragmatic literature. One is that she took my idiomatic reply literally, and the other is that she was not being ironic.

As we saw in the last chapter and will continue to see throughout this book, developmental findings have often been central to cognitive investigations. Piaget's famous research program assumed that children become more logical with age (see Chapter 5). Linguists, too, point out how children become more competent with age. For example, Steven Pinker (1997) showed how children generalize the English past tense -*ed*, as in *taked*, before mastering exceptions. Not surprisingly, one of the original findings to emerge from experimental pragmatics is that children become more pragmatic with age. Specific ages are less important than the general sequence, whose arc bends toward pragmatic sophistication. So, we will be concerned with the extent to which children access the speaker's intended meaning, and the extent to which they rely on the linguistically encoded meaning of an utterance.

Developmental data are usually demonstrative, meaning they are revealing of the emergence of pragmatic (and other) behaviors. They present us with facts whose presence inform all pragmatic theories, which are usually concerned with competent adult behavior. So, one will not find many debates in experimental pragmatics that use developmental data to argue in favor of one pragmatic account over another.

Reactions at the Millisecond Level

Some of the most common techniques involve immediate reactions to utterances, which often are presented through listening or, more often, through reading. Much of the inference-making that is called on when listening is assumed to go on when reading. Reading comes with the advantage that the experimenter can more easily control the presentation of a text. For example, texts can be presented one word, one clause, or one sentence at a time, and, with the assumption that participants will not continue before fully integrating what they are reading, latencies reflect comprehension. So, when a word or a (subpart of a) sentence reliably takes longer to process than a control item (a sentence that is as similar as possible to the one investigated), the experimenter can draw conclusions about what it is the participant is doing in the more effort-demanding cases.

A second option is to provide a type of sentence that has the potential to generate two readings and determine how each prompts different reactions. For example, as will be discussed in Chapter 6, the sentence "Some cats are mammals" can be deemed true or false as a function of the way the quantifier is understood (as "Some and perhaps all" versus "Some and not all"). Reactions to such sentences can reveal how easily one interpretation is integrated versus the other. In fact, we will see how this kind of sentence prompted researchers to come up with increasingly sophisticated sentence processing designs.

Priming and Probes

Another task that has its roots in the annals of psycholinguistics comes from Swinney's (1979) investigation of ambiguous meanings. Remarkably, he found that – despite our intuitions – participants initially consider both meanings of ambiguous words, even when a context strongly supports just one of them. For example, upon hearing the word "bugs" in the sentence "The man was surprised when he found several spiders, roaches, and other bugs in the corner of the room," both the "insect" meaning and the "listening device" meaning became available immediately. He demonstrated this through cross-modal priming, which is a complicated-sounding way to say that he tested whether associated concepts are activated upon hearing a word. There are several ways to determine this, but a straightforward one is to present a letter-string on a screen and ask participants to determine whether the string forms a word or not (unbeknownst to the participant, the suddenly appearing word is occasionally related to the meaning of the word they just heard or read). It is "cross-modal" when a stimulus (the prime) comes from one sense (e.g., hearing) and the test (probe) is presented via another (e.g., a visual one). The dependent measure is the speed with which a participant determines that the letter-string is in fact a word. In this example, the probe word could be "ant" (an associate of the insect meaning) or the word "spy" (for the listening device meaning). While both are expected to be recognized as words, the question is whether the speed changes as a function of the context. Swinney showed that immediately after the presentation of the probe, both got recognized as words at equivalent speeds. Interestingly, it is only when the probe is presented slightly later in the test sentence (three syllables downstream from the ambiguous word "bugs"), that the associate of the intended meaning is identified as a word relatively faster. This is a task that can help determine the speed with which pragmatic enrichments and inferences are activated. This technique has been used mostly with respect to words in sentences that have conventional, metaphoric, or metonymic meanings (see Chapter 10).

Eye-Tracking

Another technique that addresses sentence processing and has been used extensively in experimental pragmatics is eye-tracking, a technique in which – as the name suggests – eye movements are recorded as a participant goes about a task. The technique has actually been around for a long time as a means to better understand the mind (and more recently for understanding how Internet users interact with objects on a screen). In psycholinguistics, eye-tracking has been used most notably to follow readers as they read lines of text. Eye movements are followed as the participant reads words in a sentence, or as the participant searches for something on a screen as she hears a sentence.

One psycholinguistics area in which eye-tracking techniques have informed experimental pragmatics comes from the investigation of ambiguous garden path effects, which refer to readings that run into difficulty when an unintended syntactic parsing is applied. Let's take a closer look at such effects through exemplary work from Pickering and Traxler (1998). The question is, where in a sentence do people hesitate, and at what point do they disambiguate the sentence? For instance, participants who read a sentence like the one in (4.1a) get confused because they expect "the magazine about fishing" in (4.1a) to be an object phrase of what the woman was editing, as opposed to being a noun phrase about what amused the reporters. Given that the absence of a comma in (4.1a) can provide an implausible reading, the experimenters included a comma after "edited" in (4.1b) in order to avoid it. To create a more psychologically plausible reading, the experimenters provided a version where the verb "edited" was replaced by "sailed," as in (4.1c,) and, to round out the possibilities, the authors also had a condition that had both a plausible reading and a comma, as in (4.1d).

(4.1a)   As the woman edited the magazine about fishing amused all the reporters.

(4.1b)   As the woman edited, the magazine about fishing amused all the reporters.

(4.1c)   As the woman sailed the magazine about fishing amused all the reporters.

(4.1d)   As the woman sailed, the magazine about fishing amused all the reporters.

Researchers in this area usually define regions of interest for their analyses. In this case, Pickering and Traxler broke the target sentences into head noun (*magazine*), post-noun (*about fishing*), verb (*amused*), and post-verb (*all the reporters*) in order to determine the following: (a) the percentage of trials in which participants make regressions (look-backs); (b) the amount of time it takes to get through a region the first time; and (c) the total amount of time spent on a region (all included). It is not entirely surprising to discover that of the four (4.1a–d), (4.1a) prompts the highest percentage of regressions and the longest first-passes and total reading times at the noun and post-noun regions. This technique provides exquisite kinds of data.

Another way to use eye-tracking is by having participants seek objects on a screen (or at a real scene) as a descriptive sentence is presented. This, too, can be revealing of the way in which sentences are interpreted. This approach is more intuitive, and so I will simply describe a prominent example from the psycholinguistic literature. Altmann and Kamide (1999) presented sixteen experimental trials in which a participant visualized a scene as they heard statements such as the one in (4.2) or (4.3). The participants' task was to say whether the sentence can apply to a picture of a boy looking over a scene containing a ball, a birthday cake, a toy car, and a train set.

(4.2) The boy will move the cake.

(4.3) The boy will eat the cake.

The question Altmann and Kamide asked is the following: How soon do participants start focusing on the target object in the scene ("cake" in this case) as a function of the sentence's verb ("eat" versus "move"), in a situation where one of the objects corresponds to one verb (i.e., one object is edible), while the other three do not? Do participants wait until they hear the target or does the verb help narrow down their expectations?[1]

A typical eye-tracking graph will show the cumulative probability that a listener will look at the target item over time.[2] This means the y-axis will show the probability that the participant's eyes look at a particular target item in the scene (in this case, the cake) from the time a particular word is heard (in this case, the verb "eat"). In other words, a graph's x-axis shows time intervals that are coordinated with the elements of the utterance and the y-axis shows the probability that the participants' eyes were looking at the target. Altmann and Kamide's graph reveals that by the time the verb "eat" was completely articulated, participants began to look at the only object that was afforded by the verb (the cake) and at rates that were distinguishable from the other, more generic condition (i.e., when "move" was uttered). This advantage for "eat" came early in sentence comprehension.

Mouse-Tracking

In mouse-tracking studies, a participant's hand movements are tracked as he guides the mouse from a starting point toward a target on a screen when there are two (or more) response options. Essentially, one wants to determine the trajectories a participant's hand takes as it heads to a target. As seen in Figure 4.1 (sent to me by Jack Tomlinson; also see Tomlinson et al., 2013), the starting point of the mouse is in the bottom center and the two options here, true and false, are in the two upper corners. This representation is handy for describing a participant who is asked to answer true or false to a question such as "Elephants are not large" (see Dale & Duran, 2011). The correct response in this case would correspond with the option *false;* importantly, indications from Dale and Duran are that the mouse-tracking outcome corresponds (roughly) with the "two-stage" line on the left in Figure 4.1. When a task presents a question that is not as complex (imagine a test sentence such as "Cars have wings"), the line would be expected to go more directly to the target as part of a "one-stage – direct path" (like the rightmost line below).

To appreciate the trajectory represented by the middle line in Figure 4.1, consider a different task that requires participants to click on an image after

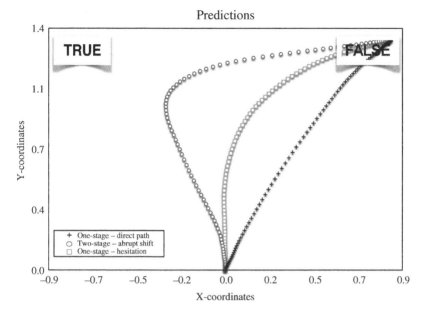

Figure 4.1. A generic representation (from Jack Tomlinson) showing three different patterns of mouse-tracking movements when the starting point is at the bottom center and when the provided options – in the two upper corners – are *True* and *False*.

hearing a word pronounced (e.g., imagine hearing the word "candy" when a picture of a candy is placed where "False" is located), as Spivey et al. (2005) did. When the alternative picture (placed where "True" is located) represents a phonetically unrelated word (such as "jacket"), participants head more or less directly to "candy." However, when the alternative image is one whose name is phonetically similar to "candy" (e.g., "candle"), participants tend to stay in the middle longer. Both eye-tracking and mouse-tracking can be found with respect to the extensive investigations on scalar utterances and on reference (in Chapters 6, 7, and 9).

Neuroscientific Methods

Functional Magnetic Resonance Imagery

Functional Magnetic Resonance Imagery (fMRI) refers to investigations of brain activity as an individual carries out a specific task. Strong magnets detect changes in blood flow and oxygenation in a participant's brain during a provided task. Nancy Kanwisher, one of the world's foremost experts of fMRI, nicely describes how to view this technique, while being interviewed by Alan Alda for a program titled, *Brains on Trial* (Chedd, 2013):

> The basic idea is that neurons are like muscles. The body needs to send more blood to supply those neurons that are active because it is metabolically expensive (to do so), just like running is with respect to muscle ... So what happens is that (as) more blood is sent to parts of the brain, the amount of oxygenated hemoglobin in that (active) part of the brain changes, (leaving) a magnetic signature that is picked up by fMRI.

More specifically, a very strong magnet lines up the hemoglobin in oxygenated blood along the poles and when one carries out a mental activity, those parts of the brain that are implicated (meaning that they especially need oxygen) will distort the alignment to varying degrees; it is the bounce back to the orderly lining that is actually captured through the technology. The usual length of time to snap (a series of) pictures of the entire brain takes about four seconds, so the activity captured by the fMRI is not very time-sensitive. That is, one cannot see how the brain is reacting at the very moment that, for example, a word is presented. Importantly, these fMRI recordings provide no meaningful feedback on their own. In order to understand what parts of the brain are implicated in a given cognitive task, one needs to compare performance to a control task that arguably lacks the activity in question. In order to appreciate how this is done, let us consider how fMRI has been used to study Theory of Mind.

Hundreds of fMRI studies have established that mindreading or "mentalizing" about others' intentions is often associated with activity in an area where the temporal lobe meets the parietal lobe (and most notably in the right hemisphere). Rebecca Saxe and colleagues refer to it as the right Temporal-Parietal junction (or right TPJ). Articles supporting this claim are numerous (see Van Overwalle, 2009). My favorite describes an fMRI experiment that has participants observe a short vignette of a film in which a person is shown walking, stopping behind a bookshelf for four seconds, and continuing to walk (Saxe et al., 2004). In order to create a control condition, the authors cleverly reorganized the series of events in the film so that the walker emerges from behind the bookcase as a first step. In this way, the control condition presents participants with an identical scene, but without showing that the walker *stopped* intentionally. One can then compare the brain activity of an observer (the participant), who has seen two identical four-second periods, and determine what areas of the brain are implicated when the walker is observed *emerging from* versus *stopping behind* the bookcase. The four-second period, with the stop behind the bookcase, prompts unique activity in the area that is now classically associated with Theory of Mind (intention-attribution) areas: the right TPJ. Notice that researchers aim to compare two activities in order to isolate brain activity that is unique to the experimental condition. As we will see, e.g., in Chapter 11, my colleagues and I extended this kind of research to utterance interpretation.

Electroencephalography and Evoked Response Potentials

Electroencephalogram (EEG) recordings are measurements of electrical brain activity that are assumed to come from post-synaptic electrical charges and that are captured on the skull of human subjects. By using tasks that allow for temporal precision (e.g., as a single word appears on a screen), studies can determine how participants react (through *Evoked Response Potentials*, or ERPs) to that word when it is part of a sentence. Actually, it would be more accurate to say that studies determine when brains react to something that is relatively unusual, because in many (but not all) cases, recordings reflect surprise or reanalysis. Importantly, any individual might react somewhat differently to stimuli, but through averaging, one can come up with a general characterization of the way the brain reacts.[3]

Scientists in this area typically speak in terms of components. These refer to specific parts of a wave that occur at a specific time. So, if a researcher speaks of a P300 effect, it means that there is specific exceptional positive activity about 300 milliseconds after stimulus onset. Note that, unlike fMRI, which captures *where* in the brain activity is taking place over the course of a long period (four seconds), ERPs characterize specific kinds of activity as they are occurring. However, the electrical activity is generalized and does not tell us what parts of the brain are implicated (certain parts of the scalp might show lesser or greater activity, but these results do not correspond with the parts of the brain below these areas). This is why many articles point out that fMRI has high spatial resolution, while ERPs provide high temporal resolution. Below, I summarize two of the main components that often appear in studies of pragmatics and the contexts in which they arise.

Kutas and Hillyard (1980a–c) have famously demonstrated how event-related brain potentials are sensitive to semantic incongruity. For example, they have shown that semantically inappropriate words (e.g., "I take my coffee with cream and *dog*") elicit a negativity that peaks around 400 milliseconds post-stimulus, which is why this is commonly designated as an N400. Kutas and Hillyard (1984) characterized the amplitude of N400 as a function of *cloze probability* of the terminal word. Cloze probability is the probability that a given word will be produced in a given context on a sentence completion task (and the probabilities are culled from other participants or corpuses). Although the precise nature of the cognitive processes underlying the N400 are not well known, it seems that the amplitude of this negative component is inversely proportional to the "semantic fit" between the target word and preceding context (Kutas, 1993). Typically, this negative component appears largest in the centroparietal region.

Another ERP component that will be relevant to us is the P600, which is a large positive-going wave that begins at roughly 500 milliseconds and reaches its peak at 600 milliseconds post-stimulus (Osterhout & Holcomb, 1992). The P600 is often linked with reactions to anomalies involving phrase structure (e.g., "The scientist criticized Max's *of* proof the theorem"; Osterhout & Holcomb, 1992), verb subcategorization (e.g., "The lawyer forced the man *was lying*"; Osterhout & Holcomb, 1992), subject–verb number agreement (e.g., "The doctors *believes* the patient will recover"; Osterhout & Mobley, 1995), and number and gender reflexive-antecedent agreement (e.g., "The woman helped *himself* to the dessert"; Osterhout & Mobley, 1995). This is why the P600 is generally considered to be a syntactic anomaly marker and its amplitude has been shown to be a function of the "severity" of the syntactic anomaly (Osterhout et al., 1994). Nevertheless, some scientists (Friederici, 2002; Friederici & Meyer, 2004) have argued that centroparietal positivity (P600) is due to the re-analyses and repair that follow from these syntactic errors. The P600 could be generalized to even nonlinguistic repairs, such as gender stereotype (Osterhout et al., 1997) and jokes (Coulson, 2004). Of all the components described, the P600 is the most likely candidate to reflect pragmatic processing. Evoked Response Potentials are used sporadically throughout experimental pragmatics, and can be found with respect to scalar utterances (Chapter 6), metaphor (Chapters 5 and 10), metonymy (Chapter 10), and irony (Chapter 11).

Crowdsourcing

To complete the panorama of methodologies, I point to a relatively new source of data collection that takes place over the Internet. *Crowdsourcing* refers to feedback collected from people who get paid for their time spent completing automated surveys remotely. This innovation, spearheaded by Amazon's *Mechanical Turk* or *M-Turk*, has been adopted for psychological and psycholinguistic studies. Researchers from all over the world can essentially count on samples from the same population of English speakers to test claims about language-related issues. While this approach does not provide the same kind of control or neural pinpointing one can find in a laboratory, it does allow for a spontaneous reaction from hundreds of participants in a single afternoon. In some cases, one can provide remote participants with just one or two questions, as opposed to a series of trials (which can ultimately reveal the purpose of the study).

When I first collaborated on M-Turk studies, I was circumspect and for three reasons. First, I was unaccustomed to *not* managing the participants' experimental environment (usually the experimenter has a face-to-face encounter with the participant before the latter begins the experiment). Second, it is difficult to ascertain whether participants are really who they say they are. Finally, I sense that participants – many of whom presumably carry out cognitive and linguistic tasks all day – might not apply themselves to a given task in the way they would if that task was a rarer, more anticipated event in their day in a laboratory. These misgivings have generally been assuaged. Papers have shown that cognitive data collected from M-Turk studies are comparable to those collected in-person in a more traditional setting (for a review, see Paolacci & Chandler, 2014). Given that the data collected from individuals sitting in front of their computers are comparable to those collected from typical subject pools, this is a fantastic way to collect a lot of data quickly.

Where Do We Go From Here?

We have now set the stage. We have introduced all of the elements – the phenomena, the theoretical approaches, the experimental attitude, and the techniques. We are ready to place theoretical accounts at the center of experimental endeavors in order to advance experimental pragmatics. We will advance by developing pragmatic tasks and by testing claims that follow from theoretical perspectives. We will begin by reviewing how Grice's theory itself affected the existing literature when it first appeared. This is what we turn to in the next chapter.

Notes

1. To see an illustration related to this paradigm, go to Altmann and Kamide (1999), Figure 1.
2. To see the graph related to Altmann and Kamide's (1999) data, see their Figure 2.
3. Magnetoencephalography (MEG) is another way to map brain activity, as it records magnetic fields produced by the brain's electric currents. So, MEG provides results that are similar to EEG. However, given that magnetic fields are less distorted by the skull, it provides better spatial resolution. That is, MEG comes with the added advantage that it allows one to identify the source of activity.

5   Early Experimental Pragmatics

Science is what you know; philosophy is what you don't know.
Bertrand Russell

In Chapter 2, I described how theorists reacted to Grice's proposal; here, I review how experimental psychologists did. Actually, one can discern two sorts of reactions. For some, Grice provided the theoretical wherewithal to describe results that heretofore remained mysterious, especially when a psychological task or question turned on an unusual presentation or test-question. For others, Grice's theory was a means to develop a psychological processing account of utterance understanding and to test its predictions. The latter provided the basis for novel experiments, on mostly figurative uses, such as metaphor, idioms, and indirect requests. We will now take a look at each of these two developments.

On the Positive Side: Grice Helps Explain Non-logical Responses

Gricean explanations nicely accounted for three sets of data with respect to experimental investigations of reasoning. The first came from developmental tasks à la Piaget, the second came from adult tasks and mostly those prone to reveal the cognitive biases made famous by Kahneman and Tversky, and the third came from studies on conditionals. The three sets of data are similar in that they are collected from tasks that make a conversationally unexpected or inelegant request. It was Grice who indirectly provided researchers with the means to address these.

Developmental Findings

Let us turn first to Piaget, who proposed that children – through interaction with their surroundings – pass through several cognitive stages in which they, to put it simply, begin by knowing little about their environment and end up being competent at formal logic by the time they reach adolescence. Each of the stages, *sensorimotor* (ages 0–2), *pre-operational* (ages 2–7), *concrete operational* (ages 7–11) and *formal operational* (ages 11–adult) is said to be marked by characteristic cognitive behaviors. So, young children were said to struggle with what is called *object permanence* in the sensorimotor stage and, when they get past that, they struggle with *conservation* in the pre-operational stage and, when they get past that, they struggle with *class inclusion* in the next stage and so on. Conservation and class inclusion will be described very shortly. Object permanence refers to an "out of sight, out of mind" phenomenon that was supposed to apply to newborns.[1] For each of these abilities, Piaget developed clever tasks that help characterize each stage. We will consider each in turn.

The Conservation Task

One task that often causes failures among children between four and six years of age is the conservation task. In this problem, young participants see, for example, two rows of five chips (called *counters*) that are equally spread out and are asked, "Is there more here or more here or are they both the same number?" Children, as one would expect, typically say that they are the same. Here comes the tricky part: the experimenter then transforms one of the rows so that its counters are bunched up next to one another making one set appear less spread out than the other. After this *intentional transformation*, children are asked the same question, "Are there more here or more here or are they both the same?" About 85 percent of the children are likely to say that the longer (non-manipulated) row has more counters. The same works with two lengths of string before and after one length of string is shaped to look like a crescent ("Is this one longer than this one or are they both the same length?").

In a paper titled *Conservation Accidents*, McGarrigle and Donaldson (1975; also see Donaldson, 1982) cited Grice's "communication of intent model" as a way to justify why children would misinterpret the question the second time it is posed. By asking a straightforward question again – and immediately after making a conspicuous change to the experimental scenario – participants (not surprisingly) reconsidered their earlier answers. To put it in Gricean terms, it would be as if the experimenter did not accept the participant's intention by asking the same question again. In addition, the testers, who are adults (authority figures), seem to be unsatisfied with the obvious answer; it amounts to a form of (nonthreatening) coercion that can compel children to focus on some other feature of the display (perhaps that the answer should be based on occupied space).

To test the idea that the children's wrong answers were due to intention-reading, McGarrigle and Donaldson set up a situation in which the second step, the one where the counters are manipulated, occurs accidentally before the test question is repeated. In the accident condition, a "naughty" teddy bear gets close to the action and risks spoiling "the game." The bear's trouble-making presence allows the experimenter to adjust the counters in a way that looks identical to the intentionally transformed row (or string) in the standard task. Once the reorganization of the counters is in place, the second question can be answered more readily. While the intentional transformation condition yielded classic results (error rates were 73 percent when presented first), the accidental transformation condition showed that kids were almost adult-like (error rates were at 13 percent when that task was presented first). An accidental reconfiguration makes it seem like the question is being repeated because of an interruption, and not because the experimenter is asking the child participant to reconsider. Note how the question is the same. What changes by virtue of the manipulation is the intention attributed to the speaker.

The Class Inclusion Task

One of the most studied developmental tasks between the 1960s and the 1980s was Piaget's class-inclusion problem. In this task, children – starting at around seven years of age – are shown, for example, five roses and three tulips, and asked, "Are there more roses or more flowers?" On its face, this question seems odd, or infelicitous to an adult because it compares a class to its subclass (it would seem odd, for example, to be asked if there are more French people or more Europeans, even if the answer is obvious). Generally, children will say that there are more roses (and I'll explain why just below). It is only when children are eight that half of the children spontaneously respond in an adult-like way.[2]

With this task one can see how researchers apply the distinction between "what is said" and "what is meant" in order to understand the errant responses. Politzer (1986) argued that while children hear, "Are there more roses or more flowers?" – they understand the utterance to mean, "Are there more roses or more flowers-that-are-not-roses?" The children turn the question into a subclass-versus-subclass comparison. To test this interpretation, Politzer (1993; summarized in Politzer, 2016) had a group of six- to seven-year-old children "point to the flowers" first and "point to the roses" second in, what I will call, the *flowers-then-roses* group, while a second group of children, in what I will call the *roses-then-flowers* group, did the same in the opposite order. While 90 percent of the children would point to all of the flowers in the *flowers-then-roses* group only about half would point to all the flowers, when asked to do so in the *roses-then-flowers* group. Interestingly, the other half, in the *roses-then-flowers* group, point to the tulips, i.e., the non-roses. For these children, *flowers* means those that are not roses. Politzer went on to show in another experiment that if five- to seven-year-old children are asked to point to the roses, the daisies, and all the flowers, in that order, before being provided with the test question, half of the five-year-olds and all of the seven-year-olds give the correct answer to the standard Piagetian question afterward. When an experimenter clarifies potential ambiguities in the test question the children are no longer confused about whether there are more roses or more flowers (also see Markman, 1978; McGarrigle, Grieves, & Hughes, 1978; Shipley & Kuhn, 1983).

These are just two Piagetian tasks that begged for a Gricean explanation.[3] When adjustments to tasks were undertaken to address the infelicities, immature reasoning performance was much reduced. Although these are arguments that ought to have undermined the Piagetian approach to development, Piagetian theory continued to hold a prominent place in developmental psychology for some time afterward.[4]

Linguistic Pragmatic Features in the Heuristics Program

In the 1970s and 1980s, Tversky and Kahneman began to document how people – when making probability judgments – do not consider normative rules but instead rely on nonlogical heuristics or shortcuts, such as *availability* and *representativeness*. Availability (as discussed in Chapter 3) refers to the way judgments are made based on the ease with which relevant instances come to mind. Representativeness refers to the degree to which an event or feature is similar to characteristics of its parent population, e.g., an engineer who likes to play chess and to solve Rubik cubes is more representative of members of his occupation than a less stereotypical member (one who likes gardening and painting).

One of Kahneman and Tversky's most impressive claims (Kahneman & Tversky, 1982; Tversky & Kahneman, 1983) came from a task, the *Linda problem*, which was designed to demonstrate how representativeness undermines normative reasoning. In this task, subjects are given a description of Linda before being asked to evaluate events about her:

Linda is thirty-one years old, single, outspoken, and very bright. She majored in philosophy. As a student, she was deeply concerned with issues of discrimination and social justice, and also participated in antinuclear demonstrations.

Subjects are asked to rank order the probabilities of several possibilities, including these:

(5.1) Linda is a bank teller.

(5.2) Linda is active in the feminist movement

(5.3) Linda is a bank teller and is active in the feminist movement.

Note that (5.3) is the conjunction of (5.1) and (5.2) and should not be judged, based on the laws of probability, to be more likely than the events in (5.1) or (5.2) alone.

Tversky and Kahneman (1983) reported, however, that most college-age subjects (about 80 percent) violate the normative conjunction rule and rank (5.3) as more probable than (5.1). Again, the conjunction of two events cannot be more likely to occur than one of the events alone (to make this clearer, consider how the number of people who have green eyes *has to be* the same or greater than the number of people who have green eyes and brown hair). Tversky and Kahneman interpreted an erroneous judgment – referred to as the *conjunction fallacy* – as evidence for the representativeness heuristic because (5.3) contains one feature that corresponds with (a stereotype of) Linda's description and (5.1) has no such matching features.[5]

You might have noticed that the request to compare (5.1) and (5.3) is conversationally inelegant in a way similar to the question in the Piagetian class-inclusion problem. This led Guy Politzer and myself (Politzer & Noveck, 1991) to argue that the class-subclass comparison, whose obviousness was problematic in Piaget's problem, similarly affects responses in the Linda problem. Specifically, we claimed that the Linda problem compels participants to transform the option in (5.1) *Linda is a bank teller* into *Linda is a bank teller and is not active in the feminist movement*. We further hypothesized that the nature of the conjunction in (5.3), which pairs a low-probability event with a high-probability event (with respect to Linda's description), obscures the set-subset relationship. We surmised that if these two task-features can be neutralized or minimized, one could eliminate the fallacy.[6]

We thus presented a version of the Linda problem along with (three) new Linda-type problems that were similarly designed, except that the conjunction of class and subclass was made more evident through nesting. To make this clear, let us consider one of our new versions in detail, the *Daniel* problem. Daniel was described as a very bright student who was strong in Math and Science and who enjoyed helping people. In one version of the Daniel problem, the critical comparison – between (5.4) and (5.6) below – used a structure (A versus A&B comparisons) that is analogical to the one used in the Linda problem:

(5.4) Daniel entered medical school.

(5.5) Daniel entered medical school and dropped out for lack of interest.

(5.6) Daniel entered medical school and graduated from medical school.

Note too that, unlike the conjunction in (5.3), both conjuncts in (5.6) are equally consistent with the provided background. In a second version of the task, we separated the explicit class-subclass descriptions in (5.5) and (5.6) by making each listed event a separate independent option. In this way, the options – now (5.8) and (5.9) – are nested under the prerequisite event (that Daniel entered medical school). This avoids re-mentioning the prerequisite event each time and obviates a need for the word *and*:

(5.7) Daniel entered medical school.

(5.8) Daniel dropped out of medical school for lack of interest.

(5.9) Daniel graduated from medical school.

Whereas our version of the Linda problem yielded error rates on the order of 80 percent (like in the original version), the two Daniel problems yielded significantly lower error rates, 53 percent for the explicit-conjunction version and 31 percent for the implicit (nested) conjunction version. Our work demonstrated that one can reduce errors by making the nesting among events increasingly clear and by avoiding explicit A&B versus A comparisons (for related findings, see Dulany & Hilton, 1991; Morier & Borgida, 1984). That said, note that these manipulations did not completely eliminate heuristic-generated effects.[7]

Individual Logical Inferences

Arguably, the first logical term to get an experimental pragmatic treatment was the conditional, "if," which is usually expressed as "if-then," as in the utterance, "If Mary goes to the cinema then she takes her bicycle." Inference-making is generated when the conditional is combined with further information. For example, if the above conditional is presented with the minor premise, "Mary goes to the cinema," one is in the position to draw the valid logical conclusion that "she takes her bicycle." This inference form is called *modus ponens*. However, this is not the only inference form related to conditionals. Another logically valid conclusion is drawn when the conditional's consequent is negated, as in, "she does not take her bicycle," which leads to the conclusion that "Mary does not go to the cinema." This inference form is known as *modus tollens*. The remaining two, which arise when the antecedent is negated or the consequent confirmed, do not provide valid conclusions. A summary of these four inference forms is presented in (5.10) below:

(5.10) Major premise: If p then q

Minor premise:	p	not-p	q	not-q
Conclusion:	q	Indeterminate	Indeterminate	not-p

Based on participants' performance with these forms however, many researchers concluded that the conditional is understood differently. That is because, instead of indicating *indeterminate* for the middle two (whose forms are called Denial of the Antecedent and Affirmation of the Consequent, respectively), participants often produce, or accept, the conclusion *not-q* after the minor premise that denies the antecedent, and they often produce, or accept the conclusion *p* after the minor premise that affirms the consequent. Many researchers (e.g., Taplin et al., 1974) were thus tempted to argue that the conditional is in fact represented as the biconditional (*if and only if p then q*).[8] With this sort of representation, reasoning outcomes conform to a different logical form and make better sense of the data.

Rumain, Connell, and Braine (1983) argued against the notion that participants' *lexical entry* (a notion equivalent to the linguistically encoded meaning) for conditionals is the biconditional. Rather, they proposed that "conversational comprehension processes" intervened so that conditional statements end up resembling biconditionals. Their Gricean argument was based specifically on a highly cited proposal from Geis and Zwicky (1971), who suggested a principle known as *Conditional Perfection* – "a sentence of the form X ⊃ Y invites an inference of the form non-X ⊃ non-Y." These authors explained it further by writing (p. 562):

This principle asserts a connection between linguistic form and a tendency of the human mind "to perfect conditionals to biconditionals" in words suggested to us by Lauri Kartunnen. This tendency is manifested in two classical logical fallacies, Affirming the Consequent (concluding X from X ⊃ Y and Y) and Denying the Antecedent (concluding ~ Y from X ⊃ Y and ~X).[9]

That is, if given the sentence in (5.11a), Conditional Perfection invites the inference in (5.11b):

(5.11)   a. If you mow the lawn then you get five dollars.
         b. If you don't mow the lawn then you don't get five dollars.

To make their point, Rumain, Connell, and Braine (1983) presented children and adults with all four conditional problems and tested performance under two conditions: (1) with standard materials, and (2) with those that block the invited inference. Thus, (5.12) below shows the standard way that the *Affirmation of the Consequent* case is tested, and (5.13) shows how the task materials were transformed to block the invited inference.

(5.12)   If the bottom of the card has a 4 then the top has a Q.
         The top of the card has a Q.

(5.13)   If the bottom of the card has a 4 then the top has a Q. But if the bottom does not have a 4, then the top may have some other letter. And, if the top has an A then the bottom may have a 4, or it may have some other number. The top of the card has a Q.

The rationale behind the manipulation was that the "expanded premise" version (in 5.13) should facilitate normative responses if the conditional ("If 4 on bottom then Q on top") conversationally invites the fallacies; on the other hand, if conditionals were indeed *represented* as biconditionals, the longer premise would only prompt confusion. To use more contemporary language, the longer premise allows for the cancellation of the pragmatic (invited) inferences. If the biconditional were part and parcel of the conditional statement, the longer expression would represent a contradiction and lead to greater difficulties. Indeed, the extra information in (5.13) generally facilitated correct performance for seven-year-olds, ten-year-olds, and adults, indicating that the pragmatic information can be canceled.

As can be seen, Grice's proposal provided a measure of comfort to reasoning researchers who were often confronted by tasks that, while respecting logical or mathematical concerns, were violating conversational ones. With respect to children, infelicitous features led Piaget to underestimate his participants' logical competence. With respect to adults, infelicitous or unclear choices can lead to judgments that allow for probabilistic or logical violations. By distinguishing between linguistically encoded readings and intended readings, researchers (such as Braine and his colleagues) could continue to argue in favor of a natural logical competence. We will return to conditionals in Chapter 8.

On the Negative Side: Extrapolations of Gricean Theory Lead to Disconfirmations

As much as the Gricean program was embraced by psychological researchers generally, it was most welcome by researchers of psycholinguistics, and especially those who were interested in figurative language, such as metaphor. Grice's philosophical proposal was particularly helpful because it implicitly proposed procedures with which one can account for metaphor comprehension. As we saw in Chapter 2, for example, Grice (1989, p. 34) proposed that metaphor works by "flouting" the Maxim of Quality that, in turn, leads the listener to arrive at a pragmatic interpretation. In the hands of psychologists, Grice's account was transformed into a straightforward three-stage processing model (see Glucksberg, 2003):

I. Derive the literal reading.
II. Recognize that the literal reading cannot be true.
III. Search for a non-literal reading that makes sense.

This depiction – which has become known (and often derisively) as the Standard Pragmatic Model (SPM) – can be applied to many pragmatic phenomena and lends itself nicely to testing on two counts. One is that metaphor processing requires extra steps (II and III) with respect to what is required to read a non-metaphorical (literal) sentence (Step I). This implies that an utterance with a metaphorical reading (such as, "Usain Bolt is a rocket") should take longer to read or should be harder to process in some way than one with a literal reading (such as, "The Ares 5 is a rocket").[10] The other is that it claims that a literal reading is practically obligatory (after all, it is Step I).

This general approach can be applied to a host of phenomena. Consider idioms. When an addressee hears "He kicked the bucket," Grice's proposal predicts that the addressee will first process the literal meaning before recognizing that the phrase was not literally true (thus violating the Maxim of Quality) and thus, by implicature, come up with an alternative, which in this case, means "to die." Likewise, understanding irony or sarcasm involves processing the literal reading before rejecting it, and accessing and recognizing the speaker's intended meaning. If a speaker says, "That was a great meeting" after what was clearly a horrible meeting, Grice implies that the encoded meaning is primary and that the ironic one is derived from a maxim violation, while maintaining the Conversational Principle. Grice's proposal was a leap forward and gave psychologists specific predictions to test and distinctions to investigate, such as the factors that encourage literal versus figurative readings.[11]

Does Metaphor Require Extra Effort?

One way to test Grice's theory is to measure reading times of critical sentences that could be read as metaphorical or literal.[12] If Grice was correct and metaphor involves processing that goes above and beyond what one would expect from the same sentence understood literally, then a single sentence – understood metaphorically – ought to take longer to process. After all, an addressee has to recognize a flouted maxim and search for the speaker's intended meaning in the metaphoric version.

There are essentially two strategies for testing this claim. One is to present a single sentence that, based on one of two contexts, is expected to be understood either literally or figuratively. For example, two different stories could conclude with "the troops marched on" with *troops* referring back to soldiers in one case or to rambunctious children in another. Most of these studies rely on reading times of the critical sentence as their measure. Another strategy is to present participants with single out-of-the-blue sentences, some that are potentially metaphorical ("Those fighters are lions") and some that are straightforwardly literal ("Those animals are lions"), among other control items, and determine whether the metaphoric ones take longer to process (or show signs of being more effortful to process) than at least the literal ones. The task could add a wrinkle by having participants read the out-of-the-blue sentences while EEG measures are collected. Let us review the findings motivated by each strategy, going roughly in chronological order. After summarizing both, we will see how the data weigh in on Grice's theory.

Metaphors in Context

The first way researchers investigated metaphor was to use statements that could be understood literally or metaphorically, depending on the context. Ortony et al. (1978) which employed a self-paced reading task, was one of the first to test Grice's model. In Ortony et al.'s study, the critical line (5.16) comes after one of two different kinds of context. In (5.14), the critical line follows a literal-inducing context and in (5.15) the critical line follows a metaphor-inducing context:

(5.14) Approaching the enemy infantry, the men were worried about touching off land mines. They were very anxious that their presence would be detected prematurely. These fears were compounded by the knowledge that they might be isolated from their reinforcements. The outlook was grim.

(5.15) The children continued to annoy their babysitter. She told the little boys she would not tolerate any more bad behavior. Climbing all over the furniture was not allowed. She threatened to spank them if they continued to stomp, run, and scream round the room. The children knew that her spankings hurt.

(5.16) Regardless of the danger, the troops marched on.

Of course, this is but one example. The participants read twenty-seven practice items and then sixteen items in one of the two *inducing* versions. The authors also included a *Short Context* version of their experiment. This contained the opening lines of stories or parts thereof, e.g., the short metaphorical-inducing condition of (5.15) presented, "The children continued to annoy their babysitter" before presenting the critical line.

Their reading-time data showed that with relatively rich context, participants have little difficulty integrating the target sentences, no matter how metaphorical they appear. While this appears damaging for the Gricean position, one could point to shortcomings in the design. For example, there was a five second pause before the critical line was presented (which gives readers an unusual amount of time to prepare for a line that is richer than a banal, literal-concluding sentence) and all the test items from the two inducing contexts followed twenty-seven (!) practice items. Also, while they reported no significant differences with respect to the reading times of the critical lines with rich contexts, they did find significant differences when the context was sparer. That is, they found slower reading times overall in the sparer condition, reporting that the target sentences of the metaphorical-inducing contexts were especially slower.

Other studies have been carried out since and these essentially showed that metaphoric sentences were read with speeds equal to those calling for literal readings (Gildea & Glucksberg, 1983; Inhoff, Lima, & Carroll, 1984). For example, Gerrig (1989) presented an example from a brief study that has made the rounds. Compare the literal construal of the last sentence in (5.17) to its metaphorical construal in (5.18):

(5.17) Joan didn't want to put her silk blanket in the automatic dryer. Although it was January, she risked putting it on the clothesline. The winter wind gently tossed the lacy blanket.

(5.18) Joan looked out into her yard with great excitement. Overnight, a layer
        of snow had covered the ground. The winter wind gently tossed the
        lacy blanket.

Gerrig reports that the reading times of the final sentence in each did not differ even though the contexts were quite different. So, with an appropriate
background a metaphoric interpretation of a sentence takes as much time as a
literal-minded interpretation. This kind of finding thus appears to be reliable.

Data like these were emblematic of a storyline that emerged with respect
to other related phenomena, such as indirect requests and irony, in which
early studies supported claims emanating from the Standard Pragmatic Model
according to which literal readings are primary to interpretation, while conveyed (intended) meanings require further work that goes above and beyond
the literal. However, later research would go on to contradict the earlier claims.
For example, Clark and Lucy (1975), in a relatively complicated paradigm,
showed participants circles (that could be pink or blue) after hearing statements of the sort: "Can you make the circle blue" (which implies that the
speaker would like the circle to be the color blue) or "Must you make the circle
blue?" (which implies that the speaker would like the circle to be non-blue).
While responding correctly to the intended interpretation of the utterance (e.g.,
determining that a blue circle confirms the first case but falsifies the second),
participants took longer to evaluate the sentences conveyed when compared to
sentences that included direct requests, such as "Please color the circle blue" or
"Please do not color the circle blue." According to the authors, at least part of
the longer reaction times in the indirect request was due to determining the literal meaning in the indirect requests. Later research would go on to show that
indirect requests can be understood as readily as, if not faster than, their literal
construals, especially if the form is conventional. In one self-paced reading
task, Gibbs (1983), who was instrumental in raising doubts about the Standard
Pragmatic Model, showed that when the same utterance could be viewed as
close to its literally encoded meaning or else as an indirect request, it is the
latter that is read significantly more quickly. For example, at the end of each of
the items (5.19) and (5.20) below, is a single utterance that could be viewed,
respectively, as a literal or indirect request:

(5.19) Rod was talking with his psychiatrist. He was having lots of problems
        in establishing relationships. "Everyone I meet I seem to alienate,"
        Rod said. "I just turn very hostile for no reason," he continued. The
        shrink said, "Can't you be friendly?"

(5.20) Mrs. Norman was watching her kids play in the backyard. One of the
        neighbor's children had come over to play. But Mrs. Norman's kids
        refused to share their toys. This upset Mrs. Norman. She angrily

walked outside and said to one of her children: "Can't you be friendly?"

Participants would read nine stories of each sort, with the final critical line being used only once per experiment, plus filler items. In fact, the experiment did not end there. The final sentence in each of the above was considered a "prime" because there was another line that followed which hewed to either the literal-inducing, the indirect-requesting, or an irrelevant interpretation. That is, participants were required to determine that a follow-up sentence was well constructed. For the "Can't you be friendly?" trial above, the three follow-ups could be 5.21 (a, b or c):

(5.21)   a. Literal: Are you unable to act friendly.
         b. Indirect: Please be friendly to other people.
         c. Unrelated: Running is excellent for the heart.

Note that these follow-up probes were all roughly the same length (at least they had the same number of words). The results showed that the "indirect" follow-ups were read faster (at roughly 1,630 ms) than the other two (literal probes took roughly 2,000 ms and the unrelated ones took 2,088 ms), regardless of context. Gibbs took this result to indicate that the immediate interpretation of the critical lines, which were designed to be conventional indirect requests, were likely to be interpreted more quickly than those that were intended to be read literally. Literal interpretations generally remained harder to access. Overall, Gibbs considered these findings as evidence against Grice's theory (i.e., when Grice's theory is transformed into a processing model). A Gricean ought to predict that deviations-from-the-literal (of which metaphor and indirect requests are two examples) should take longer to process than readings that rely on linguistically encoded sentence meanings and yet Gibbs shows (repeatedly) that such phenomena do not reliably produce outcomes consistent with that claim. As we will see in Chapters 10 and 11, Gibbs presented an alternative account to Grice based on his findings. The point for now is that his data were viewed as damaging to claims that follow from a Gricean approach.

Out of the Blue Sentences

The second way researchers investigated Grice-attributed claims was to present single (short) sentences and then determine how metaphoric ones compare to literal ones. Consider Pynte et al.'s work (1996), in which they prepared forty-eight metaphoric sentences of the sort, "Those fighters are lions" and another forty-eight that served as literal controls, e.g., "Those animals are lions." Given that one would not want a participant to get the word *lions* twice, there were two lists so that each final-word would appear only once in each list, comprising twenty-four metaphor-inducing and twenty-four literal-inducing interpretations. Critically, they used what was then a nascent technique, electroencephalography (EEG), in order to make novel discoveries. In the first of four ERP studies, Pynte and colleagues had participants read each of the sentences – one word at a time – silently and without any judgment task in order to determine whether the metaphoric-inducing final word prompts a different reaction on the scalp than literal-inducing final words. That is, the study sought to determine whether there is a difference between metaphorical and literal endings. Indeed, in their first experiment, they found that participants produced larger N400s when the last word was metaphorical, as opposed to literal[13] (see Pynte et al., 1996, Figure 1).

Follow-up experiments showed that weak metaphoric items (what the authors called *unfamiliar metaphors*, such as, "Those apprentices are lions") prompted ERP profiles that were indistinguishable from the metaphoric items used in their Experiment 1. Furthermore, context matters in such a way that relatively facilitative contexts followed by weak metaphors ("They are not idiotic"; "Those apprentices are lions") prompt larger N400s than facilitative contexts that introduce strong metaphors ("They are not cowardly"; "Those fighters are lions"). Assuming that N400s are an index of the processing effort, it appears that (1) an out-of-the-blue metaphoric sentence does require more effort than a literal one, and that (2) they are further modulated by context.

Out-of-the-blue sentences have also been used to show that one cannot help but process metaphors. This was shown through an experiment by Glucksberg et al. (1982) that was inspired by the famous Stroop task (described in Chapter 4). Glucksberg et al. gave participants short sentences of the sort in (5.22)–(5.24) and were required to say whether a sentence was *literally* true:

(5.22) Some roads are snakes.

(5.23) Some jobs are jails.

(5.24) Some roads are jails.

The first two are examples of metaphors and the third is considered a "scrambled" metaphor because it is the result of combining the previous two and is now stripped of any metaphoric import (it is nonsense). The expected response was to indicate "false" to all three. While presenting participants with these types of sentences plus two other types – trivially true sentences (such as "Some fruits are apples") and trivially false ones ("Some fruits are chairs") – Glucksberg et al. measured reaction times. Interestingly, participants took longer to respond "false" to metaphorically charged sentences when compared to the scrambled sort. This allowed the authors to argue that participants cannot inhibit their comprehension of metaphor. In other words, metaphor processing is practically automatic and requires further effort.

Taking Stock

The Grice-inspired data provide a mixed picture. On the one hand, (a) meta-phoric (and other nonliteral) readings prompt slowdowns compared to their control items when they appear with spare contexts, (b) out-of-the-blue met-aphoric sentences (without context) produce steeper N400s when compared to banal literal sentences, and (c) when participants are asked to evaluate a statement as true or false, metaphors (which are literally false) prompt slow-downs compared to more banal false statements. On the other hand, many papers have provided convincing evidence showing that literal and nonliteral readings can be carried out equally fast. Should one abandon the Gricean program then?

We first need to address another more fundamental question: Is falsifying the SPM the same thing as falsifying Grice's theory? To answer that question I turn to Marr (1982), a vision scientist who strongly influenced the cognitive sciences by distinguishing between three levels of theoretical analysis, which are referred to as the *computational, algorithmic,* and *implementational* levels. The *computational* level is the most abstract level and makes explicit the input and output of the process, as well as the constraints that would allow a spec-ified problem to be solved. The *algorithmic* level describes how to get from input to output, and specifically determines which representations have to be used and which processes have to be employed in order to build and manipu-late the representations. The *implementational* level provides a description of the physical system that should realize the process at, say, the neuronal level. Marr argued that progress could be made by keeping the three separate and complementary. Grice's theory is clearly at the *computational* level and the SPM is evidently designed to mimic Grice's account at the algorithmic level (see Noveck & Spotorno, 2013). However, resemblance across theoretical lev-els, as Marr argued, is neither necessary nor recommended. One can do theo-retical work at the computational level without recourse to the algorithmic or implementational levels and, similarly, for any level with respect to the other two. Grice's contributions remain valuable because of their import at the com-putational level and, in principle, the failed predictions of the SPM should not be considered fatal to Gricean theory.

While it may have not been deserved, Grice's monumental proposal had taken a hit in experimental circles by the late 1980s. This does not mean that Grice-inspired approaches did. Other accounts, such as Relevance Theory, which is a post-Gricean theory that is more sensitive to algorithmic analyses (see Chapter 2), was better positioned to address processing concerns. This partly explains why it has gone on to play an important role in experimental pragmatics since.

Notes

1. Spelke and many others went on to demonstrate that infants do indeed recognize that objects out of view continue to exist.

2. The Hurford's disjunctions, discussed in Chapter 3, are similar. These are the cases in which one disjunct entails another and are generally considered infelicitous. For example, "John ate all or some of the pizza" or "John is from France or Paris."

3. More recently, the sensorimotor stage, the earliest stage in Piaget's model, whose milestone is measured through performance on the A-not-B task was also taken down a notch. In a typical version of this task, an eight- to twelve-month-old child is placed in front of two upside-down containers on a table that can hide an object, such as a toy car. The experimenter will then place the interesting object under one of the two containers so that the baby will retrieve it. This procedure will be repeated a few times, while always putting the object under the same container. The task takes a turn when, on a new trial, the experimenter puts the object in the other location. Where will the child look now? It turns out that babies at this age very often persist in searching in the original (A) position and not the new (B) location. This is not the right answer, and it is referred to as the A-not-B error. The babies do not show flexibility in their search procedures even though they are witnessing where the experimenter just placed the object. Csibra, Gergely, and colleagues (Topál et al., 2008) presented an influential account for this error that argued that these young children are merely accommodating their interlocutor, who is the experimenter in this case. They claim that children are persisting in choosing A because they had generated a generalized category from the information that the experimenter had intentionally created. To make their point, they set up an experiment with three conditions. In one, children were placed in front of an experimenter (as they were in the classic experiment) in which a smiling experimenter makes a lot of eye contact as she places the object in its A (and then B) containers. In a second condition, the experimenter is present but hardly interactive (e.g., she looks sidewise from the child as she puts objects under the containers) and in a third condition, there is no interlocutor present as objects are placed – seemingly magically – by an Experimenter who is behind a screen. The results show that the A-not-B error is most prominent in the classic condition and that they hardly occur when the objects are placed non-socially – under the container between the experimenter and the young participant. The error rate in the sidewise condition was more similar to the nonsocial condition than to the classic condition. Topal et al. (2008, p. 1833) argued that their data showed that "sensitivity to ostensive-referential communication is a basic evolutionary adaptation that is fundamental to the emergence of human social cognition."

4. Probably until Piaget had his debate with Chomsky.

5. The original task asked participants to rank order eight possible outcomes and these three were included among them. A *conjunction fallacy* occurred (typically) when a participant rank-ordered the conjunction of two events (being a *bank teller* and *feminist*) above one event alone (being a *bank teller*).

6. It should be added that part of our motivation was to address a claim from Tversky and Kahneman (1983, p. 303), which said that the conjunction fallacy is not due "to esoteric interpretations of the connective *and.*"

7. It should be noted that Kahneman and Tversky were aware of these potential pitfalls – the unclear role of nesting and the "esoteric interpretations of the connective *and*" in their task, but they addressed these issues in ways that were less direct.

8. *If and only if p then q* means *if p then q* and *if q then p.*

9. Their squib did not provide a full-blown ostensive-inferential Gricean account, but rather declared a principle that would make a logical meaning consistent with intuition.

10. These examples are for illustrative purposes. They do not come from a study.

11. In the immediate post-Gricean era, one of the few developmentalists whose (early) research program consisted of investigating children's pragmatic abilities was Brian Ackerman's at the University of Delaware. He studied the factors that facilitated, among other things, ambiguity resolution, presupposition, idiom comprehension, and irony comprehension (e.g., see Ackerman, 1978, 1979, 1982a, 1982b, 1983, and Chapter 13).

12. I say "critical" because there are also filler sentences that conceal the real purpose of the task.

13. See Pynte et al. (1996), Figure 1 – available over the Internet – to see the N400 effects.

6   How Logical Terms Can Be Enriched

Exposing Semantic-Pragmatic Divergences

When you come to a fork in the road, take it.

Yogi Berra

In 1957, the Department of Welfare in New York City sued a woman named Mrs. Siebel, who was the stepmother of a boy sent – by the city – to a school for "delinquents" (to use the preferred language of the time). The suit was designed to compel her to pay a share of the costs for the boy's school along with the boy's natural father (who was able to pay about half). The Department of Welfare's claim relied on a statute (the Domestic Relations Court Act of the City of New York) that said:

If in the opinion of the department of welfare such parent or legal custodian is able to contribute ... the commissioner of welfare shall thereupon institute a proceeding ... to compel such parent or other person legally chargeable to contribute.

The critical word in the statute is "or." The Welfare Department treated the disjunction as inclusive, making the stepmom ("other person legally chargeable to contribute") a viable legal target for the request of funds. This is not surprising because nearly all uses of disjunctions in the law – and logic – are inclusive (e.g., punishments of "jail time or a fine" are often explicitly expressed with "and/or"). Mrs. Siebel objected, saying that the father was already contributing, so she did not have to. In other words, she argued that the disjunction is exclusive. Interestingly, Mrs. Siebel won the first round of this argument (see Solan, 1993). While she did go on to lose in an appeal (apparently on nonlinguistic grounds), this shows how single logical words can be open to interpretation and have real life consequences. Moreover, this is not an isolated example; the hazards of interpreting disjunctions are not limited to case law.[1]

Pragmatic theories are particularly concerned about the way logical terms are interpreted in context. This is the hottest topic in experimental pragmatics and to what we turn here. A fitting place to begin our inquiry can be found in the opening line of Grice's (1989) posthumous book:

There appear to be divergences in meaning between, on the one hand, at least some of what I call the FORMAL devices – $\sim$, $\wedge$, $\vee$, $\supset$, (x), $\exists(x)$, ιx (when these are given a standard two-valued interpretation) – and, on the other, what are taken to be their analogs or counterparts in natural language – such expressions as *not, and, or, if, all, some* (or *at least one*), [and] *the.*

This excerpt points to a distinction between formal interpretations of quintessential logical terms and their "analogues" in everyday language. Grice should not be taken to mean that these terms are used logically in math and philosophy classes, and pragmatically, elsewhere. Rather, he is pointing out that incarnations of "formal" meanings are found in everyday language. The question is, how do the two meanings line up? As we saw in the opening example, *both* meanings play a role in communication in everyday language.

By profiling the way participants understand the "analog" terms in test sentences (and in any language) one can end up in a better position to understand how they are represented cognitively and how utterances are processed. The scientific goal is to capture how pragmatic readings diverge behaviorally from semantic ones, so that we can better appreciate the distinction between *sentence meaning* and *speaker meaning*. Ultimately, experimental pragmatics can advance modern theoretical debates by, not only providing data that theories need to address but by providing novel insights. This chapter and the next provide some of the highlights on the processing of these logical terms. As will become clear, most of the work was generated by considering how a logical term in utterances has a semantic ("formal") meaning, as well as potential for refinement. We have encountered some of these refined meanings when we covered *scalar implicatures* in Chapter 2 and we will largely stick with this nomenclature.[2] In the next section, I will very briefly introduce the sort of expressions that will concern us in this chapter, along with a description of the way scholars often view enrichments before experiments on this topic got under way.

Preliminaries

In (6.1a–e), I present five examples of expressions used in actual experiments that will be discussed in the rest of the chapter. The first, in (6.1a) uses the existential quantifier *some*, which can be understood as *some and perhaps all* (its formal, linguistically encoded meaning) or as *some and not all*, its more narrowed (enriched or pragmatic) reading. The countless number of experiments on the pragmatic enrichment of *some* has turned the existential quantifier into the drosophila of the experimental pragmatic literature. The test-sentence in (6.1b) uses the disjunction *or*, which – as we have seen – has a formal meaning that is inclusive and that can be enriched to be exclusive. Likewise, the modal *might* in (6.1c) is compatible with *must*, but could be refined to exclude the necessity meaning. The same general description can be extended to the conjunction in (6.1d), which is logically compatible with "Mary getting married and getting pregnant"; however, the described order of (6.1d) could encourage a listener to consider the presented order of the conjuncts as a way to exclude the other, traditional order. In (6.1e), the speaker can be mentioning the presence of a single fork in the box, but could also be understood to mean (under the right conditions) that there is only a fork, and *nothing else*, in the box.

(6.1) a. Some children sleep with teddy bears.
       b. There is an A or a B (in the word TABLE).
       c. There might be a parrot in the box.
       d. Mary got pregnant and got married.
       e. There is a fork in the box.

What all these cases have in common is that the logical term's linguistically encoded meaning allows for an interpretation that is more specific. For example, in (6.1d) a listener who enriches the meaning of "and" in that utterance arguably prefers a more specific "and then" interpretation.

It is important to note that both specialists and nonspecialists of language often express the intuition that "some" *means* "not all" or that "or" *means* "not both." Logic professors typically have to go out of their way to inform students that, for example, "Some cabs are yellow" is compatible with "All cabs are yellow" (imagine arriving in a new city and seeing some yellow cabs only to realize that all cabs are yellow). They insist because, according to their students' intuitions, the utterance "Some cabs are yellow" implies that "not all" are (Bennett, 2004). Professors of logic have told me, on more than one occasion, that they often have difficulty convincing students that the logical meaning of disjunction is inclusive because their students quickly come up with examples that seem to indicate that disjunctions are exclusive (e.g., in the cafeteria, they can have "the main course or pizza" and the message is clearly *not both*). So, intuitions often strongly favor the generation of enrichments that might be pragmatically, but not logically, valid. At the same time, efforts to find evidence of pragmatic enrichments on, say, a reasoning task that uses a sentence such as "Some beekeepers are swimmers" provides inconsistent results (Newstead, 1995). So, at the dawn of experimental pragmatics, it was not clear whether the distinction between the semantic and pragmatic readings of logical terms would yield anything of experimental value.

The Investigation of Scalar Implicatures: A Historical Account

The experimental literature on the pragmatic enrichment of logical terms actually grew out of developmental work on epistemic modals (e.g., how *must* and *may* can be used to express necessity and possibility, respectively). It emerged

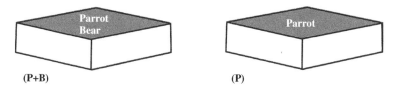

(P+B)   (P)

All I know is that whatever is inside this box (below) looks like what is inside this box (P+B) or this box (P).

Figure 6.1. Paradigm from Noveck et al. (1996) setting up a relative force experiment in which two different puppets make competing claims

as part of an investigation into another (intuitive) claim that circulated in the developmental literature, which was that deontic meanings (notions of obligation and permission) were at the root of epistemic modal understanding. This intuitive deontic-cum-epistemic claim explains (indirectly) why, for example, *must* is perceived as stronger than *might* among five-year-olds in a search task, in which children were required to find a peanut after hearing one puppet say, "The peanut must be under the box" and another say, "The peanut might be under the cup" (see Byrnes & Duff, 1989; Hirst & Weil, 1982). My colleagues and I (Noveck, Ho, & Sera, 1996) were suspicious of this claim. We argued that the relative force of epistemic modals takes a back seat to truth conditions that are, moreover, determined contextually. We thus replicated the effect first presented by Hirst and Weil, and then created a similar task, but one that provided participants with background evidence that generates necessary, possible, non-necessary, or impossible conclusions.

In the new task, children were shown the contents – toy animals – of two different boxes while a third remained covered. In one of the two exposed boxes, there was a parrot and a bear and, in the other, there was just a parrot. The experimenter then told the participant that the content of the third box resembled one of the two exposed boxes (so there is necessarily a parrot and possibly a bear). At this point, the experimenter can set things up so that two puppets presented competing modal statements that varied in terms of their truth conditions (see Figure 6.1). Participants indicated which puppet was correct.

In half the trials, the weaker-sounding one was true and the stronger-sounding one was false (see Table 6.1). The results showed that five-year-olds – as a group – were not seduced by the relative strength of a strong-but-false

Table 6.1. *A critical subset of results from Noveck et al. (1996, Experiment 2) revealing how logically correct responses increase with age (without regard to the relative force of a modal term)*

	Age			
Weaker sounding is true	5	7	9	Adult
Might be a bear/Cannot be a bear	69	75	100	100
Might be a bear/Has to be a bear	53	95	100	100
Does not have to be a bear/Cannot be a bear	41	75	94	100

statement over a weaker-but-true one and that starting with seven-year-olds, children consistently chose the true statement over the false one independently of relative force. In another condition, the two contrasted statements had the same force (e.g., "There has to be a parrot in the box" versus "There has to be a bear in the box"). Responses to these trials revealed a pattern of results that was highly similar to the ones shown in Table 6.1.

This paradigm, which can pair any kind of modal expression (*has to, does not have to, might,* and *cannot*) with a necessary conclusion (about the parrot) or a possible conclusion (about the bear), allows for a genuinely underinformative statement, "There might be a parrot in the box." This statement was not included in the Noveck et al. (1996) study precisely because it could have two interpretations, one that is formally true (since the factually true case, "has to be a parrot," entails "there might be a parrot") and another that could be interpreted pragmatically as, "There might but does not have to be a parrot," which would lead justifiably to a false response. This is the statement that would become the focus of another study.

When Children Appear More Logical Than Adults: A Seminal Pragmatic Effect

While the statement in (6.1c) – in the context of the scenario in Figure 6.1 – was not useful for studies on relative force, it has obvious appeal in itself as an underinformative test-item, and it thus beckoned investigation. This led to further studies with the hidden parrot-and-bear paradigm that focused on this underinformative item. Underinformative items could easily be investigated by having a *single* puppet present a statement while asking children whether or not they agree with it. This is what was done in Noveck (2001). Participants were asked to determine whether or not they agreed with a puppet's statement (e.g., "There has to be a parrot in the box," "There cannot be a bear in the box," etc.). Fascinatingly, that study revealed that younger children agreed more frequently than adults when the puppet said, "There might be a parrot in

Table 6.2. *Percentage of logically correct responses to the task in Figure 6.1, (reconstructed from Noveck, 2001, Table 2), revealing how an underinformative statement (see 6.1c) is unique in being understood semantically among younger participants. For this task and its number of participants (which varied by age, see original article), rates of responses reflecting chance range from around 30–70 percent. Thus, those cells that are above 70 percent (or below 30 percent) indicate a preference*

Presented statements	Logical response	Age			
		Five-year-olds	Seven-year-olds	Nine-year-olds	Adults
Concerning the necessary conclusion					
Has to be a parrot	Yes	75	90	88	100
Does not have to be a parrot	No	72	75	75	100
Might be a parrot	Yes	72	80	69	35
Cannot be a parrot	No	66	80	100	100
Concerning the possible conclusion					
Has to be a bear	No	47	65	88	100
Does not have to be a bear	Yes	66	75	81	100
Might be a bear	Yes	53	80	100	100
Cannot be a bear	No	53	80	100	100

the box" (Noveck, 2001). In the meantime, correct responses to all the control items prompted typical developmental progressions (see Table 6.2). In other words, an underinformative modal statement prompts "logical" responding among younger children and then drops with age. Adults appear equivocal, but most in this seminal study said that (6.1c) is false, making for a unique developmental curve.

As I reported in Noveck (2001), a few developmentalists in the Post-Piagetian era had run across findings that overlapped with the featured finding of Table 6.3 (Paris, 1973; Braine & Rumain, 1981; Smith, 1980; also see Sternberg, 1979). These papers showed that when a relatively weak expression is used to test reactions to a justifiably stronger claim, children tend to accept underinformative statements as true. For example, my late adviser, Marty Braine, and a student of his at the time, Barbara Rumain, had children and adults evaluate the contents of a box with statements such as, "Either there is a dog or there's a cow in the box" when there was *both* a dog and a cow in the box. This led an overwhelming majority of five- to ten-year-olds to respond by saying "Yes," whereas roughly half of the adults would say "No." While such findings were duly reported, partly because they were in each case part of a larger study that covered a range of issues on the development of reasoning,

Table 6.3. *Paradigm of anticipated reactions from Pouscoulous et al. (2007) action study, showing the starting point of the boxes on the top row and the statements in the first column. This study was carried out in French and used "quelques" as its expression for the existential quantifier.*

Scenario / Statement	Subset	All	None
I would like all the boxes to contain a token	Change (add a token to the remaining three)	No change	Change (add a token to each)
I would like some (quelques) boxes to contain a token	No change	**Logical** No change **Pragmatic** Change: (remove at least one)	Change (add at least one)
I would like no box to contain a token	Change (remove all)	Change (remove all)	No change
I would like some boxes to not contain a token	No change	Change (remove at least one)	**Logical:** No change **Pragmatic:** Change (Add at least one)

they had never been the focus of an investigation, nor had they been given a satisfying explanation. For example, Braine and Rumain (1981) noted how there was a shift from (conjunctive to) inclusive to exclusive readings of disjunctions with age; they further explained how that stumped them. One hypothesis for the reported developmental shift (which they explicitly said was unpredicted) was that the meaning of "or" *changes* with age, but they did not think this was the best explanation (and I think they were right). Critically, they did not come up with an alternative account that would involve the introduction of Gricean reasoning.

Braine and Rumain's reaction was typical for this literature (also see Paris, 1973, and Sternberg, 1979). Researchers would come across this unusual effect and express surprise but little in the way of alternative explanations, let alone pragmatic ones (Grice is not even cited in these papers). Another, slightly different example comes from Carol Smith, who studied quantifiers. She asked young (four-year-old) participants questions of the sort, "Do some birds have wings?" and *expected* them to provide an affirmative response. In Smith's case, she was "documenting" her working assumption that the meaning of *some* is equivalent to its semantic meaning and that kids would probably invoke it. However, she thought that adults would respond affirmatively too, but she never tested them.

Apropos, Smith's work was the basis of a follow-up experiment to the parrot-and-bear study summarized above in my (Noveck, 2001) paper. The idea of carrying out the Smith study with older children came about because Jacques Mehler, the Editor of Cognition at the time (and its founder), urged me to buttress my Gricean claims with further evidence. I thus asked Corinne Gruel, a Masters student who was studying in Grenoble and who lived nearby in the Alps, to find eight- and ten-year-old kids, as well as adults, to evaluate statements (not questions) with the quantifiers "some" and "all" à la Smith. For example, participants would hear Corinne make statements (in French) such as "All elephants have trunks" (true), "All dogs have spots" (false), as well as some patently absurd statements, such as "Some fruits have computers." The participants' task was to simply say whether or not they agreed with the statement. Moreover, the investigation had the advantage of being a *double blind study*, meaning Corinne had no idea why she was asked to present these specific sentences. This prevents the experimenter from unknowingly influencing the outcomes. Later, Corinne told me that she thought the focus of the study concerned the absurd trials.

Importantly, the list of statements included five underinformative sentences of the sort, "Some airplanes have wings." Whereas over 85 percent of the eight- and ten-year olds agreed with these underinformative statements, the adults were much more equivocal, as only 41 percent would agree with those statements. Ultimately, these were the data that caught the collective attention of cognitive scientists and set in motion multiple follow-up investigations into what is now a reliable developmental pragmatic effect. Once the effect was established on developmental grounds, processing investigations would go on to analyze all participants' tendencies to adopt pragmatic as opposed to semantic interpretations.

I will describe this emerging body of work in three parts. The first part deepens our understanding of the developmental progression, the second investigates whether pragmatic interpretations emerge in processing the way it does developmentally among children. After showing that there is a common thread between the developmental and adult data, the third part digs a bit deeper into the individual differences that are typically found among adults.

Follow-Up Studies on the Developmental Pragmatic Effect

Researchers replicated the developmental effect with success and with a wider range of materials and languages, and with children who were under eight years of age. For example, Papafragou and Musolino (2003) had five-year-olds and adults in Greece listen to a series of vignettes (told by an experimenter with toy-props). One of these was about three horses who all jump over a log; when a puppet then summarizes the story by saying, "Some of the horses jumped over the log," an overwhelming majority of the children agreed that it was "answered well" (*Apantise kala* in Greek), while adults did not. Guasti et al. (2005) replicated the finding from Noveck (2001, Experiment 3) with "some" and used this as a baseline before making two important points. One is that training young participants (seven-year-olds) to give a more specific description of a given situation (e.g., by pointing out that *grape* is more specific a name than *fruit*) lowers their acceptance rates (i.e., lowers rates of saying *true* to the underinformative statements, such as "Some airplanes have wings") to adult-like levels. The other is that these training effects do not persist when the same participants are tested a week later. Katsos and Bishop (2011) used a metalinguistic task (i.e., participants needed to judge whether a puppet's statement was acceptable or not) and found that five- to six-year-olds were much more likely than adults (at rates of 75 percent versus zero) to accept a statement such as, "The mouse took some of the carrots" after the mouse had been shown to take all of them.

Although the Noveck (2001) paper explicitly said that age transitions should vary as a function of the task, the paper did leave the impression that children need to be 8 or older before they begin to narrow the meaning of an utterance from "Some x" to "Some but not all x." Some researchers were determined to show that children appear adult-like at much younger ages (e.g., the Papafragou and Musolino paper). For others, the interest was not in finding a specific age, but in showing that no matter how easy a task can be, one will still find a developmental effect (Pouscoulous et al., 2007). Pouscoulous et al. (2007) invented an action study that used a puppet expressing a wish in order to make the pragmatic enrichment as accessible as possible. That task – carried out in French – had young children view a scene that always contained five boxes. In one third of the cases, two of the boxes had a token (the *Subset* scenario), in another third, each box contained a token (the *All* scenario), and in the remaining third, none had tokens (the *None* scenario). Each of these situations were presented so that a puppet could make a few statements. Critical among these was the wish, "I would like some boxes to have a token" in the *All* scenario. What was unique about this paradigm was that participants (four-year-olds, five-year-olds, seven-year-olds, and adults) needed to do something to satisfy the speaker's wish. Table 6.3 presents a summary of the paradigm.

Table 6.4. *A summary of participants' "percentage of (logically) correct responses" to the critical test utterance in Pouscoulous et al.'s (2007) action study*

		Did nothing	Did nothing	Changed
	4	64 (100)*	**32**	100
I would like some boxes to contain a token	5	67 (100)	**27**	100
	7	89 (100)	**17**	100
	A	80 (100)	**14**	100

The paradigm shows what sort of responses would be expected given felicitous responding. For the *Some statement* case in the *All* scenario (the one highlighted in the center in bold), one can note that there are two potential responses: doing nothing ("No change") satisfies a semantic interpretation of the statement, while a pragmatically refined interpretation would be expressed by removing at least one token. The same holds for the other square in bold, but it is more difficult to complete, especially for children, because it involves working in a negative context (still, "some boxes do not contain a token" is underinformative with respect to a context that describes the case "no boxes contain a token"). I will not address these more complicated negative scenarios here.

Let us focus on the "I would like some" case and begin by looking at the rates of "logical" responses in Table 6.4 and, specifically, on the *None* scenario (on the far right). One can see that all participants added tokens when the scenario began with a set of empty boxes. A similar logic-respecting finding can be found in the *Subset* scenario in the left column where two percentages are given. The bare numbers on the left show the percentage of participants who *literally* did nothing, by sitting still upon hearing the puppet's wish. The percentages in parentheses indicate that all participants respected the scenario's truth value, even when they modified the contents of the boxes (note that no one removed both tokens). By the way, none of the participants added three tokens. Interestingly, the data from this *Subset* scenario (still in the left column) show that about a third of the participants in the two youngest groups liked to move tokens into boxes, even for harmless reasons. In any case, for the two control scenarios, all the children behaved in a way that respected the request.

Now, let us look at the critical column of developmental results for the middle column's *All* scenario. One can see that a large majority of participants, across all ages, make a move to remove a token. That said, and despite the fact that the youngest children liked to harmlessly move tokens around, one continues to find the developmental effect for this scenario. The youngest children are the most likely to stand still. With age, an increasing percentage of participants remove items from the *All* scenario. All told, the developmental effect appears pretty solid as we make the task as user-friendly as possible to younger children.

The most recent (not to mention massive) replication of this developmental effect comes from a thirty-one-language study (with 768 five-year-old children and 536 adults) that I participated in. It showed that, among other things, five-year-old children accept underinformative uses of "some" more often than adults and in all thirty-one languages (Katsos et al., 2016). For example, when presented a set of five boxes, each having a turtle, five-year-olds are more likely than adults to accept "Some of the turtles are in the boxes" as true (49 percent of the children said true versus 16 percent of the adults).

This kind of developmental finding, where a minimal gloss is good enough more often for younger children but unsatisfying as a truthful statement for adults, is not reserved for modals and quantifiers. As indicated earlier, the literature reported similar findings in cases where a disjunction was used when a conjunction would have been more appropriate (Braine & Rumain, 1981; Paris, 1973; Sternberg, 1979). Papafragou and Musolino (2003) extended the effect to completions (where "start" is uttered to describe how well a puppet actually completed a task) and Noveck and Chevaux (2002) extended it to inverted-order conjunctions.

This last case, which harks back to the example in (6.1d), is important because it does not involve entailments the way that the word "all" does with respect to "some," the way that "and" does with respect to "or," or the way that "finish" does with respect to "start." Rather it concerns the way the conjunction "and" could be enriched (as a function of the context) to mean "and then." In Noveck and Chevaux's (2002) task, seven-year-olds, ten-year-olds, and adults completed booklets that included a small set of four very short stories (plus filler stories) and a comprehension question. For two of the comprehension questions concerning the conjunctions, the order of its two conjuncts respected the sequence of events in the story, and for the other two, the conjuncts were inverted. For example, one story described a girl, Julie, who had answered a phone call in the second sentence and accepted an invitation to a birthday party in the fifth. Participants were then required to respond *Yes* or *No* to one of two kinds of follow-up questions:

(6.2) a. Julie answered the phone and accepted an invitation?
       b. Julie accepted an invitation and answered the phone?

Agreeing with the utterance of (6.2b) indicates that the participant accepted the minimal meaning of the conjunctive sentence (that the two conjuncts are true). Rejecting (6.2b) would indicate that the sentence was enriched so that it was understood as something along the lines of "and then," making the order of the two conjuncts relevant. Whereas the rates of agreement to (6.2a) were high and accurate for all participants, the authors found that 85 percent of seven-year olds, 63 percent of ten-year-olds, and 29 percent of the adults responded affirmatively to (6.2b). The adults' rates of affirmation both were lower than those produced by the children and defied chance predictions. The children were evidently less fussy than adults about the conjuncts' sequence. This effect has since been replicated (Ariel, personal communication; Noveck et al., 2009). I highlight it here because it shows just how general the pragmatic-enrichment-with-age effect is and further demonstrates that it does not neces-sarily depend on the entailment relationship between two logical terms (the one that is uttered and an alternative that is unspoken, stronger, and viable). Rather, the effect relies on addressees' efforts to draw out more information based on what was presented in the context.

My contention is that the difference between young children who are less likely to enrich meanings pragmatically and older participants who do enrich meanings can be described as a distinction between an interpretation that is minimally satisfying and an interpretation that is richer and more refined. There are several alternative views for the developmental findings. One comes from (my friend) Napoleon Katsos's *pragmatic tolerance* account (Katsos & Bishop, 2011; Davies & Katsos, 2010), which harks back to semanticists' *prin-ciple of charity* (attributed to N. L. Wilson, 1959; Davidson, 1974), according to which interlocutors are assumed to make their best effort to interpret utter-ances rationally. Pragmatic tolerance proposes that children, like adults, notice an underinformative utterance's *infelicity* but that they would be less likely than adults to call it out when asked to evaluate the task's utterance for truth-fulness. They demonstrate this through tasks in which participants are asked to reward the speaker's response with a three-point scale. So, while a majority of five- and six-year-old children would answer true to a speaker who says, "The mouse picked up some of the carrots" (after it had picked them all up), they would assign the speaker an intermediate score on the scale.

Unfortunately, I do not find this account convincing and for the follow-ing three reasons. First, concerns of infelicity, truth value, and informativity are relevant for experts who analyze tasks, but they are not for – young and old – participants, who presume exchanges are felicitous to start with. Besides, the intuition that many have – e.g., that "Some cats are mammals" is just infelicitous – is arguably not as obvious in slightly more difficult cases such as "There might be a parrot" when background information indicates that there must be. Second, to expand on the first point, most of the claims for pragmatic tolerance use *metalinguistic* tasks (e.g., ratings or rewards to a "speaker" for how well something was said) that specifically ask participants to focus on the utterance's appropriateness. These are not tasks that ask participants to process an utterance, but rather to adopt a metalinguistic attitude and to evaluate it. These are not equivalent. Besides, infelicity-detection is not tantamount to pragmatic inference-making *per se*. It is, at best, a step in that direction and only if one is a strict Gricean (who says that listeners – as a second step – ought to detect whether there has been a maxim-violation) and as we saw earlier (in Chapter 5), three-step Gricean models do not have much going for them. Third, infelicity is used in myriad ways. In some cases, it is ascribed to "underinformativeness" (i.e., the utterances featured in this section) and in other cases (to be reviewed in Chapter 9) it is used to describe an utterance that has no reliable interpretation (e.g., "Point to the star" when there are two). I argue that children perform differently than adults, not because they are richer in forgivingness but, because they have fewer resources and just cannot narrow meanings as efficiently as adults.

Barner, Brooks, and Bale (2011) have a more specific claim that goes in a "lack of resources" direction. Barner et al. (2011) adopt Horn's scalar implicature account (see Chapter 2) to propose that participants go through four steps. To make the steps concrete, consider the statement "some animals are sleeping" (and a situation depicting an entire group of animals that are sleeping): (1) compute a linguistically encoded meaning; (2) generate alternative quantifiers that are compatible with the utterance ("An animal is sleeping," "All animals are sleeping," among others); (3) remove those alternatives that are entailed by the linguistic meaning of the uttered sentence (e.g., remove weaker alternatives such as "An animal is sleeping"), which leaves other alternatives that entail the spoken sentence, viz. "All animals are sleeping," and; (4) negate the remaining, more informative alternatives. These four steps provide for the more refined, strengthened meaning ("Some but not all the animals are sleeping"). They argue that children's limitations with the existential quantifier are due specifically to an inability "to generate relevant alternatives for specific scales" (p. 87). In this specific case, it concerns "some." To support this argument, they show that a majority of four-and-a half year-olds accept as true sentences, such as "Are some of the animals sleeping?" when three of three animals are shown sleeping. This persisted when the word "only" is added ahead of "some" (as in, "Are only some of the animals sleeping?"). In contrast, when Barner et al. ran similar trials in which the children heard either "Are the cat and the cow sleeping?" or "Are only the cat and the cow sleeping?" (when all three animals were shown to be sleeping), nearly all the children said "yes" to the former while nearly all said "no" the latter. They argue that the latter case allows young children to demonstrate a pragmatic ability and that the word "some" does not.

Should one take these data to mean that non-adult performance is due specifically to an inability to generate alternatives? Papafragou and Musolino (2003) would say "no." In their earlier work, they showed that five-year-olds *are* able to refine their interpretation (produce a scalar inference) if they "are provided with a context where communicative (i.e., relevance) expectations are clear and where the stronger alternative to the weaker statement is made particularly salient" (p. 277). For example, Papafragou and Musolino (2003) showed that when a child is told that a puppet is determined to put a set of three hoops around a pole and succeeds in doing so, children reject the statement "Mickey put some of the hoops around the pole." When the same sort of task did not include those expectations, children did not respond in an adult-like way. So, it seems that "alternatives" are not beyond young children's capacity; it depends on the situation.

To take their claims a step further, Skordos and Papafragou (2016) showed that other sorts of contrasts could lead to refined readings, not just those that stress the importance of an upper bound. Compare the following two experimental situations. In one, young (five-year-old) participants and adults are primed about the upper bound in a case where "All blickets have an umbrella" (and the participants see that all blickets, invented objects, indeed do have an umbrella) before being asked to evaluate an underinformative utterance, "Some blickets have a crayon" (in a scene depicting an entire set of blickets linked with a crayon). With this kind of contrast, the underinformative utterance generates a high percentage of rejections among the children (77 percent) and adults (100 percent), indicating that the computation of scalar inferences is facilitated when participants are sensitized to the meaning of "all." In the other situation, five-year-olds and adults are primed about a negative case that is described as "None of the blickets have an umbrella." To evaluate that statement, participants are shown, in one trial for example, that none of the blickets have an umbrella. This is followed by a situation that is similar to the underinformative case above, i.e., participants are asked to evaluate the statement "Some blickets have an umbrella" (when a picture shows that all the blickets have an umbrella). Interestingly, the negative prime also generates a high percentage of rejections among children (63 percent) and adults (100 percent). Data like these make it clear that children make efforts to refine the meaning of an underinformative utterance, but one would be hard pressed to link the cause to one specific feature and certainly not to sensitivity about highly specified alternatives on a predetermined scale. So, even if one adopts a Hornian model to the letter, it is hard to claim that generating alternatives is in itself what is "missing" among five-year-olds.

Processing

The developmental data reveal that readings with respect to underinformative utterances generally go in one direction with age – from a semantic (linguistically encoded) reading, which is linked to saying true, to a pragmatically enriched one, which is linked with false responses. Would on-line interpretations tell a similar story? That is, when all things are otherwise equal, are revealed enriched readings of, say, "some" and "or" linked with more intensive processing when compared to what appear to be semantic readings?

In a way analogous to the developmental data, evidence from sentence processing has shown that deeper (longer) processing is associated with arriving at more refined pragmatic interpretations. The earliest evidence comes from Bott and Noveck (2004), who used a categorization task (requiring true or false judgments) with respect to quantified statements such as "All cats are mammals" (true), "All mammals are cats" (false), and "Some mammals are cats" (true), while also including underinformative statements such as "Some cats are mammals."[3] Again, the underinformative items are critical because these can be considered true with a semantic, linguistically encoded ("some and perhaps all") reading and false with a pragmatically narrowed ("some but not all") one.

Generally, true responses to such out-of-the-blue underinformative statements occur at rates of about 40 percent (meaning false responses are at roughly 60 percent), whereas control items (correctly saying true or correctly saying false) reach rates of about 90 percent. More importantly, false responses to the underinformative items are not only slower than the true responses to these items, but are slower than all the (true and) false control statements. In the same vein, responses reflecting narrowed interpretations become more frequent as response latency increases. When participants are limited to 900 ms to respond, they provide significantly more true responses (which are indicative of semantic readings) to a statement such as "Some cats are mammals" than when the allowable response time is increased to 3000 ms, i.e., 3 whole seconds (see Bott & Noveck, 2004, Experiment 4). In other words, false responses, which point to pragmatically narrowed readings, increase as participants have more time to answer.[4] These are not isolated data. Andres Posada and I (Noveck & Posada, 2003), with admittedly less impressive controls, had similarly reported slowdowns when underinformative items inspired by Smith (1980) (e.g., "Some elephants have trunks") were compared to controls that were patently true or false. Similar to Bott and Noveck (2004), Chevallier et al. (2008) reported that underinformative disjunctive statements (where the utterance "There is an A or B" with respect to the word "TABLE" is true with a semantic reading and false with a pragmatically narrowed reading) were more likely to prompt false responses when participants were encouraged to take their time (also, true responses were highest when participants were rushed). Other effort-related psychological features can affect narrowings. For example, when participants are distracted by a demanding secondary task, they are less likely to produce narrowings of statements with "some" (De Neys & Schaeken, 2007). To sum up, much like developmental progressions show, refined pragmatic readings are associated with extra costs, even if they may be relatively light (e.g., also see Bott, Bailey, & Grodner, 2012).

One could argue that the above examples are a bit artificial. Sentences are presented in an out-of-the-blue manner or they talk about artificial situations (two letters with respect to a five-letter string). The effect would be more convincing if it occurred in a more natural (i.e., a more ecologically valid) situation. Breheny, Katsos and Williams (2006) were the first to take this step by carrying out a self-paced reading task.

In such tasks, participants are asked to read vignettes piecemeal so that parts of text unfurl with a participant's click of a keyboard's spacebar or some other button. This way a critical section can be isolated as participants read it. It is the time that it takes to read critical passages that determines whether a given prediction is supported or not. As far as scalar terms are concerned, one can test whether two kinds of context can generate different reading profiles from the moment that a weak term is read. Let us look at two examples from Breheny et al. (2006), which are illustrated in (6.3) and (6.4), and in which the slashes indicate where participants manually advance the text through a keyboard tap. Breheny et al. (2006) showed that when a disjunction (*class notes or summary*) arises in a context in which the protagonist was short on time (the Upper-bound context, in 6.3), it takes longer to read the disjunctive phrase because the context encourages a narrowed reading (*class notes or summary but not both*). In the other context, which shows that the protagonist is a bit desperate to learn what he could (the Lower-bound context, in 6.4), the semantic reading remains compatible with the disjunctive phrase:[5]

(6.3) Upper-bound context
       John was taking a university course / and working at the same time./ For the exams / he had to study / from short and comprehensive sources. / Depending on the course, / he decided to read / the class notes or the summary.

(6.4) Lower-bound context
       John heard that / the textbook for Geophysics / was very advanced./ Nobody understood it properly. / He heard that / if he wanted to pass the course / he should read / the class notes or the summary.

That the disjunctive phrase takes significantly longer to process in (6.3) than in (6.4) is consistent with results showing that narrowed readings are more effortful to process than those that do not call for this sort of pragmatic enrichment. When there is a reason for the reader to refine the disjunction's meaning (as opposed to having no reason to refine it) reading times are significantly slower.

A Focus on Eye-Tracking Studies and
What They Reveal About Scalars

In this literature, eye-tracking is used while participants are required to isolate a target (usually by pointing or clicking) as an instruction asks them to choose among presented options or while participants listen to a statement while surveying a scene. Experimenters are keen to see how quickly a listener (a participant) isolates her choice or a part of the scene as a function of the words in a sentence. Huang and Snedeker (2009a) pursued the idea that semantic readings are generally first (i.e., that a definitional reading of "some" needs to be processed and before pragmatic enrichments can take place). In order to test this claim, they cleverly set up a situation in which participants follow instructions about one of four characters, two boys and two girls, who are associated with some objects. If a speaker says, "Point to the girl who has all of the socks" when viewing the representation (c) in Figure 6.2, one should ultimately click on the one girl who has all of the socks. But, how soon do participants focus on that one girl? One possibility is that they wait for the end of the sentence, which is why objects have names that start off being phonologically similar (e.g., in Figure 6.3, the two kinds of objects are SOCKs and SOCCer balls). Another possibility (one that the authors were expecting) is that participants profit from verbal clues along the way. So, for the current example, participants should begin focusing on the appropriate girl quite soon after hearing "all" because the quantifier is a determinative clue for discerning between the two girls (keep in mind that the articulation of "girl" already removes two of the four possible targets). Huang and Snedeker's main question is, does one find a similar effect when the quantifier is "some"? When participants hear "Point to the girl that has some of the socks" with respect to Figure 6.2 (version a) below, can the target be definitively identified with "some" as a clue? After all, if the pragmatic interpretation were to be accessed automatically on-line, then one would expect the participant's eyes to alight relatively quickly on the girl with the subset of items mentioned as soon as the word "some" is uttered.

Figure 6.3 shows the *proportion of looks to target* across four different conditions. One condition presented the quantifier "some," as described above, while the three control conditions presented the quantifiers "all" (as described earlier), as well as "two" and "three." Concretely, the control item for "two," "Point to the girl who has two of the socks," would be accompanied with the representation in (b) and the control item for "three," "Point to the girl who has three of the socks" would be accompanied with the representation in (d). Of course, there are also trials that make reference to soccer balls and to the boys as well.

Huang and Snedeker found that, for each of the control conditions, participants began turning their attention to the appropriate target as soon as the quantifier "two," "three," or "all" was uttered. This was not the case for the word "some." In this critical condition, participants waited until they heard

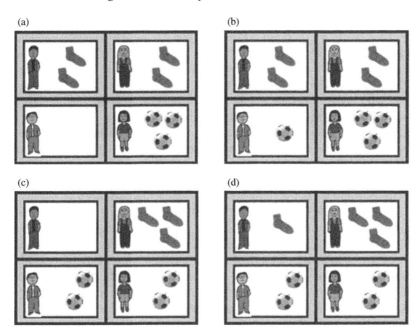

Figure 6.2. Examples of visual world displays from Huang and Snedeker's (2009a) eye-tracking paradigm. The representation in (a) is the basis for the critical trial *Point to the girl that has some of the socks*.

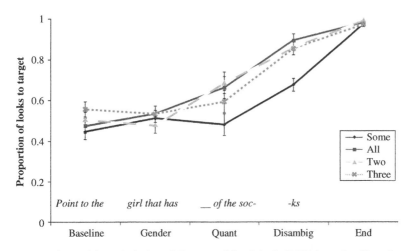

Figure 6.3. A depiction of Huang and Snedeker's (2009a) results (Exp. 1) as shared by Yi Ting Huang with the author. It shows proportional looks to Target for four quantifiers (*two, some, three,* and *all*). Unlike sentences with "two," "three," and "all," sentences with "some" (the solid black curve) lead to the target relatively late, i.e., when the sentence is disambiguated by the noun "socks"

the disambiguating word at the end of the sentence in order to head toward the intended target. They argued that the slowdown in the experimental condition was due to the presence of the *All* case (the girl with all the soccer balls), which remains an attractive alternative for "the girl with some of the socks." These effects were confirmed with similar work (Huang and Snedeker, 2009b) that involved five-year-olds and adults (in which, interestingly, the children showed no evidence of pragmatically enriching "some").

Some colleagues raised concerns about this paradigm because the study used (a) quantities that were in the subitizing range[6] and; (b) actual numbers ("two" and "three") among its control items. Unlike in previous tasks, then, the potential acceptability of "some" to represent "all" is further weighted down by the possibility that the speaker would articulate numbers such as "2" or "3" (see Degen & Tanenhaus, 2015). Although these critiques can be viewed as a weakness to the study, it also reveals an important fact: that the presence of another attractive option affects the process of enriching *some* in these utterances. This implies that slowdowns are not specifically due to the juxtaposition of two potential targets for "some" when one could be called by its scalemate "all." That numerals in clearly demarcated contexts can appear to be as (or more) attractive as the quantifier "all" lends doubt to the claim that scales are involved at all. It is arguably the case that any given paradigm encourages participants to anticipate certain words and there are some that are better fits than others.

Grodner et al. (2010) were not convinced that "some" should be exceptional and so they adopted Huang and Snedeker's eye-tracking paradigm in their own study. Critically, they made several changes to the paradigm. I will mention five. First, there are no other classes of quantifiers, such as numbers. Second, Grodner et al. (2010) expanded the presentation so that participants saw six figures, three girls and three boys. Third, when the targeted character (say, the girl) was described as associated with the partitive "some," the other two girls were represented with the two complementary quantifiers; that is, one girl would have no items associated with her and the other would have *all* items (say, four out of four soccer balls), thus providing a unique visual representation for each kind of quantifier. Fourth, items were distributed before the participants' eyes, which gives participants time to anticipate which of ten possible statements could be made.[7] Finally, Grodner et al.'s (2010) paradigm included dozens more trials, which could allow participants to create strategies. So, while Grodner et al. (2010) succeeded in pointing out that a partitive "some" can serve as a fast-acting clue in the Huang and Snedeker paradigm, and thus temper Huang and Snedeker's claims, one could also see that an experiment must go to some lengths in order to do so.

Given that any reading of a scalar expression means having access to the speaker's communicative intention and that decoding a sentence is part of accessing the speaker's epistemic state, the question that Breheny, Ferguson, and Katsos (2013a) asked is, does a listener consider a speaker's mental state *as* a scalar term is voiced? To investigate this, they had participants listen to confederates describe a simple scene after witnessing a person on film pour water into bowls. For example, participants would see a man pour an entire jug of water-containing-oranges into one bowl and only part of another jug of water-containing-limes into another bowl. The contrast between the two cases prompts test sentences such as (6.5) and the question (like in the previous studies) is, how early in the test sentence do participants naturally focus on the intended jug (while looking at a frozen slice of film on a screen) as they hear (6.5)?

(6.5) The man has poured some of the water with limes into the bowl on tray A and all of the water with oranges into the bowl on tray B.

In other words, does articulating "some" in the above context provide enough of a clue for the listener to immediately fixate on the water-with-limes? In order to answer this question, participants were provided baseline conditions too. For example, they would see the man pour part of a jug of water-containing-limes and then part of another jug of water-containing-oranges before hearing the following:

(6.6) The man has poured some of the water with limes into the bowl on tray A and some of the water with oranges into the bowl on tray B.

In this case, the word "some" ought to not help identify the intended jug of water until the word "limes" is uttered and the data confirm that. Breheny et al. (2013a) report that participants were able to anticipate their looks to the correct target in the *Some-early* condition (in 6.5) as soon as they heard the quantifier "some" and long before the disambiguating expression ("limes") was perceived. They report that scalar implicatures are accessed as rapidly as other contextual inference.

   In related work that gets much closer to the heart of Gricean reasoning, Breheny, Ferguson, and Katsos (2013b) set up scenarios similar to those above but with ad-hoc situations that lead to statements like the one in (6.7) below (as well as the one in 6.1e). Like in Breheny et al. (2013a), two people watch a scene on their own separate screens where an unidentifiable person puts objects (forks and spoons, in this case) one at a time into one of two shoeboxes marked A and B. Once the scene is over, a still image of the last frame remains on the hearer's screen, while the speaker (who is a confederate) describes the events just seen in the video. The goal (again) will be to silently follow the listener's (the participant's) eyes (on that still image), while he listens to the speaker. The statement in (6.7) is representative of one of the study's critical items:

(6.7) The woman put a fork into box A and a fork and a spoon into box B.

There are a couple of things to know about (6.7) and the experimental design in which it appeared. One is that the first conjunct of this sentence (about box A) potentially implies that nothing else went into that box (as the listener himself had just witnessed). That is, the listener (like the speaker) had first seen the woman put a fork into box B, a fork into box A, and then a spoon into box B (in that order). In this scenario, the listener can readily identify (and anticipate) that the speaker is indicating box A as soon as the speaker says "into" because nothing else followed, which is exactly what a pragmatic enrichment would describe ("a fork *but nothing else* went into box A"). Eye-movements indeed indicate that listeners made increased looks to Box A as early as hearing "into" after the first "fork" because that is the box that has the single fork. Now, let's consider the experiment's other condition.

The experiment included an "ignorance" condition in which participants were told that for some trials, the person whose role it was to be speaker (again, this was a confederate) does not see the entire video, even as the participant sees the video to its conclusion. In order to create this condition, the experimenter would literally block the speaker from seeing the end of a video (while the participant would see the entire video). In the case of (6.7), the speaker followed the scene until a fork was placed in each box, at which point the experimenter paused the video, took a big piece of board and placed it in front of the speaker's screen, then continued the video. The goal of this technique was to determine whether the participant considers the epistemic state of the speaker when processing the speaker's summary statement, which is now (6.8):

(6.8)   The woman put a fork into box A and a fork into box B.

The first part of this statement is identical to the one in (6.7), but notice that, even though the listener knows how the video ended, the speaker does not. Does the listener (as measured by his looks) consider the speaker's epistemic state? It appears that he does because his looks reveal that he does not interpret "fork *but nothing else*," upon hearing "fork into Box A," i.e., the listener does not anticipate looks to box A because, as the authors point out, pragmatic enrichment depends on gaining access to the speaker's epistemic state. Note that this is a pragmatic inference that does not depend on scales or specific words, but rather on what is considered a particularized implicature. All told, the work from Breheny's group underlines how implicatures depend on having access to the speaker's mind and not just his words.

Individual Differences

Another intriguing result from this literature is that participants are consistent in preferring one reading. Starting with Noveck and Posada (2003), who used the "Some airplanes have wings" type of materials among adults, one finds reports of two largely isolated groups of individuals with respect to scalar inferences, with roughly half seeming to prefer semantic readings and the rest pragmatic readings. Bott and Noveck (2004) also found two groups plus a smattering of "mixed" participants (whose individual data still revealed a semantic-interpretation-is-easier-to-process effect).

What are behind these individual differences? Nieuwland, Ditman, and Kuperberg (2010) showed that the moment at which underinformativeness becomes apparent is generally not noticeable to most participants on-line through EEG (see Chapter 4). Consider the word "lungs" in sentence (6.9), which is taken from Experiment 2 of their study and is arguably underinformative at the point at which it is expressed (since all people have lungs). Taking the participants as a group, "lungs" prompts an EEG profile that is indistinguishable from the word "pets" in (6.10) when it is expressed, even though the latter does not offer the same potential to be underinformative:

(6.9)   Some people have lungs that require good care.

(6.10) Some people have pets that require good care.

However, another experiment – with the same paradigm – shows that EEG profiles appear more reactive when (a) participants are broken down into two groups based on their "Communication Score" in Baron-Cohen's Autism Quotient (Baron-Cohen et al., 2001), where a higher score indicates that an individual is higher on the Autism Spectrum; plus when (b) a comma is inserted prompting a sort of "clausal wrap-up." To make this clear, consider how (6.9) and (6.10) can be presented as (6.9') and (6.10'):

(6.9')   Some people have lungs, which require good care.

(6.10') Some people have pets, which require good care.

With these sentences, those participants who are considered more "pragmatically skilled" (with low AQ scores) had EEG profiles with an N400 of greater magnitude to the underinformative item in a sentence such as (6.9') when compared to (6.10'). This indicates that some sort of expectation was violated on-line among this half of participants. Those who scored higher on the scale had N400s that were less remarkable in that their reactions to (6.9') and (6.10') were comparable. The upshot here is that it can be demonstrated that a subgroup of participants who appear to be more pragmatically skilled go further in narrowing the meaning of a sentence on-line. The rest do not.

Summing Up

The studies in this chapter show that the narrowing of (an utterance containing) a weak scalar term (e.g., to interpret "some" as "some but not all") is not a common occurrence nor is it automatic. Children are generally less likely to do so than adults, adults do not necessarily carry them out routinely and context is critical to making them occur. It is hard to argue – based on a wide range of data – that scalar enrichments arise automatically. This provides the grounds for discharging Levinson's account, which argues that the enriched reading (the narrowed one) occurs by default and that it can be potentially cancelled later. This is an important development. Moreover, one sees that accounts that place a focus uniquely on linguistic features (proposed scales and a role for entailment relations between proposed alternatives) cannot anticipate some of the findings from experiments that place an emphasis on the particularities of a given context. That said, such findings have not dampened others from applying grammatically inspired models to account for pragmatic data. This leads to the scalar literature's other concurrent phase of research, which we turn to in the next chapter.

Notes

1. The biblical injunction declaring what sort of meat is fit for consumption, i.e., kosher, is expressed with a conjunction embedded in a universal quantifier. The categorical rule can be translated roughly as "These are the living things one may eat: All creatures that both chew their cud, i.e., are ruminants, and have split hooves." This permits, for example, cows, which are ruminants that have split hooves. Interestingly, the Bible goes on to explain – with a disjunction – which sorts of animals are *not* kosher ("those that either chew their cud or have split hooves"), at which point pigs (and other curious examples) are specifically mentioned as having one feature but not the other. Missing from the list is a specific restriction against eating animals that neither chew their cud nor have split hooves (e.g., horses). For medieval rabbinical authorities, it was unclear how one can account for the prohibition against eating horses if one adopts an exclusive disjunctive reading of "or" in the stated prohibition. This was a conundrum for the authorities because another important rabbinical law prohibited punishing people corporally for offenses based on mere inferential derivations. While medieval rabbinical authorities intuited that animals with neither feature were unkosher, their justifications varied widely and depended on their view of the disjunction as inclusive or exclusive. (Apparently they also wanted to maintain the strong disincentive for members of the tribe who would dare eat horses.) Bernhard Rohrbacher, a labor lawyer and a linguist, whose article (Rohrbacher, 2015) brings this interesting medieval case to light, makes some fascinating insights about the authorities' knowledge of logic and disjunctions; he also argues that one occidentally influenced authority saw the issue non-problematically as semantic (while treating "or" as inclusive), thus avoiding the conundrum. In my view, an inclusive reading of the disjunctive rule would be problematic because (rather than prohibit horse-eating) it would make cows unkosher. I think the reading is indeed intended to be exclusive and on pragmatic grounds (see Chapter 7). That is, the two biblical rules combined essentially say, "while creatures that are ruminants and that have split hooves are kosher, those that are ruminants *or* have

split hooves are not." To determine whether or not horses are kosher, it would have behooved the authorities to complete the truth table for the *conjunction* and, yes, infer from it that an animal that is neither a ruminant, nor split-hooved is unkosher and stop there.

2. Although I have become convinced – through much of the work described here – that scalar implicatures are neither scalar nor implicatures, this is the term that gave birth to this area, and so we are essentially stuck with it.

3. Noveck and Posada (2003) made similar points with an EEG study, but I find the materials in Bott and Noveck (2004) to be superior.

4. People often remark that responding *false* necessarily takes longer than responding *true*. I consider this a myth. There are many papers that include cases showing false responses as faster than true ones (e.g., see Prado & Noveck, 2006; Chemla & Bott, 2014). In my view, important factors are the task and the strategy of the participant.

5. Steven Pinker (2015: Sense of Style) complains about the overly technical, mathematical terminology such as "upper-bounded" and "lower-bounded" for describing "*some*," while expressing a preference for the "only" and "at least" senses, respectively. However, as this example makes clear, the terminology works because it can be applied to a wide range of cases. That said, if the reader prefers, one could describe these cases as having "exclusive" and "inclusive" readings, respectively.

6. This range refers to a low number of items that are easily perceivable and countable even with brief stimulus times, up to three or four.

7. There are eighteen possible ways to distribute objects among the six Figures (from each of the six having "all the x" to each of the six having "none of the x" and anything in between). Instead, about ten are used.

7   Grammatical or Semantic Approaches to Scalar Implicatures

> Don't say that Aretha is making a comeback, because I've never been away.
>
> *Aretha Franklin*

After studying scalar inferences for some time, I had become convinced that there was no support for default accounts. As the previous chapter described, data from my lab (e.g., Bott & Noveck, 2004) and others' (e.g., Breheny et al., 2006; De Neys & Schaeken, 2007; Huang & Snedeker, 2009, to mention a few), had clearly shown that (a) utterances containing scalar terms do not provide uniform interpretations (roughly half of participants appear to respond with an enrichment and half do not); (b) *when* scalars are enriched, they require extra effort and, moreover; (c) scalar inferences are often linked with individual differences on a scale involving mindreading abilities (Nieuwland et al., 2010). With more and more people reporting similar findings that countered default accounts, I was even sanguine about my belief that no one could continue to maintain an account that resembles a default position. I could not have been more wrong.

Over the course of the last ten years or so, specific semantic analyses of scalar-inference-related phenomena have driven many (mostly formally trained semanticists) to argue – and with a vengeance[1] – in favor of the idea that scalar inferences result essentially from a *grammatical* process. Determined at least in part to account for pragmatic phenomena through non-Gricean analyses, theoretical analyses from Landman (1998) and Chierchia (2004) would ultimately bring about accounts of scalar terms that make Horn's scalar implicature account and Levinson's GCI proposal seem quaint in comparison. In any case, these semantic approaches have become part of the experimental pragmatic enterprise because their advocates have sought verification of their claims through experimental studies.

Before turning to these semantic proposals, it is important to highlight a recognized weakness in Grice's original proposal, which had (even forty years ago) led either to modifications (among sympathetic Griceans) or to calls to abandon the Gricean program (among the less sympathetic). This will be followed by a summary of two experimental phases aimed at investigating scalar phenomena based on semantic-cum-grammatical proposals. Along the way, we will see how semanticists, in general, formally address phenomena related to scalar inferences.

On Gricean Claims

Before identifying the weakness, let us quickly summarize five features of a properly Gricean pragmatic inference as it emerges from an input sentence (as underlined by Recanati, 2004).[2] The first important feature is that an utterance's extra-linguistic information comes from, say, facts, background knowledge, or information gathered from an ongoing conversation at the time of the utterance. This leads to the second feature, which is that the enrichment process is a top-down rather than a bottom-up affair – one that helps make sense of the communicative act performed by the speaker. The third is that listeners can reconstruct how they draw their conclusions from an utterance because it is a matter of speaker meaning. While the conversational protagonists must be consciously aware of what the speaker means, they need not be consciously aware of the grammatical meaning of the expressions used, nor of the processes through which the meaning of the whole is determined on the basis of the meanings of the parts. Fourth, the enrichment is global rather than local; that is, enrichment is not part of a step-by-step process of compositionally determining a semantic interpretation for the sentence, but takes place *after the global interpretation of the sentence* has been calculated. Finally, there must be a way to maintain the option of using the same form of words so that it carries the plain, unenriched interpretation; an enriched interpretation of an utterance is one possibility, but not the only one.

My italicization above might have cued you in. Early criticisms of Grice's proposal concerned a weakness with the fourth point, the notion that an enrichment relies on a global process. Theorists argued that if Gricean enrichments are predicated on the idea that they are generated by hearing an entire utterance, there should be no enrichments of a given clause or even *locally* on a specific word (independently of the rest of the sentence). Let us consider this more carefully.

Embedded Implicatures

According to a Gricean view, an utterance leads to the emergence of a logical skeleton of a proposition. Let us call the emerged proposition p. Subparts of the utterance (e.g., an individual word) should not need to be pragmatically enriched *in order to* arrive at that proposition p. That proposition p should remain unenriched as pragmatic inferencing is carried out on the entire sentence. If one could show that *local* enrichments are actually critical to arriving at that p, it would undermine this one critical feature of Grice's proposal.

Cohen (1971), soon after Grice's William James lectures, pointed to cases where one critical (embedded) *part* of a sentence appears to call for enrichment as part of a listener's attempt to come up with his truth-evaluable proposition. Antecedents of conditionals quickly captured linguists' attention because (as we will see below) this is a linguistic environment in which enrichments should be held at bay in order to come up with minimal truth evaluable propositions (i.e., an enrichment here could affect the way the proposition is articulated). Consider this example of a perceived local enrichment, (7.1) from Wilson (1975):

(7.1) If the King dies of a heart attack and a Republic is declared, then Tom will be quite content.

Logically speaking (as far as truth conditions go), the order of the conjuncts should not matter for understanding the entire utterance. The point of this example, however, is that the implicit order in the antecedent is critical (as if the speaker's intended reading calls for a specific order in which the King dies of a heart attack *first* and *then* a Republic is declared) and this is information that goes above and beyond the "what is said" meaning of "and." To scholars who have analyzed (7.1), it seems reasonable to assume that Tom's contentedness would not be guaranteed (to the same extent at least) in the event that the King dies after the Republic is declared. So, it was argued that there are potentially cases that include the local enrichment, which in this case encourages an "and then" reading for the conjunction.[3] Other examples of this kind of observation come from Carston (1988) and Wilson and Sperber (1998), (7.2) and (7.3), respectively, as inspired by Cohen (1971):

(7.2) Eating some of the cake is better than eating all of it.

(7.3) It's always the same at parties: either I get drunk and no one will talk to me or no one will talk to me and I get drunk.

In (7.2), the enrichment of "some" to "some but not all" is necessary *in order to* make sense of the utterance. A paraphrase that keeps a "some and perhaps all" reading would make the second part of the sentence redundant. In (7.3), like in (7.1), the order is critical, which means that "and" (used twice) needs to be enriched with "and then" or "and because of that"; without such an enrichment, this utterance, too, would appear redundant. So, it does appear that enrichments can arise as part and parcel of the uttered *sentence meaning*. These enrichments are referred to as *embedded implicatures, local implicatures,* or, more generally speaking, as *conventionalized implicatures*. Is this a reason to abandon the Gricean program?

In reaction to these examples, investigators went generally in one of three directions (Carston, 1988). Some argued that Grice was simply wrong and that critical terms (such as "and" and "some") are in fact ambiguous (Cohen,

1971). Some suggested that there is a Gricean explanation and one just needs to come up with it. For example, Levinson would eventually devote a part of his classic book (2000) to "intrusive constructions," like those in (7.1) through (7.3) and argue that the "Obstinate Theorist" could say that the "what is said" reading of the utterance yields an interpretation that violates a maxim (such as Quality or Manner), which is the source itself for generating an implicature that yields the speaker's intended reading. Others, still, made modifications to the Gricean program and suggested that there are not two levels of analysis ("what is said" versus "what is meant") but three, with the new one being intermediate between the two. For example, Relevance Theorists propose that the linguistically encoded meaning serves as a skeleton upon which one can arrive at an *explicature* level.[4] Explicatures are logical forms that listeners use to work out the speaker's communicative intention along with genuine implicatures in Relevance Theory (moreover, both explicatures and implicatures are assumed to be worked out in parallel). The latter two approaches maintained Grice's overall program, which envisions a cooperative speaker who aims to get at the speaker's intended meaning.[5]

Chierchian semantic accounts come closest to the first approach and assume that the linguistic code ultimately *provides* the means to be cooperative. While these accounts begin with observations similar to those raised by Cohen (1971) and Wilson (1975), they either aim to describe how specific syntactic features generate (or do not generate) enrichments or they stipulate syntactic features that would make sense of the range of scalar inferences. There were in fact two phases in the more recent semantic approach. The first phase focused on the way specific grammatical environments, such as negations or question forms, affect pragmatic inference-making. Let's call this the *syntactic environment* approach. The second phase, which is the center of much current attention, focuses on the way scalars are locally enriched. Let's call this the *embedded cases* approach. This more recent approach has generated much heated debate (Chierchia, 2004; Chierchia, Fox, & Spector, 2012; Geurts, 2010; Russell, 2006) and no single chapter in this book could do justice to the intensity of the exchanges. Given that the goal of this book is to present and evaluate the experimental claims that such approaches produce, my aim for now will be to largely summarize the findings from each of the semantic approaches. Let us take a look at each of these phases in turn.

The Syntactic Environment Approach

In the earlier foray, Chierchia and his colleagues (Chierchia, 2001; Chierchia et al., 2012) noted that weak terms such as "some" or "or" appear to get enriched in specific grammatical contexts, while they do not in others. What are these contexts? The best known of these is *downward entailing* contexts, which I will describe briefly. If I say, in (7.4a), that "John is not eating ice cream," it entails, in (7.4b), that he is not eating strawberry ice cream (nor chocolate, vanilla, pistachio, etc.). The entailment relationship is *downward* from the universal to the particular.

(7.4)   a. John is not eating ice cream.
        b. John is not eating strawberry ice cream.

Downward entailment has been investigated in order to describe negative polarity items (NPIs), such as the word "any," which appear seamlessly in certain contexts. These contexts, illustrated in (7.5a–d), situate "any" under negation (7.5a), in the antecedent of conditionals (7.5b), in questions (7.5c), and in what are called optative operators (7.5d), which describe desires, beliefs, and wishes:

(7.5)   a. Steve does not want any of your money.
        b. If Marlene has any biscuits, her dog would know.
        c. Does Bernie have any chance of winning the nomination?
        d. Send me any pictures showing children eating ice cream.

These same sentences do not appear to "license" the use of "any" outside of these contexts. Consider the cases of (7.6a–d) that are (1) part of an affirmative statement, (2) in the consequent of a conditional, (3) in an assertion, and (4) non-optative, respectively, which explains why examples like these appear ungrammatical:

(7.6)   a. Steve wants any of your money.
        b. If Marlene takes her dog out for a walk, she carries any biscuits.
        c. Bernie has any chance of winning the nomination.
        d. Michael sent me any pictures showing children eating ice cream.

Interestingly, downward entailing (or uses of "any") contexts appear to coincide with cases in which scalars appear to be *not* readily enriched (i.e., they retain a semantic reading), as in (7.7a–d):

(7.7)   a. Eliana does not want a cat or a dog.
        b. If Jonathan hikes or dances, he brings sneakers.
        c. Does Matt enjoy rollerblading or bicycling?
        d. Send me videos of people speaking Catalan or Spanish.

In each of the above cases (7.7a–d), it is argued that an *A or B and perhaps both* interpretation appears to be most appropriate. Compare that to cases in upward-entailing contexts (7.8a–d), where an *A or B but not both* can be considered more salient:

(7.8)   a. Eliana owns a cat or a dog.
        b. If Jonathan is wearing sneakers, then he is hiking or dancing.
        c. Matt enjoys rollerblading or bicycling.
        d. The people are speaking Catalan or Spanish.

Note that these are largely observations. It would be more convincing if there were data to support these claims.

In a collaboration I carried out with Gennaro, Noveck et al. (2002) presented participants a series of syllogisms concerning letters written on a hidden blackboard. To anticipate, syllogisms were prepared with disjunctions in either the antecedent of a conditional, in its consequent, or else with disjunctive conclusions as questions or assertions. For example, imagine a participant who is asked to draw a conclusion (below the line) from the syllogism in (7.9):

(7.9) If there is a P then there is a Q and an R.
       There is a P.
       There is a Q and an R.

Evaluating this syllogism (7.9) is straightforward for participants (nearly everyone agrees it is correct). However, if one were to present the conclusion in (7.10), "There is a Q or an R," most people (75 percent) balk and say, "No" (meaning that 25 percent say "Yes"), indicating disagreement.

(7.10) If there is a P then there is a Q and an R.
        There is a P.
        There is a Q or an R.

Likewise, when a participant is given the syllogism in (7.11), participants say "No" 70 percent of the time.

(7.11) If there is a P then there is a Q or an R.
        There is a P.
        There is a Q and an R.

Now, consider a syllogism whose disjunction is in the antecedent (7.12):

(7.12) If there is a P or a Q then there is an R.
        There is a P.
        There is a Q.
        There is an R.

In this case, participants appear to have less difficulty accepting the disjunction – what is implicitly a conjunction – as true, because a large majority (85 percent) agree with the conclusion. Thus, one can see a reversal of interpretations for the disjunction. When the provided conclusion is a disjunction but the premises prompt a conjunctive conclusion, participants treat the disjunction exclusively (7.10). Likewise, when the disjunction is initially in the consequent and the basis for a conclusion (7.11), participants treat it as exclusive when the provided conclusion is a conjunction. When participants are presented a disjunction in the antecedent of the conditional and it turns out that both disjuncts are asserted (7.12), participants accept the disjunction as true and allow the conditional to go through. The disjunction in the antecedent is compatible with an inclusive interpretation. This seems quite remarkable. Similarly, when disjunctions are in question form, as in the concluding line of the syllogism in (7.13), participants' responses (80 percent saying "Yes") indicate that disjunctions are more likely to be treated as inclusive under such conditions:

(7.13) If there is a P then there is a Q and an R.
        There is a P.
        There is a Q or an R?

As I indicated above, responses to this syllogism (7.13) in its more standard form (7.10), with an assertion as a conclusion, yield "Yes" responses at a 25 percent rate. So, there is some indication that question form encourages inclusive readings.

This is nice support for claims stressing grammatical overlap with scalar inference-making. But, before continuing, let me point out that there are two caveats and an alternative account for these sorts of findings. One caveat is that we presented another syllogism that was almost identical to the one in (7.12), except that the conjunction was made explicit in the minor premise (see 7.14). In this case, participants responded less convincingly.[6] That is, with a syllogism such as (7.14), participants accept the conclusion just 60 percent of the time, which is closer to chance levels (i.e., this rate of acceptance is – statistically speaking – not dissimilar from the rates one would expect when flipping a coin):

(7.14) If there is a P or a Q then there is an R.
        There is a P and a Q.
        There is an R.

Thus, by making the contrast between "or" and "and" more apparent participants are more likely to apply an exclusive reading to the disjunction in the major premise of (7.14), even though it is in the antecedent.[7] That said, it does appear that disjunctions in antecedents do make participants more open to inclusive interpretations than disjunctions outside of it. The second caveat, which concerns disjunctions in question form (e.g., 7.13), is that a follow-up experiment (Noveck et al., 2002, Experiment 4) showed that participants seek consistency in their responses and to such a degree that when provided both (7.10) and (7.13) in the same experimental session, i.e., with a conclusion as an assertion in one case and as a question in another (separated within the experiment and among many filler items), participants are influenced by the answer they give during their first encounter. When conclusions are provided as assertions first, participants' interpretations to conclusions-as-questions later are more exclusive too.

The alternative explanation is that these grammatical "contexts" overlap with another – more global – feature, which is that participants (listeners) extract the most informative interpretation possible from a statement. In the above syllogisms, an exclusive reading in the consequent provides for a more informative reading overall than an inclusive one; likewise, an inclusive reading in the antecedent of a conditional renders the entire proposition more potentially informative than an exclusive reading there.[8] How can one see that? By comparing truth tables for the conditional statements when the disjunctions are treated inclusively or exclusively.

Below are two truth tables for "If there is a P then there is a Q or an R." The one on the left shows the outcomes (those below the sign for implication ultimately define the truth value of the proposition) when the consequent is treated as an inclusive-*or* (as per classic logic) and the one on the right is the truth table when the disjunction in the expression is treated as (a pragmatically enriched) exclusive. As per the truth table on the left, the conditional (->) is the determining connective for the entire statement on the right.

One can see that the first row is true when one considers the disjunction inclusive (on the left), while it is false when one considers the disjunction exclusive on the right (the truth values for the disjunction are noted in those places where changes arise when the disjunction is treated inclusively versus exclusively; the assigned truth value affects the evaluation of the sentence only in the first row). The main point of this exercise is to show that the exclusive reading of the disjunction in the truth table on the right renders the sentence more informative, by ultimately providing fewer true conditions.

Table 7.1. *The truth tables for a conditional when a disjunction is in the consequent and understood inclusively (left), as opposed to exclusively (right). Truth values in bold italics indicate differences across tables. Note that only the first row leads to a different conclusion, determined by the sign for conditionals (→). The remaining rows are included for the sake of completeness.*

P	→	(Q	or	R)	P	→	(Q	or	R)
T	*T*	T	*T*	T	T	*F*	T	*F*	T
T	T	T	T	F	T	T	T	T	F
T	T	F	T	T	T	T	F	T	T
T	F	F	F	F	T	F	F	F	F
F	T	T	*T*	T	F	T	T	*F*	T
F	T	T	T	F	F	T	T	T	F
F	T	F	T	T	F	T	F	T	T
F	T	F	T	F	F	T	F	F	F

Although I have included all possible rows, do keep in mind that the bottom half of the rows (in both tables) represent irrelevant or uncommon situations (because the antecedent is false). In any case, one is increasing the likelihood of finding a false evaluation with an exclusive disjunction in the consequent. This is what it means to be more informative (Carnap & Bar-Hillel, 1952).

Let's do the same exercise with "If P or Q then R." In this case, there are more false possibilities when the disjunction is inclusive (on the left), as opposed to when the disjunction is exclusive (on the right). In other words, an inclusive reading (on the left) provides for a more informative statement because it ultimately increases the number of false cases. It removes from consideration a greater proportion of true cases.

The Noveck et al. (2002) experiments were conceived with Gennaro, soon after the maiden *Experimental Pragmatics* workshop in Lyon in 2001 and are exemplary of what Kahneman had called an *adversarial collaboration* (Mellers, Hertwig, & Kahneman, 2001). The idea behind this cool-headed expression is to pair colleagues who have opposing points of view in order to work out experiments (and ideally with the help of a judicious arbiter who determines who, of the two, is correct, or which side better accounts for the data). In this case, we were investigating whether Gennaro's observations could be supported through experiments and to see the extent to which these findings are compatible with other (e.g., Gricean) accounts. As far as I was concerned, this work showed that the grammatical approach provided insight in that it confirmed that specific communicative acts could account for some of the narrowed (exclusive "or") readings in proper reasoning experiments. On the other hand, the data did not show that grammatical features are independent of

Table 7.2. *The truth tables for a conditional when a disjunction is in the antecedent and understood inclusively (left), as opposed to exclusively (right). Truth values in bold italics indicate differences across tables. Note that only the second row leads to a different conclusion, as determined by the sign for conditionals (→). The remaining rows are included for the sake of completeness.*

(P	or	Q)	→	R	(P	or	Q)	→	R
T	T	T	T	T	T	F	T	T	T
T	T	T	*F*	F	T	F	T	*T*	F
T	T	F	T	T	T	T	F	T	T
T	T	F	F	F	T	T	F	F	F
F	T	T	T	T	F	T	T	T	T
F	T	T	T	F	F	T	T	T	F
F	F	F	T	T	F	F	F	T	T
F	F	F	T	F	F	F	F	T	F

other factors. For example, participants' prior encounters were determinative as one can see with respect to the question forms in examples such as (7.13) and explicit contrasts between two connectives mattered, as one can see when one compares (7.12) and (7.14). Overall, predictions converge in that both explanations, Gricean and grammatical, underscore how listeners tend toward more informative readings. These data are revealing of a potential compatibility between grammar-inspired, Ideal Language explanations and Ordinary-Language explanations that take information-gain into account (Bar-Hillel & Carnap, 1953; Levinson, 1983; Sperber & Wilson, 1986).

Phase II: Embedded Cases

At the top of the chapter, I explained how one feature of Grice's original account – the claim that enrichments occur over entire utterances – prompted some pushback. Griceans as well as anti-Griceans began to consider cases that showed how a listener needs to enrich specific components *in* an utterance in order to arrive at a truth-evaluable proposition. The statements in (7.1) through (7.3) illustrated how one needed to enrich the meanings of "some" (in 7.2) and "and" (in 7.1 and 7.3) locally (not over the entire utterance) *in order* to make sense of the speaker's utterance. Without a local enrichment, these utterances would be contradictory or redundant. Before we get to the way grammatical accounts took a second stab at scalar implicatures, it is relevant to review how formal semanticists accounted for implicatures more generally before this subfield took a grammatical turn.

Inspired by Horn and his default account, semanticists assumed that a weak scalar expression generates alternative and stronger possible ones that are considered and summarily rejected (see Chapter 2). By considering a step-by-step account of the way a listener would do this, semanticists propose, with greater precision, how one can get from 7.15a to 7.15b – a relatively standard scalar case. For the sake of this illustration, consider that (7.15a) is uttered by Noemi to Isaac and that Isaac pragmatically enriches the utterance so that it means (7.15b):

(7.15) a. Jeremy brought some of the basketballs.
   b. Jeremy brought some but not all of the basketballs.

Before we begin, notice three things. First, the expression in (7.15a) can generate a linguistically encoded meaning, "Jeremy brought some and perhaps all of the basketballs" and, according to semanticists, two kinds of implicatures. One kind is the added information traditionally associated with a weak "Gricean" implicature, which would be "It is not the case that Jeremy brought all of the balls" (where a negation takes scope over the entire, stronger alternative). The other kind is stronger and is expressed in (7.15b), where the negation is limited to the existential quantifier "*some*," rejecting the stronger "all." Second, the two implicatures are not equivalent. The Gricean one does not entail (7.15b), although (7.15b) entails the two others. Third, it would take some sort of assumption to get from the Gricean implicature to the strong one in (7.15b).

The goal for semanticists is to explain how one can get from a weak Gricean implicature to one embedded into beliefs attributed to the speaker, so that it ends up like (7.15b). The *Standard Recipe* (Geurts, 2009, 2010) breaks down this transformation into four steps. Step 1 is that, rather than saying (7.15a), Noemi could have made a stronger alternative statement (assuming it is relevant), something like (7.16a):

(7.16) a. Jeremy brought all the basketballs.

Step 2 arises when Isaac (the listener) wonders, "Why didn't Noemi say the stronger statement?" The most likely explanation is that Noemi doesn't believe that (7.16a) is true, which is presented as (7.16b):

(7.16) b. Noemi does not believe that Jeremy brought all of the basketballs.

Step 3 arises when the listener (Isaac) assumes that the speaker (Noemi) has an opinion as to whether (7.16a) is true. In attributing an opinion to the speaker, one assumes that the speaker is aware that one of two opposing possibilities is true. The creation of this disjunction relies on what is called the Experthood Assumption (Sauerland, 2004) or the Competency Assumption (Van Rooj & Schulz, 2004), and is expressed as (7.16c):

(7.16) c. Noemi believes that Jeremy brought all of the basketballs or that Jeremy did not bring all of the basketballs.

Step 4, the conclusion, arises through the combination of (7.16b) and (7.16c), which yields – through disjunction elimination – (7.16d):

(7.16) d. Noemi believes that Jeremy did not bring all of the basketballs.

It is the Competency Assumption that ultimately provides a bit more specificity than the weaker Gricean implicature (which only negates the stronger potential alternative).[9]

This preamble provides us with a listener's representation of (7.15b) and provides the backdrop for the grammatical approach. Why would this formal Gricean account not be considered satisfactory? Basically, Chierchia and colleagues consider newer cases that do not provide outcomes that are entirely consistent with standard treatments and that do not comply with an expert's pragmatic intuition. To appreciate how this is so, consider the sentence in (7.17):

(7.17) George believes that some of his advisors are crooks (Chierchia, 2004).

If (7.17) were to be enriched with the Standard Recipe, in which the listener assumes that the speaker could have said something stronger but did not, at Step 2, the enriched utterance would end up looking like (7.18):

(7.18) It is not the case that George believes that all of his advisors are crooks.

While this seems minimally satisfying, it is, according to Chierchia, too weak. Pragmatic intuition accords better with (7.19), which is a stronger inference:

(7.19) George believes that some but not all of his advisors are crooks.

Consider another case, this time with an existential as part of a disjunction:

(7.20) Howie either had a baseball bat or some of the balls.

Given the standard approach, one should first consider stronger alternatives, which include (7.21):

(7.21) Howie either had a baseball bat or all of the balls.

However, were (7.21) to be negated, one would end up with Howie having no bat, nor all of the balls, which means no bat. This could not be a conclusion that one would want. Given this series of unexpected or unwanted inferences in embedded contexts, Chierchia started a second grammatical phase with new explananda, a new formalism, and eventually new experimental findings. As before, Chierchia and colleagues were convinced that grammar must play some role with respect to pragmatic inference-making. What would a grammatical account look like?

The argument goes that there is a covert operator *in the syntax* that provides words such as "some" with a lexical add-on at any sentence node. The covert operator is known as EXH, for exhaustivity, or as a covert "only" so as to render "some" as equivalent to "only some" (represented sometimes with a sign resembling an O). The operator provides a strengthened meaning much like default accounts have argued, by negating certain alternatives, but at a more local level. Sauerland (2014) presents the following example (7.22a), which can be represented as (7.22b):

(7.22) a. Either John is familiar with some of Beethoven's symphonies or he is familiar with all of them.
      b. Either [*EXH* [John is familiar with some of Beethoven's symphonies]] or [John is familiar with all of them].

In embedded cases like in (7.22a), a listener is obliged to come up with a local inference in order to make sense of the sentence. Again, as in (7.2), a listener needs to locally enrich the word "some" in (7.22), otherwise the expression, "He is familiar with all of them" becomes redundant.

There are actually a wide variety of proposals among those who pursue this line (for a summary, see van Tiel, 2014). In some accounts, the "exhaustifier" *EXH* is applied to all sentences (Chierchia, 2004), in others it is said to apply when it yields a more informative sentence (Chierchia et al., 2012) or if it helps avoid a contradiction, as in Sauerland's example (7.22) above. This has led to a very rich discussion about the nature of these proposed covert operators among grammaticalists; what seems not to be controversial among them is whether an operator exists.

Notably, there are semanticists who expressed doubt about this family of proposals (e.g., Geurts, 2009, 2010; Russell, 2006). Russell (2006) made the point that it is doubtful that the stronger pragmatic inference, (e.g., see 7.19), would be expected to go through. According to his analysis, a weaker Gricean reading (see 7.18) would arguably be more justified. Geurts (2010, see Chapter 7) has vehemently argued against grammatical proposals on the grounds that, among several other things, the covert operator is highly unconstrained, the weak implicature is no longer accessible, and that it makes false predictions (based on his own self-generated examples). For example, consider the utterance in (7.23):

(7.23) I hope some of my relatives will remember my birthday (Geurts, 2010, p. 154).

According to a grammatical account, (7.23) ought to prompt a local "some but not all" reading, but this does not accord with Geurts's intuition.

There are two other reasons to be doubtful about this family of grammatical claims. The first is that sentences such as (7.20) require understanding the speaker's intention. If one better understood the speaker's intention when she said, "Howie has a bat or some of the balls," it would help determine whether or not an enrichment of "some "(or of the disjunction) is called for. For example, if the utterance were made so that a coach can be informed that Howie has a portion of the equipment necessary for the coach to run a drill, then arguably neither scalar term would be enriched. The speaker is just providing information that would allow the coach to start gathering what he needs. On the other hand, if (7.20) was uttered in response to another coach who uttered, "Where's my bat and who took all the balls?" then it is arguably more likely that "some" would be enriched, even in its embedded position (for similar arguments, see Noveck & Sperber, 2007). The second reason to remain dubious at this point in the narrative is that these claims are, again, based on armchair observations. As I emphasized earlier (see Chapter 3), it is not advisable to trust one's own introspection with respect to pragmatic inference-making, partly because one cannot rid oneself of the tendency – even among the best intentioned – to confirm one's own theory.[10] This is exactly why experiments are called for. At the very least an experiment can demonstrate that a phenomenon exists as a kind of proof of concept; once that is satisfactorily accomplished, a second step would be to determine whether the proposed mechanism, as opposed to other factors in an experiment, is responsible for effects as claimed. This is why we now take a look at the experimental literature that this approach has spawned and evaluate how well the evidence supports the grammaticalist's strong claim.

Experiments with Embedded Scalar Terms

Geurts and Pouscoulous (2009) launched experimental investigations into these special cases. They ran three different experiments, but the one that generated most discussion involved presenting participants with rather difficult graphs and asking them to evaluate (as true or false) sentences that have the potential to provide embedded implicatures. For example, Figure 7.1 shows a trial in which participants need to evaluate, "Every square is connected with some of the circles." Given that there are two squares that are connected with just two (out of three) circles and one square that is indeed connected to all three, the correct answer – with a local implicature (with a reading of "Every square is connected with some but not all of the circles") – should be false. Meanwhile, with both a linguistically encoded meaning and a weak "Gricean" reading ("It is not the case that every square is connected with all of the circles"), it is accurate to say true.[11] All participants responded true to this particular test item and the other test-cases provided similar outcomes (i.e., Geurts and Pouscoulous found no evidence for the existence of local implicatures).

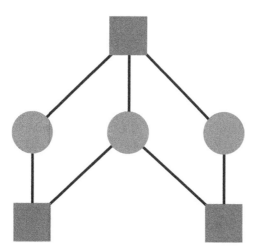

Figure 7.1. An exemplary test item in black and white (of an embedded case) from Geurts and Pouscoulous (2009). Participants were required to answer *true* or *false* to, "All the squares are connected with some of the circles"

As can be seen, this type of problem is particularly difficult (in my view, it resembles a reasoning problem). Nevertheless, given Geurts and Pouscoulous's challenge, others were motivated to modify the task in order to make local interpretations appear more readily. Chemla and Spector (2011), as well as Potts et al. (2016) reacted to the Geurts and Pouscoulous paper by keeping the paradigm but by making it more user-friendly. Let's consider each.

Chemla and Spector made two major modifications. First, they asked for, not true/false judgments, but judgments of appropriateness that ranged from 0 to 100 percent (where 0 percent on a mouse-driven scale meant "No" for *not appropriate* and 100 percent meant "Yes" for *highly appropriate*). Second, Chemla and Spector came up with individuated, simplified representations so that the test sentence could be more readily assessed. Instead of a common set of circles that connect with an overlapping set of squares, the tested rule became, "Every letter is connected with some of its circles," so that the relationship between each of the six letters and its own set of circles could be clearly represented.

Let me first describe the general structure of each trial. Imagine a 3 × 2 table in which a letter (imagine A through F) inhabits each cell. One would see A through C in the top row and the letters D through F in the bottom row; furthermore, each letter is surrounded by six little circles (see Figure 4 in Chemla & Spector, 2011). Given that Chemla and Spector were interested in the way participants modify "some" when it is embedded in "Every letter is connected with some of its circles," they were in a position to determine the extent to which participants judge, as *appropriate*, the three readings below:

> Literal: Every letter is connected to some and perhaps all of its circles.
> Global: It's not the case that every letter is connected to all of its circles.
> Local: Every letter is connected to some but not all of its circles.

There were four relevant conditions. One control condition yields a false response no matter the reading. In this *False* condition, just two of the six letters are connected (by a line) to half of its circles; the rest of the letters remain unattached (imagine an A connected to three of the six little circles and an E connected to three of the six; otherwise one sees four letters, each surrounded by floating, concentrically organized circles, like a star surrounded by six well-organized planets). In the *Literal* condition, each of the letters is connected to all six of its little circles. With this set-up, the picture is true by way of a Literal reading but false with respect to the two others. In what they call the *Weak* condition, each of four letters is connected to all of its little circles, while the remaining two are connected to only half of its circles. This makes the statement true according to the Literal and Global readings but false according to the local reading. Finally, in what they term the *strong* condition, each of the letters is connected to half of its circles. This makes the statement true according to all three readings.

The upshot is that one can better see how a distributed set of circles are, or are not, connected to a single letter (over the course of several trials). Note how the negative space is made explicit. Whereas in Geurts and Pouscoulous (2009), a circle that is unconnected to one square might still be connected to another, every circle in Chemla and Spector's (2011) design clearly is, or is clearly not, connected to a letter. Their modifications allow participants to distinguish between the three kinds of reading better.

The results showed that, out of 100 percent (which indicates that participants judge a sentence as fully appropriate), the mean rating was 12 percent for the *False* condition, 44 percent for the *Literal* one, 68 percent for the *Weak* one and 99 percent for the *Strong* one. So, while three scenarios are literally true, ratings vary and the scenario for which the test-sentence is most satisfying for participants is the one where a local reading of it is true (i.e., in the *Strong* condition). These results appear to support the claim that participants can distinguish local readings from weak Gricean (global) ones.

In a second experiment, the authors presented a test-sentence whose interpretations are based on non-monotonic relationships (i.e., readings that do not have entailment relationships among them). With the test sentence "Exactly one letter is connected with some of its circles," one can again draw out three readings: (a) a linguistically encoded meaning in which "some" can be understood as "some and perhaps all"; (b) a reading with a weak implicature in which the sentence is the basis for denying a global, stronger alternative; or (c) a reading with a strong implicature in which "some" is locally enriched to mean "some but not all." These amount to the following readings:

> Literal: Exactly one letter is connected to some and perhaps all of its circles.
> Global: It's not the case that exactly one letter is connected to all of its circles.
> Local: Exactly one letter is connected with some but not all of its circles.

For these cases, the paradigm works with just three boxes containing letters surrounded by a constellation of circles. The *False* condition shows two letters that are connected to three of six circles while the third is unattached to circles. The *Literal* condition shows one letter being attached to all six of its circles while the remaining two are not attached to any of their circles. The *Local* condition shows one letter attached to just half of its circles while the other two letters are connected to all six of theirs. The fourth condition, which Chemla and Spector labeled *All*, makes all three readings true, as it shows one letter connected to half of its circles (while the other two letters remain unattached to theirs).

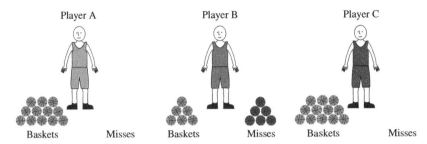

Figure 7.2. A (black and white) example of an item inspired by Potts et al. (2016). This one comes from a follow-up experiment by van Tiel et al. (in press); this item investigated rates of *true* responses to "Exactly one player hit some of his shots"

Much like the earlier example above, a local implicature would account for those scenarios in which there is a single box that depicts a "some but not all" representation (the *Local* and *All* conditions). Indeed, these two generate ratings of 73 percent and 99 percent (as being "appropriate"), respectively. The False and Literal conditions prompted ratings of 7 percent and 37 percent, respectively. Taken together, these two experiments were the first to present evidence indicating that participants, at least while evaluating appropriateness, preferred interpretations that called for local "some but not all" readings.

It was Potts et al. (2016) who refined the Geurts and Pouscoulous paradigm further so that it allowed for direct true/false judgments (as opposed to judgments of appropriateness). They transformed the task so that participants would see three basketball players who succeeded to different extents with respect to 12 foul shots and they collected their data through a crowd-sourcing study (that included dozens of different test-sentences). For the sake of brevity, I will mention two examples that use the test sentence "Exactly one player hit some of his shots." In one critical trial, Potts et al. presented a scenario in which one player always succeeded, a second player who never succeeded and a third who succeeded half the time (see Potts et al., 2016, Figure 3, for a representation of this trial). According to a linguistically encoded meaning, there are two players who have hit at least some of their shots, so participants should say false. Likewise, one should say false with a weak Gricean implicature ("It is not the case that exactly one player hit all of his shots"). But one should say true if there is a local reading, as in "Exactly one player hit some, but not all, of his shots." Potts et al. reported that 50 percent of participants responded true to the sentence. The same analysis generalizes to the representation in Figure 7.2, which shows two players who hit all their shots and one who hit only some. Potts et al. (2016) reported that nearly the same percentage of participants answered true to this one as well.

What Have the Experiments on Embedded Implicatures Accomplished?

Taken together, the Chemla and Spector (2011) data and the Potts et al. data (2016) have shown that participants can be encouraged to provide local enrichments to a term like "some." Findings like these have dynamized the sector of the experimental pragmatic literature that takes a formal semantic approach to scalar implicatures. That said, it is another matter to consider such findings as *positive* evidence in favor of a covert grammatical operator. The main source of hesitation is that small changes made to the format can profoundly change responses – as one looks at the task as it passed from Geurts and Pouscoulous (2009) to Chemla and Spector (2011), and on to Potts et al. (2016). This is an indication that there is probably more to this task than a hidden operator that readily allows for an "only some" reading. This explains why non-grammatical accounts could lay claim to these effects (see van Tiel, 2014, for a discussion and summary of experimental data that make this point). It will take some intricate follow-up experiments to verify that the proposed mechanism, a covert operator, is itself responsible for the effects as claimed.[12] In the last chapter, we will take another look at these claims as we place this set of findings in the general corpus of scalar implicature work and, more generally, in the context of the experimental pragmatic enterprise.

Notes

1. This is based on a comment made to me by David Beaver at the XPrag conference in Chicago (2015).
2. What follows are liberal paraphrases from Recanati (2004).
3. In my view, this remains an intuition that has yet to be experimentally investigated. While I have shown that adults – unlike children – are sensitive to the reordering of conjuncts in unembedded cases (Noveck & Chevaux, 2002; Noveck et al., 2008), I know of no data that show that adult participants, for example, consistently answer "false" or "can't tell" when the provided "rule" is A&B->C, and where background information indicates that B occurs before A.
4. Bach has a similar notion called *impliciture.*
5. As will be seen, what is different about current attempts at addressing embedded implicatures, from Chierchia (2004) and onward, is that they are conceived as a challenge to the Gricean program. Before that, attempts to account for localized implicatures were not presented as inconsistent with the Gricean program. It should also be noted that Grice (1989, p. 375) conceded "to the view that what are implicatures of simple sentences (hence non-truth-conditional aspects of utterance meaning) can become aspects of the truth-conditional aspects of utterance meaning" (Carston, 2004, p. 20).
6. Another technical caveat is that, according to classical logic, conditionals having a false antecedent are true no matter what, so if one were to assume that a participant treats the disjunction exclusively in (7.12), one can argue that a (hyper-logical)

participant would respond true anyway. That said, participants rarely respond true to conditionals having a false antecedent; they are wont to treat conditionals with falsified antecedents as false (Evans, 1973) or by making an inference that negates the consequent, i.e., *If p then q* often leads participants to accept that *if not p then not q* (see Chapter 8).

7. This is arguably one of the bases of later efforts to grammaticalize scalars.

8. I am indebted to Dan Sperber for sharing this observation with me in 2002.

9. I do not want to give the impression that this is a representation that is universally accepted. For one thing, it involves two very precise assumptions, neither of which has ever been shown to be justified, and in order to account for an inference that is not carried out with regularity (see Noveck & Sperber, 2007).

10. French has a nice expression for this: *Déformation Professionnelle*.

11. Grice did not talk specifically of *scalar implicatures*; these neo-Gricean notions of scalars are derived from Gricean principles.

12. A recent line of neuroimaging work (Shetreet, Chierchia, & Gaab, 2014a, b, c), which includes a developmental study, presents data appearing to support the claim that the main site responsible for scalar inference-making ought to be found in language areas (viz. left Inferior Frontal Gyrus); there are two reasons to doubt this specific claim. First, the part of the left IFG that was found activated in Shetreet et al. in 2014 (i.e., Brodmann Area [BA] 47) does not subserve linguistic functioning exclusively. For example, Monti, Parsons, and Osherson (2009) showed – through the juxtaposition of two very similar tasks that aimed to determine the neural underpinnings of logical inference-making and of linguistic inference-making – that BA47 is implicated in both linguistic inferencing *and* logical inferencing. Second, Shetreet et al.'s most discerning isolating case (one which compares an underinformative "some" statement to their task's two other "some" statements) points to BA 10, i.e., the region of the Rostro-Lateral PreFrontal Cortex (RLPFC) that is underlined in other pragmatic tasks (see Politzer-Ahles & Gwilliams, 2015). The neuroimaging literature, including Shetreet et al.'s, points to the bilateral RLPFC as being involved in inference-making generally.

8   Conditionals

> If you can't get rid of the skeleton in your closet, you'd best teach it to dance.
> *George Bernard Shaw*

With the benefit of hindsight, it is a bit surprising that "some" and "or" are the drosophilae of modern experimental pragmatics because the conditional (*if-then*) was primed to be the most studied logical expression. Researchers in the psychology of reasoning – even as far back as the 1970s and 1980s – were focused on the way children and adults represent and reason with conditionals. These efforts raised questions about the role associated with pragmatic enrichments. In the meanwhile, theorists in the linguistic-pragmatic literature, as we just saw in the last chapter, were taken by the way pragmatic enrichments arise when embedded in the antecedent of conditionals. Theorists also considered how the connective "if" often appears to mean the more informative "If and only if" (see Chapter 5). Interestingly, the reasoning and pragmatics literatures hardly intersected with respect to conditionals (e.g., the developmental data that enlisted the notion of *invited inferences* in Chapter 5 from Rumain et al. [1983] represent an exception rather than the rule).

What did each of these two literatures report? The psychological literature largely treated conditionals as a set of two valid and two invalid inferences (as described in Chapter 5). As a reminder, the two valid inferences are Modus Ponens (*If P then Q; P//Therefore, Q*), as represented in (8.1), which is generally carried out routinely (children and adults evaluate the conclusion, below the line, as true at rates of at least 90 percent)[1] and Modus Tollens (*If P then Q; not-Q//Therefore, not-P*), which is shown in (8.2), which is not carried out with ease and leads to middling rates of correct responses.

(8.1) If the fish is red then it is striped.
       The fish is red.
       ‾‾‾‾‾‾‾‾‾‾‾‾‾‾‾
       The fish is striped.

(8.2) If the fish is red then it is striped.
       The fish is not striped.
       ‾‾‾‾‾‾‾‾‾‾‾‾‾‾‾‾‾‾‾
       The fish is not red.

Modus Tollens is difficult because in order to evaluate the conclusion one needs to first make the supposition that the antecedent *P* (*the fish is red*) is true and notice that this would lead to a conclusion (*the fish is striped*) that is in contradiction with the minor premise. This amounts to a *reductio ad absurdum* argument that prompts the rejection of the supposition *P*, the conclusion in (8.2).

The two invalid (fallacious) inferences amount to two pragmatic inferences that will concern us in this chapter. These are *Affirmation of the Consequent* in (8.3) and *Denial of the Antecedent* in (8.4), which were described in Chapter 5 when I mentioned Geis and Zwicky (1971).

(8.3)   If the fish is red then it is striped.
      The fish is striped.
      The fish is red.

(8.4)   If the fish is red then it is striped.
      The fish is not red.
      The fish is not striped.

The conclusion in the Affirmation of the Consequent (AC) argument is accepted as true by anywhere from 20 percent to 80 percent of participants and across a range of conditional reasoning tasks (for slightly out of date summaries, see Evans, 1993, or Girotto et al., 1997, but newer data are within this range too). One finds similar rates with respect to the conclusion in the Denial-of-the-Antecedent (DA) syllogism. From a logical point of view, the minor premises in (8.3) and (8.4) are non-starters for prompting further inferences. That is, once a participant encounters one of these sorts of minor premises (in the context of a conditional), the argument is invalid and the logical response is something along the lines of "nothing follows." However, as the data indicate, that is not how participants see things. Participants often carry out the invalid inference and are, at best, mixed about responding logically.

As we saw in Chapter 5, Geis and Zwicky (1971) suggested a principle known as *Conditional Perfection*, which would explain how a conditional (*if-then* sentences) could be seemingly interpreted as a biconditional (*If and only if*, see Chapter 5, *fn 8*), which justifies the pragmatic inferences in (8.3) and (8.4).[2] Over the years, pragmatists aimed to better account for "perfection" and they would invariably start by employing a familiar approach – Gricean maxims and scales. The thinking was (and largely continues to be among linguists) that the conditional implicitly generates another proposition that can be considered more informative than the uttered conditional (and that can ultimately be rejected). The question has been, what are the more informative renderings of *if-then*?

One suggestion came from van der Auwera (1997), who, in a review that covers 25 years of discussion, argued in favor of his own (and what he called tongue-in-cheek the "correct") view. As can be seen below, he begins by defending an ideal based on scales before presenting his suggestion:

In my view, the explanation of the conditional perfection phenomenon is Gricean. We are dealing with a scalar Quantity implicature. The type of scale involved is [the one represented in (8.5)]. The higher assertions entail the lower ones. Standard scalar implicatures arise as negations of the higher assertions and this is what we find here ... One thus implicates that only p will do and that if p is not fulfilled, q will not ensue.

(8.5) ...
    if p, q and if r, q and if s, q
    if p, q and if r, q
    if p, q

van der Auwera's idea is that when one *says,* for example, "If the fish is red then it is striped" in (8.1), this is relatively underinformative; instead, according to van der Auwera, the speaker could have said, "If the fish is red then it is striped and if it is blue then it is striped" but did not. This more-informative assertion can then be rejected (it would become "if blue then not striped"), putting one in the position to draw the conclusion that the speaker's only condition for stripedness is the color red. This turns the conditional into the biconditional "If and only if the fish is red then it is striped." While many share van der Auwera's approach, other theorists (including Horn, 1972, and Matsumoto, 1995) consider his choice of "higher assertions" to be too complex (too "prolix"), which would violate another of Grice's maxims (compare this to the case of "some," where the rejected more-informative-alternatives are other highly frequent words). Horn (2000) later suggests that a better higher assertion might simply be q or, alternatively, as von Fintel (2001) put it, *q no matter what* (see also Ducrot, 1972; Haspelmath & König, 1998).[3] As can be seen, the distinction between van der Auwera's account and the others concerns the nature of the scale, but the adherence to scales is obviously a strong one.

A relevant side note is that there was universal agreement about *discounting* the idea that one might be tempted to consider the biconditional as a more informative alternative. After all, it entails the conditional (much like *All* is a good entailing alternative for *Some*):

(8.6) if and only if p then q
    if p, then q

The problem with this possibility is that – if one assumes that the higher assertions are there to be negated – one would actually be *negating* the very proposition that theorists are seeking to justify. The way theorists justify this non-move is to say, for example, that this scale is ill-formed (e.g., Atlas and Levinson say that this scale relies on a higher assertion that is complex) or that *if-and-only-if* is not a word, so it cannot serve as an alternative.

In light of these objections and complications, Horn (2000) eventually proposed that, unlike the scalar terms *Some* and *Or*, which rely on a Quantity- (Q-) based maxim, a conditional is *strengthened* to a biconditional through a different, Relevance (R-) based maxim. That is, the weak conditional gets *narrowed* to *mean* the biconditional, much like the way the general term *drink* is used more specifically to describe an alcoholic beverage or the way "I don't believe that p" is meant to be understood more narrowly as "I believe that not-p." In the case of conditionals, enrichments do not occur due to a trimming off of stronger terms, they are simply narrowed directly to a more refined meaning.[4]

Although the two classes of linguistic proposals are at odds about the way the interpretation comes about, theorists end up with some form of conditional perfection – i.e., the conditional is transformed into a biconditional. In its original form, the antecedent in the conditional is simply sufficient for the consequent; once the biconditional transformation is complete, the antecedent acts as a necessary and sufficient condition for the consequent. Note that theorists are trying to come up with an explanation that will account for, what strikes me as, an intuition. Again, this reliance on intuition is exactly what an experimentalist guards against and what I will address later. Before getting to relevant experiments, I first want to quickly address another question.

Why did the two (linguistic-pragmatic and psychology of reasoning) literatures fail to seriously engage with one another? My humble take on this question is that, while there were a number of people who individually recognized an interesting overlap across the two literatures (e.g., Leo Noordman and Martin Braine), there was not a critical mass of investigators asking the questions that would sustain interest among both fields. The reasons for this are twofold. On the psychological side, most specialists of reasoning (those who would be concerned with *if-then*) did not take linguistically oriented concerns seriously enough. Instead, they feuded over cognitive representations ("Are inferences carried out by logic-neutral models or through logical schemas?") that did not speak to linguists. Moreover, psychologists became interested in non-linguistic factors, such as the way low-level strategies can undermine logical inference making.[5] On the linguistics side, scholars did not sustain their interest in conditionals and when they did they rarely cited psychological data, as far as I can tell. The time was just not ripe, I suppose.[6]

If the two literatures had collaborated earlier, the way linguists and psychologists do now about scalars, conditionals could very well have overshadowed scalars as the main topic of experimental pragmatics. After all, the conditional has much to offer. The equivocality among adults in the psychological literature on conditionals showed promise just like the early scalar data. Conditionals also prompt reliable developmental data. Conditionals could have engendered a linguistic debate between several opposing Gricean-inspired theoretical descriptions of conditional enrichments as well as discussions among those who rely on scales (and the quantity maxim) versus those who rely on R-based accounts.

Imagining an alternative history is fun to think about, but it is just that – a counterfactual. The upshot is that much research remains to be done on conditional processing and we have a large set of data from scalars that can now serve as background. In the next section I summarize the data on conditionals that went largely overlooked by pragmatists. Along the way, I turn to work carried out in my own lab since and partly to show how a concerted group of experimentalists can attack a relevant pragmatic issue. I think the experimental pragmatic literature on the semantic/pragmatic divide on conditionals would look very different today if other groups were to pursue this difficult case.

Enrichments Linked to Conditionals Do Not Line Up With Those of Scalars

Although much of the data collected on the comprehension of conditionals are not recent, they use familiar techniques (involving development, reading times, and individual differences) and varied paradigms. In some cases, participants are asked to evaluate conditional rules based on presented evidence and at other times participants are required to evaluate conclusions from syllogisms. I will review some of these studies to provide flavor and, where relevant, I will juxtapose results with those reported in the previous chapters about scalar terms. By the time we get to the end of the section, it should be clear that conditional perfection (enriching *if* to *if and only if*), when it occurs, is actually a different kind of pragmatic enrichment, despite accounts that liken them to scalars.

The Development of the Comprehension of Conditionals

We have seen that the semantic meaning of scalar terms is often acceptable for young children and that pragmatic enrichments become evident with age (while keeping in mind that tasks vary in their difficulty). If this phenomenon were applied to conditionals, one would expect younger children to apply a logical reading with relative ease (e.g., correct evaluations to Modus Ponens arguments) and to increasingly apply pragmatic readings – to accept AC and DA arguments – with age. This is hardly the story. In fact, advancing age and further effort are linked to *fewer pragmatic* interpretations with conditionals (Barrouillet et al., 2000; O'Brien et al., 1989; Taplin et al., 1974). These studies reveal that children are more likely to accept AC and DA inferences

Figure 8.1. A schematic representation of four boxes containing toy animals and fruits that serves as basis of a conditional inference task

when they are younger before becoming more circumspect with age by being more likely to reject the conclusions in arguments such as (8.3) and (8.4). Ultimately, adults end up in both columns by providing both logical and non-logical responses.

To give one example in detail, consider O'Brien et al. (1989) who showed how conditionals are understood among seven-year-olds, ten-year-olds, and adults. Imagine you are a participant who is shown four boxes, each containing one animal and one fruit, as schematically represented in Figure 8.1; there is one box with a toy cat and banana, one with a toy dog and an orange, one with a toy dog and an apple and, finally, one with a toy horse and an apple. Actually, participants were shown two sets of these four boxes. One set was covered and placed on the side momentarily while the other would remain uncovered in front of the participant as a reminder of what the covered boxes could look like. During the test phase, a single, randomly chosen covered box would be presented. This was the basis for (what could be) dozens of true or false conditional statements. About a single box, one can truthfully say that, "If there is a banana then there is a cat" as well as the inverse "If there is a cat then there is a banana." Dissimilarly, one can truthfully say that, "If there is a horse then there is an apple," but not the inverse. Developmental trends show that nearly all seven-year-olds, who answer control sentences correctly (e.g., by saying false to "If there is a horse in the box then there is a dog"), say true (incorrectly) to "If there is an apple in the box then there is a horse" and "If there is a dog in the box then there is an orange." Adults answer these correctly and the ten-year-olds are intermediate. It is as if younger children treat "If there is an x in the box then there is a y" as "There is a box that has an x and a y," which means that they do not readily apply a conditional relationship between the objects.[7] Younger children understand "If" as a conjunction which mimics the acceptance of the AC arguments above.

These data also show that the youngest children do not treat the conditional as a biconditional. If they did, they would say false to "If there is an orange then there is a dog" because the inverse is false; they say true, because they notice that "an orange" is joined with "a dog" in a box and that is good enough evidence for saying true. This research on conditionals shows that, as kids get older, they better consider the range of evidence that the antecedent calls upon, which leads to improved performance.

Reaction Time Data

As far as I know, no one in the conditional perfection literature has made a claim that says *if-then* is understood by default as a biconditional.[8] On the other hand, it is plausible to suppose, based on our prior findings on scalars, that theorists would not object to a proposal that says conditional perfection is more effortful than a reading that does not call for it. Arguably, pragmatic enrichments of conditionals can be processed in a way similar to enrichments linked to scalars, where good-enough semantic readings of *Some*, for example, are typically processed more easily than those that are revealing of pragmatic enrichments.

This is the hypothesis we investigate here. To keep things simple, from here on I will focus on participants' reactions to AC arguments as in (8.3) and Modus Ponens (MP) arguments, as in (8.1) because these two arguments have many of the same elements and they come with no negations (while the minor premise of MP is the conditional's antecedent and its conclusion is the consequent; the minor premise of AC is the conditional's consequent and its conclusion is its antecedent). The only difference between the two arguments is that saying true to MP does not require conditional perfection, while saying true to AC does. In other words, I will consider participants' performance on MP as a control for performance with AC. The other option for a control would be the normative (logical) answer to AC – "can't tell" or "insufficient information to decide" – but these are clearly harder to capture quickly when compared to a simple "yes" or "true." That said, I will continue to note the rates of logically correct performance on the AC argument, which remains an important reference.

With this in mind, let's consider two of the older reaction time studies that concern conditionals. First up is Marcus and Rips (1979, Experiment 2), who presented the four sorts of conditional syllogism – Modus Ponens, Affirmation of the Consequent, Denial of the Antecedent, and Modus Tollens– and recorded their participants' reaction times. While all of their participants endorsed MP conclusions and only about a third of them endorsed AC arguments, their data showed that the speeds at which the two are endorsed are statistically comparable (1,813 ms to endorse MP and 1,907 ms, to AC). Importantly, rejections of AC arguments, coinciding with a logical interpretation of the conditional, were more common and took noticeably longer to carry out (2,437 ms).[9]

In contrast, Barrouillet et al. (2000), who investigated the endorsement patterns of all four conditional arguments, found rates of AC endorsements (79 percent) that are among the highest in the literature; more importantly, the associated response times (2,355 ms) were slightly, but significantly, *slower* than MPs (2,018 ms). Notably, their experimental design, in which participants were required to hold a conditional premise in memory as a series of minor premise-conclusion combinations were presented, was slightly different. Also, reaction times of those who rejected conclusions from an AC argument were not reported (probably because there were not enough of them to produce statistically reliable means). So, while this experiment's design is more complex than Marcus and Rips's, it draws the conclusion that *affirming the consequent* can appear to be more effortful than Modus Ponens.

This means that the data by the turn of the century was mixed on the question of whether or not an invited inference is effort-demanding. Note that the early efforts in the scalar literature were unequivocal. As noted in Chapter 6, *all* the early attempts showed that enriched readings came with longer reading times. As will become clear in the next section, work conducted by my colleagues and myself aimed to, among other things, determine which of the two empirical claims is better supported.

Individual Differences

When individual differences have been reported with scalars, they concern distinctions between those who are more or less skilled pragmatic hearers (e.g., through Theory of Mind measures). Dissimilarly, individual differences linked to performance with conditionals concern other cognitive factors such as memory abilities and IQ (De Neys et al., 2005; Evans et al., 2007, 2008, 2009). For example, De Neys et al. (2005) gave participants a memory task (developed by La Pointe & Engle, 1990), in which participants were given a mathematical operation followed by a word (15 trials all told). The mathematical operation would be, for example, $(4/2) - 1 = 5?$ and the word would be BALL. Participant memory scores were based on how well they recalled the words and in their presented order. After removing participants who made too many errors on the math problems or who took too long to carry them out, De Neys et al. took participants from the highest and lowest quartiles and gave them conditional reasoning problems in the format exemplified by (8.7) before asking them how sure they are about drawing the conclusion by using a seven-point scale:

(8.7)   Rule: If Ann turns on the air conditioner, then she feels cool.
        Fact: Ann turns on the air conditioner.
        Conclusion: Ann feels cool.

Remarkably, those with high-memory spans were generally more likely to give ratings reflecting greater normativity. That is, compared to those in the lowest quartile for memory, those with the strongest memories were more sure about (provided higher ratings for) properly logical inferences, Modus Ponens (MP) and Modus Tollens (MT), while being less sure about the pragmatically valid Affirmation of the Consequent (AC) and Denial of the Antecedent (DA). Once again, superior normative reasoning performance on a basic conditional task

is linked with enhancing logical tendencies and suppressing non-logical (pragmatic) ones.

Overall, the data concerning pragmatic enrichments with respect to conditionals tell a different story compared to those linked to scalars and across
three sections of literature: (1) whereas children lean toward semantic readings
of scalar terms and become progressively "pragmatic," children's early interpretations of conditionals appear compatible with pragmatic interpretations
but become progressively logical (at which point the pragmatic interpretations
appear to be blocked, discarded, or unconsidered); (2) whereas processing
times of scalar items among adults are linked with the presence of pragmatic
enrichments, extra effort – when it makes itself known – appears linked to
avoiding the so-called invited inferences that often appear with conditionals
(in one of two studies, one notes a longer reaction time to an endorsed AC
argument, when compared to MP, but in another study, longer reaction times
are linked to the rejection of an AC argument, as opposed to its acceptance);
and (3) whereas differences in scalar enrichment have inspired investigations
into measures of Theory of Mind, enrichments linked to conditionals deal with
memory abilities or intelligence scores.[10] When viewed through the prism of
pragmatic enrichment behavior described in Chapters 6 and 7, the pragmatic
enrichment of conditionals seems characteristically different, even though
many linguistic-pragmatists use the very same tools – the Quantity maxim and
scales – to describe both phenomena. Something has to give.

Doing Experimental Pragmatics on Conditionals

With this paradox as background, I turn now to work on conditional processing
that my colleagues (principally Mathilde Bonnefond and Jean-Baptiste Van der
Henst) and I carried out in Lyon. It is work that has not received nearly as much
attention as the work on scalar terms, but is based on the very same approach
that helped make "some" and "or" the focus of so much attention. Plus, we
conducted many of these studies with the benefit of hindsight about the processing of scalar terms with the express purpose of determining whether the
lessons drawn from scalars can be generalized to the case of conditionals. One
of our main goals was to resolve the contradictory findings concerning reaction times (as a reminder, we decided to focus uniquely on the AC argument
because it is negation-free). Assuming that AC confirmations are pragmatic
enrichments, should they not prompt extra effort compared to controls (in this
case, Modus Ponens)? Before I get to the findings, it is useful to describe our
approach, which relied on perseverance and great teamwork.

Our lab in Lyon wanted to come up with a paradigm that would put us in a
position to accomplish three things. First, we intended to set up an EEG experiment on conditional processing, which entails a word-by-word paradigm. So,

we needed to come up with a way to eventually isolate, not only each line, but each word in a syllogism and we wanted to be sure that such a presentation would not be detrimental to our data collection. When we began, our focus was on the last word of each syllogism, because we had figured that a participant makes a final judgment then. Second, we intended to use reaction times, too, to make hypotheses about how participants evaluate the MP and AC arguments, and this is best done in more naturalistic settings (i.e., outside the EEG chamber without electrodes on the head and without a focus on individual words). This implies a more ecologically valid sentence-by-sentence (as opposed to word-by-word) presentation. Finally, we wanted to see whether participants differ in the way they answer and to determine how reading times pattern with these individual differences.

We also kept in mind the prior studies (described earlier), which measured reaction times from either entire syllogisms (Marcus & Rips, 1979) or from the last two lines, the minor premise and the conclusion, while the major premise was committed to memory (Barrouillet et al., 2000). We, obviously, were taking this progression several steps further by breaking down the arguments into single lines and eventually words. As part of this intensive undertaking, Jean-Baptiste came up with syllogisms that looked like the Modus Ponens argument (8.8) below:

(8.8) If Jean goes to the cinema then he travels by bicycle.
        Jean goes to the cinema.
        He travels by bicycle.

These sorts of slice-of-life syllogisms made it easy to come up with control conditions that could keep participants honest through the replacement of a single word; that is, we also presented control items with conclusions that can render a syllogism false, such as, "He travels by bus," which would replace the conclusion in (8.8). Of course, it makes sense to provide the AC argument too.

(8.9) If Jean goes to the cinema then he travels by bicycle.
        Jean travels by bicycle.
        He goes to the cinema.

This type of argument could be presented with a thoroughly anomalous conclusion such as "He goes to the gym," which is inconsistent with the invited inference. We called (8.8) and (8.9) Modus Ponens-Consistent (MP-Consistent) and Affirmation of the Consequent-Consistent (AC-Consistent), respectively. Through the replacement of the last word, we came up with conditions that were "Inconsistent" for each.

Our first efforts addressed our preoccupation with carrying out an EEG study. We presented the four kinds of conditional arguments to two groups, either sentence-by-sentence or word-by-word, as we wanted to make sure that the presentation did not unduly affect participants' evaluations. To give an idea of how we went about this, the sentence-by-sentence group saw a left-justified cross midway up a screen to indicate that the upcoming line was a premise and, likewise, an arrow in the same place in order to signal a conclusion. Participants then had to make a choice between two options on the keyboard: *logical* or *not logical*. The word-by-word condition was also presented in the middle of the screen, but in the center; as before, a syllogism began with a cross to signal a premise and an arrow for the conclusion. This technique is known as Rapid Serial Visual Presentation (RSVP). Aside from the presentation, the main difference between the two was that the sentence-by-sentence condition gave two full seconds per line (with a 200 millisecond pause after each sentence) and the word-by-word condition showed each word for 400 ms (followed by a 200 ms pause after each word). In light of the fact that the materials were provided in French, the first sentence always contained 10 words and both the minor premise and the conclusion had 4. This translated to a difference in terms of uptake. The sentence-by-sentence condition gave participants 2.2 s to read each line (6.6 s in total) while the word-by-word condition gave participants 6 s to read the first premise and 2.4 s read the minor premise and the conclusion each (10.8 s in total).

To our mild surprise, there was one major difference between the word-by-word condition and the sentence-by-sentence condition. While participants correctly evaluated the two Modus Ponens arguments at rates approaching ceiling and they correctly rejected the thoroughly anomalous AC-Inconsistent condition, more people rejected what we called the AC-consistent condition when it came in the more measured word-by-word condition.

We considered these results an indication that the extra uptake time was encouraging more logically correct evaluations. This was interesting in itself and led to a short paper (van der Henst et al., 2006) and, as far as paradigm-development was concerned, we concluded that our word-by-word technique did not undermine the performance that is usually found. While rates of correct performance shifted, we still found that participants treated the AC argument in one of two ways and that participants generally stuck to one of those ways throughout. I will refer to those participants who consider the AC-Consistent conclusion as "logical" as *Endorsers* and those who consider the AC-Consistent conclusion as "non-logical" as *Rejectors*.[11] We were convinced that the word-by-word presentation could provide us with a way to study conditional arguments "on-line" through EEG without compromising typical performance. We held off from reporting the reaction time results because we began to realize that the conclusion, our intended target, was not providing the most interesting results.

As part of a Masters project in Lyon in 2004, Kinga Bujakowska, who now works as a molecular geneticist at Harvard University, tested participants with the above word-by-word paradigm while using EEG. Kinga's work provided us with a second mild surprise because she found that participants' reacted differently to the second word of the second premise (the 12th word overall in French) of the AC syllogisms when compared to the 12th word of the MP syllogisms. For example, the word "travels" in the minor premise in (8.9) prompted negative going activity on the frontal area of the scalp 200–300 ms after its onset with respect to the word "goes" in the minor premise in (8.8). Note how this is the first word that indicates the direction in which the argument goes. I will address what this negative-going activity indicates in greater detail below, but for now I'll say that it shows that participants detected something unexpected about the minor premise in the AC syllogism. All in all, we succeeded in isolating the very moment that distinguishes MP and AC inferences with a straightforward task. With this astounding finding in hand, we were ready to refine the paradigm further.

That was when the baton was passed to Mathilde Bonnefond, a biologist who had given up working with animals due to the onset of a severe allergy and who had, and has, an enduring passion for EEG (and MEG) technology. For her PhD thesis (under Jean-Baptiste's direction), Mathilde began by further simplifying the materials in the above paradigm in the interest of having an even cleaner signal. Instead of having conditional arguments that present slice of life scenarios (about Jean's plans), participants now saw MP-Consistent and AC-Consistent problems as (8.10) and (8.11), respectively:

(8.10) If there is a B then there is a D.
There is a B.
There is a D.

(8.11) If there is a G then there is a K.
There is a K.
There is a G.

This way participants could ignore any extraneous information that can be construed from even trivially thematic premises and, as before, the Inconsistent problems could be created with a small change – the substitution of a letter. For example, a MP-Inconsistent problem could result from changing D in the conclusion of (8.10) to an E, and an AC-Inconsistent could be created by changing G in the conclusion of (8.11) into a T. Afterwards Bonnefond et al. (2012) ran two experiments.

One was a behavioral study that was carried out sentence-by-sentence. This time, however, the task was self-paced, meaning that participants moved the argument along with a press of the spacebar of an ordinary keyboard and answered "logical" or "not logical" through a single key (one labeled on the right side and another labeled on the left). As we had become accustomed, this

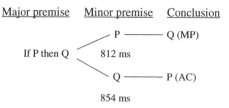

Figure 8.2. This summarizes the behavioral finding from Bonnefond et al. (2012) showing that even Endorsers, who fallaciously accept Affirmation of the Consequent (AC) arguments, take longer to process the minor premise of AC than they do the minor premise of Modus Ponens (MP)

produced two sorts of participants. There were participants who consistently endorsed the AC-Consistent syllogism and others who did not (there were also "mixed" participants, but for the sake of simplicity, I will not address their data here). Remarkably, again, Endorsers process the minor premise in the AC syllogisms significantly more slowly than they do the minor premise in the MP arguments (see Figure 8.2).

Why is this finding relevant? Because none of the existing linguistic-pragmatic theories proposed can account for it (no matter what Gricean maxim is used as part of the explanation). If one assumes that the conditional gets enriched (so that it is interpreted as a biconditional), this should occur when the Major Premise is processed beforehand. Once enriched, it should not matter whether the conditional's antecedent or consequent serves as a minor premise. Yet, it appears that it does matter, even for those participants who routinely endorse the AC argument. Also, one cannot assume that the enrichment of the conditional is akin to our other storied enrichment, viz. the scalar. Another finding from Bonnefond et al.'s first experiment (one that is not new) is that those who provide "logical" evaluations to the AC-Consistent syllogisms (Rejectors) take a longer time to get through the Minor Premise than those who endorse the AC-Consistent syllogisms (Endorsers). Thus, one cannot say that logical interpretations at this crucial juncture are more basic than the *pragmatic* one. No matter how one slices it, the Affirmation of the Consequent argument, which is the most ideal test of conditional perfection, appears to behave in a way that is unlike anything we have seen so far.

Capturing relative speeds of response allowed us to infer where extra processing is taking place. It did not allow us to determine the *nature* of the extra effort, which is what we turned to next. Bonnefond et al.'s Experiment 2 was practically identical to Experiment 1, except that it was designed for an EEG study and was thus modified slightly to save time as well as to come up with a cleaner signal. Compared to the paradigm of Experiment 1, it (a) had more trials, (b) further reduced wordiness (i.e., "If there is an *A* then there is a *C*" became "If *A* then *C*" and "There is an *A*" became "*A*") so that participants read while keeping eye movements to a minimum; and it (c) added filler items whose minor premise had nothing to do with the conditional so that participants would not come to expect either the minor premise for MP or AC (e.g., *If P then Q; U*). Our goal from the beginning was to develop a satisfying and thorough EEG experiment to investigate conditionals. We finally landed on our final paradigm after years of refining our methods.

The EEG study further supported what Kinga's study had indicated earlier. Namely, the minor premise of an AC argument prompts what we would eventually determine to be an N200. What is an N200 (or an N2)? It is an ERP component that is related to the violation of expectations (for a review, see Folstein & Van Petten, 2008). To give an example of an N2 from another cognitive area, consider a working memory task that requires participants to determine whether a second stimulus (S2) is similar or not to an earlier stimulus (S1) presented a few milliseconds earlier; a mismatching S2 elicits a larger N2 component than a matching S2 component (Wang et al., 2002; Zhang, Wang, Li, & Wang, 2003). As in Experiment 1's self-paced study, we found that the arrival of the minor premise for an AC argument prompts a universal reaction, an N2 that reveals a dispreference. Not only do we find it among participants who ultimately reject the AC argument, we find it among those who will later endorse it. That said, it is even stronger among Rejectors.[12] This result is noteworthy because it is an indication that the minor premise of the AC argument is to some extent disruptive to all participants. Below (in Figure 8.3) is one of nine measures taken that captures the difference across conditions from the moment that the second premise of MP and AC is presented. The one on the left represents the midline frontal site among Endorsers, who ultimately accept the MP-Consistent and AC-Consistent arguments, and the one on the right captures the same site among Rejectors.

My view, as developed over the course of several generations of students and experiments, is that participants note that the minor premise of AC arguments is a source of conflict (Noveck et al., 2011). To wit, *all* participants (Endorsers and Rejectors) react similarly to (what is essentially) an unexpected minor premise; profiles differ only with respect to degree. There is thus little reason to suppose that the conditional premise lends itself – in any way, shape, or form – to conditional perfection, which presupposes a seamless enrichment. Once something goes awry (because one did not get a minor premise for MP at the moment it was expected), one can react in one of two ways. A generous reaction can ultimately lead to finding ways to endorse the argument (dashed expectations notwithstanding) while a strict reaction is to recognize the flaw and to not budge.

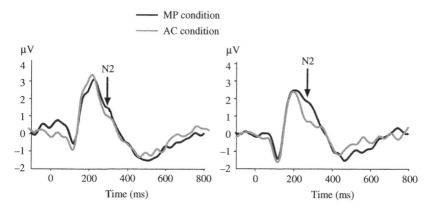

Figure 8.3. Stimulus locked grand-average waveforms evoked by the appearance of the letter representing the Minor Premise of the MP (black line) and AC (gray line) conditions on the frontal midline site for Endorsers (N = 17) and Rejectors (N = 23). The N200s are shown with an arrow and indicate statistically significant effects (from Bonnefond et al., 2012)

When one turns to scalars (see Hartshorne et al., 2015; Noveck & Posada, 2003, Nieuwland et al., 2010), one finds nothing like what we found here. Data from EEG studies with scalar inferences prompt very different reactions. Those who respond "logically" to "some" do not prompt steeper ERP components and when one finds something to report with respect to scalar enrichments, the component described is weaker, later, or requires relatively rich contextual information. In contrast, the logical responses with respect to AC (the Rejectors) prompt the steepest N200s (even when compared to Endorsers).

This brought to a close a very intensive period of joint work. Our behavioral and ERP studies showed that conditionals prompt reactions that are categorically different from the intensively studied scalars. We could safely conclude that the notion of conditional perfection and its concomitant invited inferences are linguistic proposals that have no support. We are better off thinking about the pragmatic import of conditionals very differently, perhaps as a means to heighten expectations about the antecedent.

Notes

1. Modus Ponens can be "disabled" if an argument presents a second conditional premise. For example; Modus Ponens will not be carried out mindlessly in the following set of premises (Byrne, 1989):

   If she meets her friend then she will go to a play.
   If she has enough money then she will go to a play.
   She meets her friend.

2. While a biconditional interpretation accounts for both AC and DA, a conjunctive interpretation could account for AC. In fact, the conjunction entails the biconditional, which entails the conditional. This chapter will focus on AC but will continue to test linguists' classic notion that the pragmatic enrichment of conditionals involve a "perfection" to a biconditional interpretation.

3. In my view, this would not encourage the acceptance of invalid arguments (and the production of *perfection*) but the opposite; it would encourage valid evaluations of "can't tell." Assuming that the conditional *If P then Q* prompts the rejection of (the higher assertion) Q, the minor premise Q (for example, in 8.3) would be cause for a contradiction and the immediate breakdown of the argument.

4. Note that this can apply to *Some* too; "only some" is a narrowing of *Some*.

5. Consider *Matching bias*, which refers to the non-normative performance that occurs when elements mentioned in a rule do not correspond with those in a test item (e.g., consider the double mismatch between the rule "If there is a not a T on the card then there is not a 4" and a card showing *H6* (see Evans, 1998; Prado & Noveck, 2007).

6. For the record, investigations into conditionals remain vital to several lines of reasoning research. One concerns the way logically valid conditional inferences, such as Modus Ponens in (1), are processed on-line (see Lea, 1995). This has carried over to the neuroimaging literature, where conditionals are one of the main connectives used to determine the neural centers of logical processing (see Monti et al., 2009; Noveck et al., 2004; Prado et al., 2010; Reverberi et al., 2009). Other approaches to conditionals come from Mental Models (Johnson-Laird & Byrne, 2002) as well as the "new paradigm" (Baratgin et al., 2015), which couches conditional reasoning in probability.

7. O'Brien et al. (1989) argued that children do not appreciate the quantified aspects of *If-then* sentences. When given a sentence of the sort "All the boxes that have a dog have an apple," performance was much more adult-like for the 7-year-olds. In this respect, children's performance here does share something with scalar terms in that a test question such as "Some of the boxes have animals" can be understood as, "There is a box with an animal" or "There are at least two boxes with animals."

8. One of my early lessons as an experimental pragmatist came from Larry Horn who told me that I should not so readily place all neo-Griceans into one basket because, he said, he himself did not make the claim that scalar enrichments should be considered effortless default inferences the way Levinson did. It is with that in mind when I say, "As far as I know." If someone did make this proposal and I failed to find it, I apologize in advance.

9. The authors did not report statistical tests, so this point is based on eyeballing the presented data. For other data that point in the same direction, the reader is directed to van der Henst et al. (2006), to be described later.

10. As Jean-Baptiste Van der Henst points out, it could be that no one has considered testing Theory of Mind abilities with respect to conditional reasoning performance. That said, it appears that the two sorts of phenomena afford different kinds of studies on individual differences.

11. This is akin to the labels Bott and Noveck (2004) used when participants' *Some-and-perhaps-all* reading was called "logical" and their *Some-but-not-all* "pragmatic," except that here the Rejectors are "logical" and the Endorsers are arguably "pragmatic."

12. We also reported a P3b with the arrival of the minor premise of the MP inference, which is an indication that an expectation was satisfied (Bonnefond & van der Henst, 2009).

9   Referring

Pointing is ... not only easier to use but more efficient.

Steve Jobs

Imagine you and a friend, a journalist, are strolling through Times Square in New York City. While facing a newspaper stand, which has dozens of periodicals on display, she says, "I used to work for that paper." You – seeing the plethora of possibilities – respond by saying, "Which one?" She looks at you quizzically until you realize that she wasn't pointing to the newspaper stand, but to the New York Times building behind it.

Some amount of intention-reading is needed to close the gap between "that paper" in the example above and what the journalist meant by uttering it. Such resolution is another phenomenon that naturally calls on pragmatics because a verbalized reference ("the tall glass," "the man with a hat") provides only part of what is needed to pick out the intended object from what could be a crowd. This chapter reviews the reference-resolution findings with respect to experimental pragmatics. As will become clear, the studies and the claims with respect to reference resolution do not coalesce around one paradigm or even one (shared or disputed) notion. Experimental studies on reference resolution range widely.

We begin by presenting developmental studies, where we examine the nomenclature of reference in order to bring this phenomenon in line with other pragmatically oriented tasks; while reference-resolution requires less structure than, say, scalar inference enrichment, the two still have much in common. This will make the terrain clear. The chapter then looks at babies to determine the extent to which pointing and direction-gaze-shifting are linked to accessing communicative intentions. The second half of the chapter turns to adults, which allows for investigations about processing.

Developmental Studies

One can break down developmental referring into two groups. One set emphasizes the role of language and the way the linguistically encoded meaning of an utterance is enriched, much like the way scalars are. These studies can be considered to be a developmental version of the adult studies that inspired them. The other set investigates pre-verbal or barely verbal children in order to demonstrate just how strong they are at communication through, say, pointing. Let us look at each of these sets in turn.

Linguistically Based Reference and
the Semantic/Pragmatic Distinction

Chapter 6 underlined the semantic-pragmatic distinction in order to explain how listeners enrich a sentence that is potentially underinformative with respect to the context in which it was uttered (a speaker says something like, "Some of the boxes contain a dog" with respect to a set of boxes that each have a dog). The reference resolution literature also sports what is called an underinformative condition, which is when a speaker requests a single object by name (e.g., *the star*) but the context shows two objects of this kind. However, it is important to make clear that this is not underinformative in the same way as the scalar case (in fact, the utterance itself is overly specific since the object is referred to with a definite determiner) making the seeming analogy across the two an illusion. An "underinformative" referential remark is infelicitous.

Let's consider how referential remarks are categorized more generally. In Figure 9.1, one finds a sample trial from Davies and Katsos (2010) that contains four items. Now, let's assume that the speaker wants you to pick up the big ball that is on the left upper corner of the array. If the speaker says, "Pick up the ball," the addressee would not know which ball is the speaker's intended one, despite the speaker's use of a definite article. This is where the speaker is being *infelicitous* (in terms of helping the addressee find the intended item) because the speaker is referring to one object but there are two potential referents. While *ball* allows the addressee to narrow down the reference set's possibilities from four to two, it is not clear which of these two is the intended one by uttering "the ball." One *optimal* way for the speaker to make the addressee clarify which of the two balls is the intended one is to distinguish it from the other ball. For example, she can call it "the big ball" by contrasting a feature that distinguishes the two objects.[1] This is why some consider such reference resolution as being the result of a *contrastive inference*.

To complete the range of referring expressions, consider a slightly different paradigm that has a single ball, and that is called "the big ball" by an interlocutor (see Figure 9.2). The adjective here makes the utterance seemingly *overinformative* because *"big"* is essentially gratuitous for identifying the intended object; "the ball" would do. Another way to view it is that

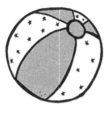

Figure 9.1. A sample trial from Davies and Katsos (2010), as generously shared by the authors. The speaker can isolate one of the balls by saying, for example, "Pick up the big ball"

the speaker is prompting a contrastive inference when there is nothing to contrast.

All told, we have three levels of informativity – underinformative, optimal, and overinformative. This seems well and good. Let me point out again, however, that the way we use underinformative in the referential domain differs from the way we used underinformative with respect to scalars. It is important to clear up any potential for confusion.

The two underinformative utterances – in the scalar case and the reference resolution case – generate very different outcomes in their respective situations. In the scalar inference tasks, an underinformative utterance allows an addressee to make a relevant interpretation based on its linguistically encoded meaning (it is formally true to say that "Some dogs are in the boxes" when all are).[2] In reference-resolution tasks, the speaker's choice of words leaves the addressee nonplussed. The different natures of the scalar inference and reference-resolution tasks also explain why the tasks from these two literatures could end up appearing so different. In scalar tasks, participants make truth-judgments or read a passage; in reference resolution tasks, a participant is typically required to find a single item after receiving a request. While one can turn

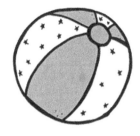

Figure 9.2. Given that there is just one ball in this trial, the speaker could simply refer to it as "the ball"

a scalar inference task into a reference-resolution task (Huang & Snedeker, 2009a, b), one would be hard-pressed to incorporate a truth-judgment request into a reference-resolution task. Furthermore, in reference resolution, one can make a contrast out of just about anything in nature. While big was used, an investigation could set up a situation in which a "white ball" is singled out from a second "red" ball, or in which a "striped" ball is isolated from a "solid" one. The possibilities are endless. Scalars are investigated with a more limited set of cases in which an underinformative expression could be rendered more precise. This is why scalar inference studies typically employ utterances that use *some* (where *all* would be tempting) or, less typically, *start* (when *finish* would be appropriate). In typical scalar tasks, the test-statement is weak with respect to the evidence; this can encourage participants to interpret the statement more narrowly (e.g., by transforming *some* to *only some*).

With these caveats in mind, I will nevertheless adopt the reference-resolution literature's nomenclature in its use of terms such as *underinformativity* and *overinformativity*, mostly because those expressions are already "out there." However, I will be careful when I use these expressions by adding scare quotes to these *infelicitous* or *ambiguous* referential cases. Despite heightened attention to these labels, at the end of the section I will explain how scalar tasks and reference resolution tasks are indeed comparable, but not in the way the nomenclature allows us to assume. First, let us review the data.

In a study that predated Grice-inspired analyses, Ironsmith and Whitehurst (1978) showed that five- to eight-year-old children rarely ask for clarification when an experimenter instructs them to select one item through a request that could in fact refer to two; for example, the experimenter would say, "I am thinking of the person with antennae" when there were two (funny) representations of people with antennae. Meanwhile, nine- to twelve-year-olds ask for clarification ("Which one?") reliably more often in such situations (see also Ackerman, Szymanski, & Silver, 1990; for a review, see Flavell et al., 1981). This was taken to mean that young addressees do not readily notice that an utterance is "underinformative."

In more modern Grice-inspired studies Davies and Katsos (2010), whose paradigm I described above (and whose Figures I borrowed), had five-year-olds evaluate referential expressions by asking the children whether the speaker asked for the object in "a good or bad way." When a cartoon character said, "Pass me the ball" when there were two such depictions in front of the child (see Figure 9.1), roughly 75 percent of the children considered the instruction "good," which was a significantly greater proportion than adults (roughly 40 percent) who considered the request natural. These results are comparable to those described about scalar inferences in the last chapter – children were more likely than adults to find an underinformative scalar statement to be "right" (Katsos & Bishop, 2011). However, this does not mean that children are entirely oblivious to non-optimal instructions. Davies and Katsos (2010) also had the same five-year-olds in their study carry out a similar task in which the children were asked to essentially reward the speaker by giving "as many strawberries as he deserves for the way he asked for the object." In the underinformative referential task Davies and Katsos reported that, with these instructions, children are much more adult-like.

With younger children, Morisseau, Davies, and Matthews (2013) presented three- and five-year-old children with a nearly complete grid (see Figure 3 for an imaginary example trial) and a series of instructions, such as, "Pick up the orange motorcycle" (to be put in the empty space) to see how the children reacted when they received optimal, (infelicitous) "underinformative," or over-informative utterances (note how the grid contains pairs of contrasting items, as well as unique items). They found that both the three-year-olds and five-year-olds asked for further information when given "underinformative" instructions (by looking at the experimenter or by asking for clarification) and, even if the five-year-olds did not ask about the bizarre "underinformative" cases, they took longer (compared to the optimal case) to move their preferred piece in

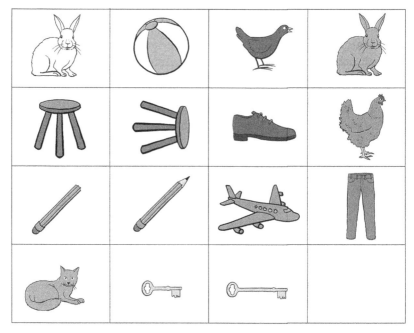

Figure 9.3. A potential set up before a trial from the Morisseau et al. (2013) paradigm. Here, the participant's task is to listen to an instruction so as to identify a described object and move it into the empty slot. They could receive instructions that are ***optimal*** (e.g., "Pick up the white rabbit"), ***"underinformative"*** (e.g., "Pick up the key") or ***overinformative*** (e.g., "Pick up the plane with wings"). The author is indebted to Tiffany Morisseau for creating this example for the purposes of the book.

such situations. While the three-year-olds showed no sensitivity to the over-informative items, the five-year-olds slowed down a bit (again, with respect to the optimal instructions). Overall, very young children (three-year-olds) notice when an utterance is infelicitous but addressees need to be a bit older before they profit from sentences that contain cues that potentially call for further narrowing.

As described at the beginning of this section, the "underinformative" referential case is ambiguous between two objects and so it is not analogous to underinformative scalar terms, which have two related (linguistically encoded and enriched) readings. On the other hand, the overinformative referential cases *are* akin to scalars in that (1) the linguistically encoded meaning can suffice for making an effective interpretation, i.e., "the small star" could describe "a single star that qualifies as small" (just as *some* could be understood as *some and perhaps all*); and in that (2) an enriched reading provides an interpretation that ultimately allows the listener to narrow his or her focus, i.e., "the small star could be understood as the small star and not other (large) stars" (just as *some* could be understood as *some and not all*). Once viewed in this way, the overinformative referential cases are analogous to the scalar case and the data generated by the two phenomena are in-line with one another (as they ought to be). In both cases, the younger a participant is the more oblivious she will be to an utterance's pragmatic potential when its linguistically encoded meaning can suffice.

To make my case clearer, consider a fun task that Edmundo Kronmüller and Tiffany Morisseau created (see Kronmüller, Morisseau, & Noveck, 2014, Experiment 3), in which children and adults can potentially exploit an adjective as a source of pragmatic enrichment. In the task, a participant is shown four cards, each showing a picture. Critically, only two of the picture-cards were from the same category (e.g., two rabbits, one brown and one white). The cards were shown face up before they were turned upside-down (and the participant kept an identical set of the cards as a reminder of what was face-down). Now, in front of the participant were two people – the experimenter, who will be the speaker, and a silent partner, who will simply respond to the experimenter's request by revealing a card. The participant's job is to listen to a (felicitous) request and to see the ostensible reply. This "exchange" will become the basis for the participant's own test question.

To make this concrete, imagine that the experimenter randomly takes two of the overturned cards from the table, shows them to the silent partner and then asks him to "show me the brown rabbit" (see Figure 9.4, panel a). The silent partner (the addressee) obliges and takes the brown rabbit card from the experimenter's hand (b) and puts it face up on the table (c). The experimenter then asks the participant (d), "In your opinion, what is on the other (remaining) card (in my hand)?" Given that the experimenter first asked the silent partner for the "brown rabbit," the participant is in a position to infer that the experimenter was making a contrast in order to isolate what must have been two rabbit cards, which means that the other remaining card is the white rabbit. The question is whether participants, including seven- and ten-year-olds, can profit from such a clue.

Note that "the brown rabbit" could also be an innocent description of a bunny. It is not obvious that a participant can take the adjectival modification as a means to make a contrast. That is why Kronmüller et al. (2014) predicted that pragmatic enrichment would develop with age because, for relatively younger participants (in this subtle game), there is enough information in

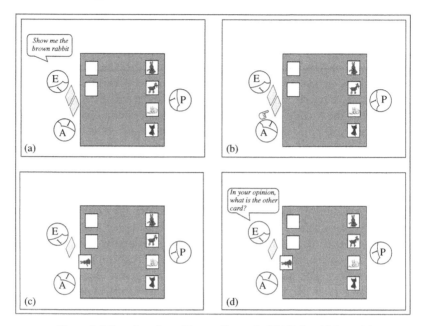

Figure 9.4. Paradigm from Kronmüller et al. (2014), in which participants are asked to identify the remaining card in the experimenter's hand, based on the statement provided to the experimenter's silent partner. In this trial, "Show me the brown rabbit" is an indication that the other card in the speaker's hand is the remaining (non-brown) rabbit.

the linguistically encoded meaning to come up with a good-enough interpretation; that is, the linguistically encoded meaning suffices for interpreting the experimenter's utterance to the silent partner and all that is left to do is to guess between the remaining cards. Indeed, Kronmüller et al. report a developmental effect showing that younger children (e.g. seven-year-olds) do not benefit from the adjectival modification to infer a contrast. In our most refined version of the task (using just three cards), seven-year-olds chose the contrasting object at chance levels (50 percent correct guesses), ten-year-olds say that the other card is the white rabbit at above chance levels (73 percent), as do the adults (81 percent). So adults are not distinguishable from the ten-year-olds in answering this subtle test question nor are the adults at ceiling levels. When features of an utterance need to be exploited in order to come up with a narrowed reading and when the context is less-than-optimal (in this case, the make-up of the cards in the holder's hand is derivable but not ostensible), then one almost routinely finds developmental effects.[3]

Some of the Most Interesting Work on Reference Is in Its Infancy

Developmental investigations into reference go beyond merely underlining very young children's referential abilities. Several attentive researchers have noticed inconsistencies among reports about young children's communicative abilities (e.g., see Breheny, 2006) and these differences need to be reconciled. On the one hand, young children – and for the sake of argument let's say those under 4 years of age – appear sufficiently talented in multiple areas, including word-learning, and yet these same children seem to be relatively weak at carrying out tasks that involve some amount of mindreading. Two notable examples of such impoverishment are the Sally-Anne task and the scalar inference task described earlier,[4] which show that children become more proficient at pragmatic inferencing with age (see Stiller, Goodman, & Frank, 2015, for some interesting data on similar tasks with children two years of age and older). Working backwards to younger participants, then, should one expect pre-verbal children (say twelve-month-olds) to possess the wherewithal to do genuine ostensive-inferential communicating? This has led to studies that investigate the roots of communication by looking at infants.

I will focus on pointing here because it is a form of reference that even very young, pre-linguistic humans do. While early work had suggested that pointing reflects imperatives of the sort "Give me that" or "Look at that" (Bates, Camaioni, & Volterra, 1975), more recent work views pointing much differently by putting it in line with Gricean theories. The two accounts I will cover (cf.; Csibra, 2010; Tomasello, Carpenter, & Liszkowski, 2007) consider young children as hard-wired for communication and they both present convincing evidence that infants possess a communicative intention while pointing. With respect to receptive communication, both highlight the importance of actively looking toward the object and to the infant while pointing in order to create a triad – a form of common ground. They differ with respect to what they view as the purpose of early adult–infant communication. Let's turn first to work coming out of Michael Tomasello's group when he was based in Leipzig.

Michael Tomasello has been one of the leading figures in both the animal cognition literature and the developmental literature with respect to communication. Part of his research program is devoted to showing how very young children, including pre-verbal toddlers, use ostensive-inferential communication and how their abilities compare to nonhuman primate communication. He argues that humans use "a cooperation model" in which communicators create joint intention for prosocial communication. Nonhuman primates fall far short of this. Tomasello (2010, p. 108) writes:

(Non-human) primates do not structure their communication in this same way with joint intentions, joint attention, mutually assumed cooperative motives, and communicative conventions; rather they simply attempt to predict or manipulate the individual goals, perceptions, and actions of others directly.

When studies from his group look at pre-verbal or minimally verbal children, they find that these miniature humans possess the intentional force of
their adult selves (minus language). This becomes especially evident when it
comes to pointing. Several different studies have been carried out to show the
extent to which pointing is a profoundly intentional act in which the pointer
(the speaker, so to speak) directs the recipient's attention to something in their
shared space.

Tomasello and colleagues specifically view pointing as a form of pre-
linguistic communication. Their theory "posits that when young infants point
for an adult they are in some sense trying to influence her intentional/mental
states" (Tomasello et al., 2007) and that this is revealing of a form of ostensive-
inferential communication. Their main evidence comes from studies where
experimenters accidentally misplace an item (while doing some uninteresting
task) in front of a twelve-month-old who (1) *does* know where the misplaced
item is, and (2) indicates through a point where to find it. This shows that
twelve-month-olds are trying to be informative to the experimenter. Liszkowski
et al. (2006) also showed that children can understand the specific meaning of
a point (e.g., that a point indicates that a sought-after toy is under one of two
buckets). While this might seem trivial to our adult minds, apes – our evolutionary cousins – are not able to use at least distal pointing[5] reliably as a cue
(for a review, see Miklósi & Soproni, 2006). The main difference between
chimpanzees (even those who are raised by humans) and ourselves is that we
use pointing cooperatively, while they do not operate with such assumptions.
On the other hand, chimpanzees are able to make inferences so that if they saw
a human attempt to *reach* toward a box, the chimpanzee would infer that there
must be something of value in it and turn it over (Hare & Tomasello, 2004).
Pointing has all the elements of ostensive-inferential communication. Let me
present two experiments in greater detail in order to show how powerful pointing is. In one experiment, the participant receives information through pointing, and in the second, children communicate through pointing.

Experimenters in Grassmann and Tomasello's (2010) study interact with
two-year-olds and four-year-olds as they point to one of two objects. One object
is familiar (e.g., a car) and the other is a novel object (e.g., a U-shaped door
stopper). Children are known to infer that a novel name ("Give me the modi")
ought to refer to a novel object and that is what both groups of children generally do. But, if one adds natural pointing (from the speaker), the outcomes are
highly modifiable. When the pointing is "ostensive" (this means that pointing
is done "with the whole forearm [and index finger])" and while repeatedly
"alternating [the] gaze between the child and the object"), children are liable
to ignore their knowledge of common objects and follow the point. So, when
the experimenter ostensively points to a familiar object (the car) while saying

"Give me the modi," both the two-year-olds and the four-year-olds hand over the familiar object nearly every time. Similarly, when the experimenter points to the novel object and says, "Give me the car," the children will pass along the novel object (on over 70 percent of the trials), even though there is a real toy car in view. The only time when children show hesitation is when there are two familiar objects and the experimenter points to one while using the wrong label (the experimenter says "Give me the car" while pointing to a shoe). In that case, the children choose the mislabelled (the pointed to) object about half the time.

In Liszkowski et al. (2007), one-year-olds were brought into a room that had an elaborate set-up in which objects or lights would suddenly appear to elicit pointing. More specifically, a baby would be facing the experimenter, who would be sitting in front of a screen; behind that screen was a second, hidden experimenter. On occasion (and when the baby was attentive to the visible experimenter), this second experimenter would either use a hand puppet that would protrude from behind the screen or activate some device (lights or a fan) that were in the baby's view and not necessarily in view of the (visible) experimenter. The "magical" appearance of puppets or the activation of toys were designed to elicit pointing by the baby. The main manipulation behind the experiment was actually the visible experimenter's reactions. In the *Joint Attention* condition, the baby's interlocutor (the first experimenter) would respond very positively (through a gaze that alternated between the stimulus and the infant's face while talking excitedly). In the *Misunderstanding* condition, the experimenter would react similarly but to the wrong source of the baby's attention. In the *Uninterested* condition, the experimenter correctly identified the source of the baby's pointing, but reacted neutrally (without excitement). In the *No Sharing* condition, the experimenter reacted to the wrong source and neutrally. This amounts to a 2 × 2 design with "Attitude" on one axis and the experimenter's focus on the other, and the question was, "How does it affect participants' reactions?" Do they point more or less when the experimenter has engaged with them enthusiastically or mistakenly? If Liszkowski et al. are correct, and children's pointing is a form of communication (and not, say, just a self-satisfying reflex), then one ought to find that they point most when their interlocutor shares their joint view or when the infant is aiming to correct a mistaken impression. There were two different kinds of measures – the number of trials that elicited pointing and the number of cases with repeated pointing. The authors found that the *Joint Attention* condition encouraged pointing the most (in terms of proportion of trials with pointing), indicating that the babies wanted to share in the Joint activity. Interestingly, the Misunderstanding condition prompted the most *repeated* pointing, as if the baby wanted to inform the experimenter of a mistaken impression.

All told, preverbal infants and minimally verbal toddlers show that they understand and use pointing for communicative purposes. Pointing is a fundamental form of ostensive-inferential communication and the receptive data show that pointing is a privileged form of communication. The production data show that even babies are sophisticated users of pointing and that their gestures are affected on-line by their interlocutor's reactions.

A second hotbed of infancy communication research comes from Budapest (Csibra & Gergely, 2009). Work on *natural pedagogy* aims to show that early efforts at communication are driven by an innate system in which infants gain information from interlocutors, e.g., benevolent caretakers, who are naturally viewed as important sources of information. Central to this mechanism are communicative cues that make a child ready to receive informative cues. Csibra and Gergely (p. 148) argue that:

Human infants are prepared to be at the receptive side of natural pedagogy (i) by being sensitive to ostensive signals that indicate that they are being addressed by communication, (ii) by developing referential expectations in ostensive contexts and (iii) by being biased to interpret ostensive-referential communication as conveying information that is kind-relevant and generalizable.

As part of an effort to provide support for natural pedagogy, Csibra and colleagues have carried out a host of studies, some of which are designed to show that a bias towards accepting ostensive-intentional cues are at the very root of communication. I'll provide two examples.

Senju, Csibra, and Johnson (2008; Experiment 1) followed nine-month-olds' looking time as the babies observed a screen showing a loop of a scene that showed a face, followed by a cartoon fish appearing on one of two sides of the face for roughly a quarter of a second. In the *congruent* condition, the pupils in the face's eyes moved towards the object, and in the *incongruent* condition, the pupils moved in the direction away from the side containing the fish. The looping would continue until the children would turn away. Interestingly, the children looked at the congruent scene for significantly longer loops than the incongruent scene. According to the authors, this gaze is a preparatory step for the infants *in order to* anticipate novel information.[6]

Another study investigated six-month-olds as they were given two different ostensive cues, i.e., signals designed to get a baby's attention, before an experimenter shifts her gaze toward one of two objects. One cue was a motherese-inflected (as opposed to an adult's) "Hello," and, by the way, while the experimenter was looking down. The other cue was simply a direct (versus a looking-down) gaze. The dependent measure was the infants' first object-directed saccade, as measured through eye-tracking. In short, when a gaze-shift to the experimenter's preferred object is preceded by what are arguably built-in ostensive-communicative signals – direct eye contact or infant-directed speech – the infants' first move (the object-directed saccade) is toward the experimenter's indicated object. In the absence of such cues, they do not follow the experimenter's gaze.

Clearly, young children are sensitive to ostensive cues that capture their attention as part of a communicated message. Whether the innate purpose of these cues is general (to be viewed straightforwardly as pre-verbal communication) or specific (for pedagogy) is a concern that goes beyond the purposes of this book (see Kovács et al., 2014, for a study that compares the two). The main point is that both sets of studies show that when prelinguistic human primates react to an ostensive cue (think pointing), they reveal the rudiments of a natural ability to carry out reference.

Referring Adults

We can better understand current debates about referring by looking at two strands of research that have reference resolution in its sights. I'll call one *conventionality-creation* because, as it was developed by Clark and his colleagues, it aimed to demonstrate that interlocutors work together to arrive at agreed-upon labels in conversation. The other can be referred to as *context-as-a-constraint*, which started out by investigating sentence-processing through inventive eye-tracking techniques before ultimately turning to pragmatics. I refer to the latter in this way because these online investigations progressively revealed that syntactic representations are not processed independently and need to rely on context. I'll take a look at each of these areas in turn so that we can address some ongoing debates in contemporary experimental pragmatic investigations.

Finding Common Ground

In Chapter 2, we saw how Clark had cited Lewis and his notions of *common ground* (or *mutual knowledge*) to determine the speaker's meaning when using reference. His basic approach has been that referring and naming do not respect Gricean-like maxims. Rather, interlocutors are more concerned with finding links in joint activities for the length of the activity. Clark's account is particularly relevant when accounting for reference (to both conventional and unconventional objects). According to Clark (1996), reference is a matter of two people working out an agreed-upon name for a reference for the duration of an exchange. Whether one is talking about "you know, the guy we talked about last week," the "upside-down funnel," or "the golden retriever," interlocutors need to work together to figure out what they are referring to. To provide one early example from this influential work – inspired by studies by Robert Krauss and Sam Glucksberg (e.g., see Krauss & Glucksberg, 1969) – consider a piece of dialogue between two people who are not sharing eye contact as they are organizing two sets of twelve (pictures of) tangrams so that the two sets are arranged in a like manner (Clark & Wilkes-Gibbs, 1986).[7] One person, who is called the "Director," has her cards set up in a predetermined order because she needs to describe to the other, the "Matcher," how to position his tangrams. In the example below, the Director is identifying one of the cards:

Director: Okay, the next one looks, is the one with the person standing on one leg with the tail.
Matcher: Okay.
Director: Looks like an ice skater.
Matcher: Okay.

As this example shows, referring is part of an exchange that comes peppered with confirmations such as "okay" from the Matcher. As can be gathered, investigations in this genre put the emphasis on the way two interlocutors come to agreement on a referent. Another general finding is that, over the course of the experiment, the referent gets shorter. For example, it would not be surprising if the *ice skater* eventually becomes the *skater*. Two general theoretical points have been made from data generated by this paradigm.

The first is that conventions take precedence over being informational at each step. This claim is supported by a study (Brennan & Clark, 1996) that used *repeated references* as a measure of production. As in the Clark and Wilkes-Gibbs (1986) study described above, two interlocutors without eye contact – a Director and Matcher – exchange descriptions and information in order to organize their (identical) sets of twelve pictures in a particular fashion. This time, the twelve pictures represent basic objects (dog, toy, car, etc.) and participants, as expected, refer to these with their common names. However, when a second slightly modified set of twelve pictures is introduced, which now include four objects of the same category (e.g., four dogs), Directors are likely to use more specific references (e.g., *Labrador* instead of *dog*), indicating that the specificity of reference is modified by context. This much is Gricean because references are at increasing levels of informativeness as context calls for it. Interestingly, when the exchange returns to the first phase – i.e., the one containing single examples of basic objects – participants continue to use the more specific reference they established in the earlier round (they keep *Labrador* instead of returning to *dog*). This demonstrates that once a convention between two people is engaged, it remains for the duration of the exchange. This sort of conventionalizing avails itself to concepts too. For example, if, upon entering a traffic circle, a car passenger instructs the driver with "we enter at 6 o'clock and we go out at three," the driver – even if he has never heard such a description before – will very likely use that sort of language at the next traffic circle.

When novel expressions are baptized, so to speak, a process of *lexical entrainment* occurs. This expression refers to the way interlocutors attribute names to novel objects and maintain them for the length of a conversation (Brennan & Clark, 1996; Garrod & Anderson, 1987). It is also assumed that a *conceptual pact* is "partner specific" among interlocutors and that it takes precedence over being just informative enough on each occasion. These are important findings showing that shared language even early in a dialogue takes precedence over the particular informational value that a new word in a situation can offer at any instant. For Brennan and Clark (1996), the interactive process – the joint activity between interlocutors – is crucial and determinative for labeling and much more so than "solitary choices on the part of the director."

The second claim that has been attached to Clark and colleagues' approach is that common ground is so central to conversation that the identity of the speaker is also part of the joint process. Given that memory representations of the speaker's epistemic states are among the sources of information (these are considered to be simple *one bit* representations; see Brennan & Hanna, 2009), it is argued that speaker-specificity emerges from the earliest moments of interpretation (Brown-Schmidt, 2009). This explains why Metzing and Brennan (2003) argue that once a term is coined among interlocutors as a referent, it would be odd if the same speaker were to come up with a new name because the speaker is part of the common ground. I'll call this view the *perspective-dependent account* because it assumes that pragmatic expectations are linked to specific partners in a conversation and that interpretation involves some representation of the partner's epistemic states (E. V. Clark, 1990; Brennan & Hanna, 2009; Brown-Schmidt, 2009; Metzing & Brennan, 2003). Once the referent has a name, it preempts the listener from adopting any new coinage from the same speaker.

This led to a prediction about *recovery-from-preemption*, which refers to the difficulty that arises when a single speaker suddenly does give a new name to a previously named object. Concretely, they predicted that a listener would find it difficult to recover from preemption, but that he would *not* have such difficulty when it comes from a speaker who is herself *new* to the exchange. In testing this claim, Metzing and Brennan (2003) adopted an eye-tracking paradigm in which a confederate "Director" would provide a participant (the "Matcher") with instructions to move small objects to new locations among cubbyholes in a grid (this experimental innovation was developed by Keysar and colleagues and will be presented in greater detail below). By measuring the duration of time between the onset of a referring expression and first-looks to the target (as well as touches to the target), experimenters could determine how fast a listener makes referential commitments when the same ("original") Director comes up with a new name for a previously named object as opposed to when a new Director does so. As predicted, they reported slowdowns (only) when the same Director came up with a new name for a previously named object.

Keysar and Egocentric Processing

One conclusion to draw from Clark and colleagues' conventionalizing paradigms is that naming an object is associated with the speaker who designated
it and to such an extent that perspective taking is practically automatic. Keysar
and colleagues (Barr & Keysar, 2002), while using eye-tracking techniques,
have challenged Clark's interactive view by arguing that listeners are more
naturally *egocentric*. By that, they mean that listeners make interpretations
without immediately considering the speaker's perspective. The implication is
that Clark's interactive view is not so "joint."

   This led Keysar and colleagues to develop a new paradigm in which several
objects are distributed in the slots of a 4 × 4 grid (Keysar et al., 2000). While
an addressee can see all 16 of the grid's slots, the speaker (the "Director")
can see only 12 and thus not all of the objects (see both the Director's and
Addressee's perspective in Figure 9.5). Keysar et al.'s (2000) eye-tracking data
indicate that – for situations where a speaker's intended reference could only
be an object that is commonly viewed – listeners cannot prevent themselves
from first fixating on a non-intended item (one that matches the speaker's
description even though it is out of the speaker's view) before fixating on the
intended target. Concretely, when a "Director" asks for "the small candle" (see
the Director's "small candle" in Figure 9.5), she is contrasting two candles.
For the addressee, there are two relatively small candles to consider: one is the
smallest of three and the other is the middle-sized one. Keysar et al. (2000)

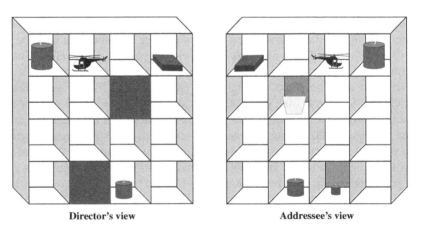

Director's view   Addressee's view

Figure 9.5. A hypothetical set of objects in a display from the point of view
of the Director (the Speaker) and Addressee based on Keysar et al. (2000)
paradigm. Note how there are just two candles from the Director's perspective. The author thanks Boaz Keysar for sharing this previously unpublished
illustration.

data show that listeners cannot help but look at the smallest of the three at first. This finding has been replicated multiple times and the paradigm has been the source of many follow-ups that pursue new lines of thinking, e.g., Wu and Keysar (2007) demonstrate how Chinese students in America appear to be less egocentric than American students are.

Barr and Keysar (2002) also proposed that egocentrism lies at the heart of speaker-specific preemption (i.e., they challenged the Brennan and Clark claim that says that recovery-from-preemption is difficult only when the original speaker, who coined the referent, also decides to change its name). According to Barr and Keysar, changing the given name of an object is difficult for listeners generally, irrespective of who appears to make the change in name. To make their point, they presented a form of the Brennan and Clark paradigm (the one described earlier in which a dog is described as such early in the task – when it was the only dog – before context encourages a subcategory name, e.g., as a *Labrador*). When the experimenters came to the last round, they found that listeners were delayed in finding the target when they heard the basic-level category name "dog" once again, no matter who the speaker was (the original speaker or a new speaker). So, while Barr and Keysar found support for the general effect that shows that listeners prefer the entrained name, the recovery-from-preemption effect is not linked to a specific speaker.

What Is at Stake?

Once again, researchers are debating the role of intentions in utterance interpretation. One side defends the position that shared intentions (about a given label) play a role in interpretation very early in utterance processing (this is the full-fledged Common Ground view). The other position is that, while intention reading is ultimately essential, it is not necessarily the directing force from the start; linguistic decoding can also be an (early) source of interpretation (the Egocentric view). This is why current debates continue to focus on how quickly participants find a target when there are two speakers and more than one name for an object. Researchers want to investigate the interaction between the linguistic unit (the referential utterance) and the common-ground that a listener establishes with a specific speaker. If a novel-looking object has been labelled the *upside down funnel* this name will pre-empt searching for another. The debate between defenders of the full-fledged Common Ground view and the Egocentric view continues unabated (Brennan & Hanna, 2009; Brown-Schmidt, 2009; see also Kronmüller et al., 2017).

The corpus of studies that address this debate typically have four conditions: in the *Same Director-Maintain* condition, reference would be made to an object three times in the same voice and with the same name; in the *Same Director-Break* condition, a single speaker would introduce a new name for a previously named object on the third occasion; in the *Different Director-Maintain* and the *Different Director-Break* conditions the third trial would be presented by a different voice and would maintain or break with the prior uses. Again, Metzing and Brennan reported slowdowns only when the same Director came up with a new name for a previously named object.

To re-evaluate Metzing and Brennan's (2003) claims, Kronmüller and Barr (2007) carefully tracked the time course of participants' emerging preference for a target item as they followed instructions from two recorded speakers, one having a male voice and the other female (and participants were told that the two had nothing to do with one another). The task would use eight pictures of unusual objects as participants were required to move them around a computer-generated grid. Participants would hear the same object referred to three times but under the four conditions described above. Critically, Kronmüller and Barr – while carefully analyzing eye-movements in the wake of the third reference – showed that the earliest reaction was a *main effect* for Maintaining versus Breaking the precedent (regardless of speaker). That is, any break in precedent prompted participants to look at the target less (cumulatively compared to other targets) and this effect began to emerge 300–600 ms after the reference was made. While there was a speaker-specific interaction (between the Same Speaker-Break and Different Speaker-Break condition), it was a late-occurring phenomenon (at around 1,500–1,800 ms). In other words, hearing the same voice use a new expression did lead to distinctive results (slowdowns in choosing the intended object), but participants' eye-movements indicated that any change in label prompted looks away from the target nearly as soon as the new name arose.

Given that ten studies using a similar visual-world paradigm had been carried out, Kronmüller and Barr (2015) were inspired to carry out a meta-analysis. Despite some discrepancies among individual studies, the meta-analysis largely echoes what these authors reported in their (2007) paper, which can be summarized in three parts. First, when object-names are maintained, there is an early advantage for locating objects when they come from the same speaker. Second, when an object is given a new label, there is an advantage for locating objects indicated by a different speaker. Third, there is a strong preference for precedent, meaning participants in general expect labels to remain unchanged. While it appears that addressees internally adopt labels from their conversation partners, the identity of that interlocutor does not remain an indelible part of that label. Essentially, object names, once christened, are privately held.

When Context Is Viewed as a Constraint

While the *convention creation* literature was taking shape, a related eye-tracking literature was emerging about the way utterances are interpreted on-line. This work is extremely important for both theoretical and methodological

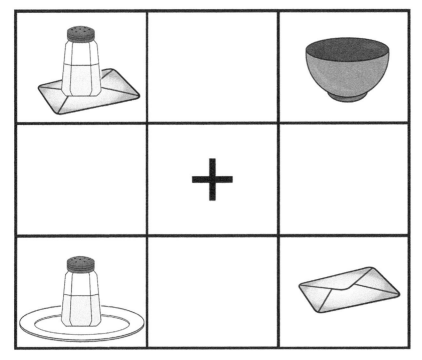

Figure 9.6. An example of a trial from Eberhard et al. (1995). I am indebted to Kathleen Eberhard for sharing her previously unpublished slide with me.

reasons. Theoretically, this work grew out of investigations that emphasized the role played by context when deciphering ambiguous sentences (see Chapter 3), so it is directly relevant to concerns of experimental pragmatics. For example, consider a sentence such as the one in (9.1), which is intended to mean (9.2):

(9.1) Put the saltshaker on the envelope in the bowl.

(9.2) Put the saltshaker that's on the envelope in the bowl.

This kind of sentence was investigated because many predicted that – based on the assumption that syntax processing was modular (i.e., independent of context) – "on the envelope" would be treated as a goal rather than as a modifier. If that is the case, the sentence ought to appear confusing. However, Eberhard et al. (1995) showed – through live presentations schematized in Figure 9.6 – that when context disambiguates among potentially underspecified sentences, participants have little difficulty using the prepositional phrase in order to distinguish between two saltshakers, of which only one is on an envelope (see Eberhard et al., 1995, for further descriptions).

Work in this tradition led to a reference resolution task that would become critical to questions in experimental pragmatics. Methodologically, these studies add a level of sophistication to psycholinguistic research because they show how – and when – language integrates features of context.

Back to Adjectival Modifications

Imagine looking at a different grid (much like the one in Figure 9.6) that contains four different objects: a tall glass, a short glass, a water-pitcher, and a key (see Figure 4 in Sedivy et al., 1999). For this task, the critical trial asks the participant to pick up one of these four objects as per the instruction in (9.3):

(9.3) Pick up the tall glass.

Remarkably, for such trials, listeners' eye-movements reveal that they make referential assignments (measured by looks to the tall glass when it was one of two differently sized glasses) as soon as the adjective was uttered and even before hearing the noun "glass" (Sedivy et al., 1999). Between surveying the scene and hearing the utterance, participants are practically anticipating which object will be the speaker's fancy.[8] How is one to account for such findings? Don't participants first have to hear the whole utterance?

Like nearly all the work in this book, this finding on reference resolution prompts a debate that compares the influence of form versus pragmatic inference. On one side are those who would attribute these results to structural form (for a summary, see Grodner & Sedivy, 2011). One such formal view would be that knowledge of the semantics of the adjective *tall* triggers a search for a pertinent comparison class, which provides for an early integration of contextual information. This kind of analysis ultimately leads to distinctions among types of modifiers because Sedivy and colleagues would go on to find that not all adjectives prompt similar behaviors. For example, Sedivy (2003) investigated prenominal color modifiers when there was (or was not) a contrasting object. When "yellow banana" (whose modifier is highly predictable for the noun) was used in these (eye-tracking) studies to distinguish between two bananas (say one yellow and one green), it helped listeners identify the target item. However, when "yellow" was used to modify the word *cup* in order to distinguish it from a green one, it provided no advantage. So, on first blush, it appears that the effect initially described by Sedivy et al. is confined to scalar adjectives and is not a general one. Moreover, other work does show that color could be used. Kronmüller et al. (2014) findings, based on the paradigm described in Figure 9.3, used color successfully as a contrasting adjective.

Grodner and Sedivy (2011) came around to the idea that there is more to enriching a reference than the linguistically encoded meaning when they fascinatingly explored the role played by speaker attributions in referential cases. They did so by essentially replicating the Sedivy et al. (1999) study but with both scalar (e.g., "tall glass") and material, non-scalar ("the plastic spoon") modifiers and to two groups of participants. One group was provided the standard sort of (presumably cooperative) speaker. The other was presented an "unreliable" speaker who was said to "have an impairment that caused language and social problems." The unreliable speaker would, for example, call a *toothbrush* a *hairbrush*, introduce non-necessary (overinformative) adjectives, or ask the participant to move an object to a nonexistent location. As expected, when participants were listening to the reliable speaker, Grodner and Sedivy found results similar to those reported in Sedivy et al. (1999), with more early looks to the target (e.g., to *the tall glass*) and fewer looks to the contrasting object (e.g., the small glass). They even found similar effects with material modifiers. Most interestingly, however, is that they found that these effects disappear with the unreliable speaker. Grodner and Sedivy (2011) drew the conclusion that "characteristics particular to a speaker are taken into account in the generation of referential contrast inferences."

Summing Up

Similar to other pragmatic phenomena, the processing of a referential utterance's linguistically encoded meaning may be all that participants use. However, we also saw that a referential utterance can be enriched much like scalar terms, that pre-verbal infants use pointing as an ostensive signal to share an informative intention, and that interlocutors use words to construct common ground together. Of all the phenomena reviewed in this book, pointing out something to one's interlocutor in the form of a reference is arguably the most simple – and richest – of pragmatic acts, making reference resolution a quintessential pragmatic phenomenon.

Notes

1. Csaba Pleh pointed out to me how this type of question resonates with questions in De Renzi and Vignolo's Token test (1962), which is used as a diagnostic of comprehension in neuropsychology.
2. See Ferreira, Bailey, and Ferraro (2002) for a similar notion.
3. The absence of a modifying adjective, as in "Show me the rabbit" (which is then revealed to be either the white or brown one) is also a clue that the card remaining in the experimenter's hand is the goat. When this sort of utterance served as a clue, adults are stronger than the ten-year-olds.

4. The Sally-Anne task was reviewed in Chapter 3.
5. Apes are adept at using proximal distance as a cue so if one were to point while standing close to the target, then they are stronger.
6. It is hard to argue that it is due to dishabituation because the more boring of the two is arguably the congruent case.
7. Google *tangram* to see a sample of them and specifically *tangram ice skater* to appreciate the upcoming example.
8. In my view, the fast-acting contextual influences described in Sedivy et al. (1999) result at least partly from the fact that the objects (which were real objects) were placed on the grid before each set of trials. So, participants had time to become familiar with the four objects and to note that two of them differed from one another in a specific way. Sedivy et al. (1999) were, of course, aware of this and aimed to address this concern. This is why they included one condition in one of their studies in which the experimenter set up the grid while the participant had his eyes closed; test sentences were presented as the participant opened his eyes. In these cases, looks to non-target objects increased substantially, indicating that the initial findings (anticipated searches for targets before the utterance is completed) relied on participants doing referential work prior to the presentation of the utterance.

10 Speaking Falsely and Getting Away with It

Post-Gricean Accounts of Metaphor
and Other Lexical Adjustments

Life is a great big canvas, and you should throw all the paint on it you can.

Danny Kaye

We saw in Chapter 2 how Grice devoted space to metaphor, a prominent pragmatic phenomenon. He argued that speakers flout the Quality maxim ("to tell the truth") and that listeners use the violation to prompt a search for an alternative, so that the Cooperative Principle is maintained. We also saw that metaphor was one of the first pragmatic phenomena to get an experimental treatment. In Chapter 5, I reviewed how researchers transformed Grice's proposal into what has since been called the SPM (the Standard Pragmatic Model), an algorithmic account that reduces Grice's approach to three serial steps (process the literal meaning, notice a violation, and come up with an alternative interpretation). This approach was often made generalizable to a host of figures of speech (especially metaphor and irony) because many researchers treated figurative language as a category. This chapter will not do likewise. Rather, I will focus on metaphor and other lexical transformations in the present chapter and turn to irony in depth in the next.

In reviewing some of the earliest experimental work on metaphor, we saw in Chapter 5 that, with enough background information, a novel metaphoric phrase can be read as routinely as a non-metaphoric one. This appeared to undermine Grice's account. While out-of-the-blue metaphors might prompt slowdowns and more intensive reactions in EEG investigations when compared to literal controls (compare "Those soldiers are lions" to "Those animals are lions"), indicating an impact on processing, these eccentricities in time disappeared when metaphors were folded into a richer context (for a review, see Ortony, 1993). Similarly, one can process whole sentences, such as "The winter wind gently tossed the lacy blanket," either metaphorically or literally as a function of context and with equal ease. These kinds of data would set the stage for one of the longer running discussions in the literature concerning the role and contours of linguistically encoded meanings in metaphor processing.

The Advent of Post-Gricean Accounts on Nonliteral Language

The rejection of the literal-first notion demystified accounts of metaphor processing and prompted a metamorphosis in the cognitive literature. It would soon become commonplace to find articles whose introductions resembled the following: "Revered scholars have thought that there is something special, unique, or exceptional about metaphor and now we know that this is not the case." For example, Giora (2008) opened a chapter with, "Is metaphor unique as assumed by Aristotle (350 BCE) and more recently by Grice (1975) and Searle (1979)?" before arguing that there is nothing particularly unusual about metaphor. Sperber and Wilson (2008) wrote a pointed paper titled, "A deflationary account of metaphor," which argues that "there is no mechanism specific to metaphor, no interesting generalization that applies only to them." Importantly, both of the above papers rely on experimental findings to make their arguments, thus representing a victory of sorts for experimental approaches. Not surprisingly, this change in perspective also gave rise to new accounts of nonliteral language processing, with a particular focus on metaphor and irony.

There are arguably two post-Gricean lines of research on the pragmatic processing of figurative language that have had a lasting impact on experimental pragmatics. One line, which aimed to answer a *psycholinguistic processing question*, focuses on the extent to which the literal meaning of a given figurative word or phrase plays a role in processing. In the next section, I will describe two opposing accounts that are concerned with this line. One is the *Direct Access* view (Gibbs, 1994), which claims that one can access a nonliteral (e.g., metaphoric, ironic, idiomatic, or indirect) meaning of a word or phrase without considering that phrase's literal meaning. The other account, the *Graded Salience* hypothesis (Giora, 2002), claims that one cannot help but consider literal meanings. Though both accounts are considered pragmatic in nature, they are less concerned with integrating their approaches with Gricean (i.e., ostensive-inferential) theoretical concerns, arguably because they both forcefully disowned the Standard Pragmatic Model. This leads to the other line, which is exemplified by Relevance Theory. As an ostensive-inferential account, Relevance Theory is concerned with the way intentions are called into play in order to better discern the utterance but still concerns itself with the process that transforms a prototypical concept behind a word into a metaphoric one. We will consider each line in turn.

The Psycholinguistic Processing Question

The Direct Access View

The Direct Access account (Gibbs, 1992; 1994; 2002) defends the position that a listener need not consider the linguistically encoded meaning when processing a metaphor, irony, idiom, or an indirect request. According to Gibbs and

Colston (2012), "the 'direct access view' simply claims that listeners do not automatically analyze the complete literal meanings of linguistic expressions before accessing pragmatic knowledge to figure out what speakers mean to communicate" (p. 63). From the mid-1980s on, Gibbs has carried out a host of studies that point in this direction.

To give a flavor of Gibbs's technique with respect to metaphoric reference, consider an experiment in which Gibbs (1990) presents participants with eight lines, constituting a little story (what we in our lab refer to as a *vignette*) before presenting one of three different concluding sentences that vary with respect to their referential content. As one might imagine, this was a self-paced reading task where each line appeared on a screen and disappeared with the arrival of the next line. The story in (10.1) below concerns a character who goes out to see some boxing matches; one of the fights featured a weak boxer. Lines (10.2–4) were potential concluding sentences:

(10.1) a. Stu went to see the Saturday night fights.
        b. There was one boxer that Stu hated.
        c. This guy always lost.
        d. Just as the match was supposed to start, Stu went to get some snacks.
        e. He stood in line 10 minutes.
        f. When he returned, the bout had been canceled.
        g. "What happened?" Stu asked a friend.
        h. The friend replied,

(10.2) The creampuff didn't even show up.

(10.3) The fighter didn't even show up.

(10.4) The referee didn't even show up.

Sentences (10.2) and (10.3) are, respectively, metaphoric and synonymic references to the same character, the hated boxer. Sentence (10.4), which makes reference to a previously unmentioned referee, served as a control. Gibbs found that the average reading time for control sentences such as (10.4) was not significantly different from the reading times of (10.2) or of (10.3). In fact, the mean reading time for the control sentence fell between the two others. Gibbs concluded that this amounts to a null effect. Given the theoretical environment that assumed that metaphors are effortful, Gibbs remained convinced that metaphors do not call for extraordinary effort to process.

He also gave prominence to a probe task, in which the participant was required to determine quickly whether a particular word appeared previously in the story. A relatively quick "yes" response to the earlier-instantiated referent of the metaphoric term could be a measure of processing benefit. For example, a "yes" response to the word "boxer" after reading (10.3) above would signal that the metaphor served to prime the referent. Although Gibbs found a facilitation for probes following metaphoric conclusions (on average, 1,118 ms) compared to the control condition's conclusions (1,331 ms), he also found that the synonymic condition's probes led to latencies (1,229 ms) that were statistically comparable to the metaphoric condition's probes. Thus, he took the metaphoric references to be as efficient as synonymic ones.

Gibbs (1980) made the same point with respect to idioms (such as "He's singing a different tune") and indirect requests (Gibbs, 1983). If these results can indeed be generalized, these data provide a strong basis for claiming that one does not need to go through a literal step in order to access a speaker's meaning or for claiming that the literal meaning need be even triggered at all in metaphoric contexts. However, it also pays to point out that many of the results are based on a null effect, which simply means that the experiment failed to reject the null hypothesis. This could mean that the null hypothesis is true. But it could also mean that the test was not sensitive enough to reject the null.

Graded Salience

The *Graded salience* hypothesis (Giora, 1997; 1999; 2003; Peleg et al., 2001; 2004) also addresses issues on figurative language as a category (metaphor, irony, and idioms are treated as a group) by focusing on the way a critical word (or a word in a phrase) generates its most salient meaning. According to Giora's model, comprehension involves bottom-up and top-down processes working in parallel. The bottom-up process is "sensitive only to linguistic stimuli" (Giora, 2008, p. 146), the top-down process integrates linguistic and extra-linguistic information. The concept of salience is critical to the bottom-up process in that literal meanings are always accessed. However, a word could generate a figurative alternative, especially due to background information, but it is not coded to do that. The alternative meaning can essentially compete for "most salient" status with the literal one. As Giora put it (2008, p. 146):

The graded salience hypothesis assumes that the bottom-up, modular mechanism is salience sensitive: more salient responses [to the stimulus] – responses coded in the mental lexicon and foremost on our mind due to, for example, conventionality, frequency, familiarity, or prototypicality – are accessed faster than and reach sufficient levels of activation before less salient ones. Accordingly, such responses would be accessed upon encounter, regardless of contextual information or authorial intent. Low salience responses, however, may not reach a threshold and may not be visible in a context biased toward the more salient meaning of the stimulus. Non-salient meanings are not coded. They are constructed on the fly as a result of top-down processes.

If I were to call my friend Mary a *fish*, the conventional meaning for fish will persist through bottom-up processes; meanwhile the listener's top-down processes will help discern that I had a figurative meaning in mind (perhaps that she is a good swimmer). So, according to Giora, the important distinction is between, not literal and figurative meanings but, the salient and the less salient meanings related to a word.

As far as experimental work on metaphor goes, Giora's support comes mostly from reinterpretations of others' data with respect to familiar versus non-familiar metaphors. For instance, Lai et al. (2009) showed that conventional and unconventional metaphors differentially modulate the P600 ERP component. That said, much of the original work from the Graded Salience view focuses on irony (which we will turn to in the next chapter), and to a lesser extent, idioms (Filik and Moxey, 2010; Giora, 1997; Giora and Fein, 1999; Giora et al., 1998). The account remains the same across these different phenomena. Consider the relatively familiar idiom, "to step on one's toes." According to graded salience, concepts related to both the literal (e.g., *foot*) and figurative (e.g., *offend*) meanings readily become available (Giora and Fein, 1999). If a speaker were to use an unfamiliar (or obsolete) expression, such as the "black ox has trod upon my toe" (this is an obsolete idiom indicating that the speaker has been visited by misfortune; the black ox refers to the devil) then only the literal meaning of *toe* is salient and should hold sway because the figurative meaning related to the idiom is likely beyond the listener's ken.

As this brief review of the Direct Access and Graded Salience shows, the two accounts provide diametrically opposing predictions. Gibbs, by dismissing the importance of "literal meanings," predicts and shows that linguistically encoded meanings prompt responses or readings that are similar to metaphors. Graded Salience emphasizes that – at least at some level – addressees need to consider the linguistically encoded meaning of a critical word in a figurative utterance. The work on metaphor from these two perspectives appears to be at an impasse because, as we saw since Pynte and Ortony, there are data that support both sides.

Relevance Theory's Account of Metaphor: Loose Use

In Chapter 2, we saw how Relevance Theory conserved key Gricean concepts, such as an integral role for intention-reading, and radically expanded on it. It distinguished between communicative and informative intentions and outlined a procedure that takes into consideration effort and cognitive effects as part of the listener's attempt to optimally apply relevance in order to discern the meaning of an ostension. This means that listeners aim to arrive at an interpretation while balancing between cognitive effects and cognitive effort.

In Chapter 1, we saw that one of the important issues for (experimental) pragmatics is to understand lexical meanings. I cited Searle's remark that showed how a concept for *cut* has overlapping meanings so that one could both *cut a cake* and *cut the grass*. Yet, one would not bring a lawnmower to divvy up a wedding cake or go down on hands and knees in order to use a cake knife to manicure a lawn. There is a concept, CUT, that is a common denominator for both. According to Relevance Theorists (Sperber and Wilson, 2008; Wilson and Carston, 2008), these concepts are prototypical encoded lexical meanings that are given more specific meanings through context. These can take on a range of more subtle, and sometimes, seemingly original meanings; and they come about through a process of *narrowing* or *broadening*.

Narrowing occurs when a concept gets a more specific meaning. For example, Sperber and Wilson (2008) describe how the word *temperature* in (10.5) has a conceptual meaning (which is denoted in Relevance Theory with capitals as TEMPERATURE) and that to understand the speaker's intended meaning it gets *narrowed* to mean a relatively high temperature (for average human beings) or a feverishly high temperature.

(10.5) I have a temperature.

This narrowed reading is represented as TEMPERATURE*. The asterisk indicates there is an intended meaning that is derivable from the prototypical concept. One may notice that this kind of narrowing is what was applied to *Some* when I covered the RT account with respect to scalar terms. The narrowed interpretation effectively entails the prototypical concept in these cases.

Meanings can be derived by *broadening* a concept, too. In broadening, the extracted meaning retains some element of the prototype but does not necessarily entail it. To make this concrete, consider these two statements:

(10.6) The gas tank is empty.

(10.7) John is an empty chair.

In (10.6), the lexical concept EMPTY refers to an entirely empty tank. On the other hand, it can be used as an *approximation*, EMPTY*, when a speaker wants to indicate that the tank is nearly empty and it is time to get gas. We often use concepts in such approximate ways. Imagine a scenario in which a car's signal indicates that the gas tank is extremely low on fuel; while it is not literally empty (there are probably a couple of litres left to find a gas station), it is not a far cry from saying that the tank is empty. So, EMPTY* in this case means nearly empty, not entirely EMPTY. Notice that the intended meaning (*nearly empty*) in such a case is not a subset of EMPTY, unlike the concept TEMPERATURE in (10.5). The two are hardly compatible (a tank is empty or not). One can go further still. The speaker's statement in (10.6) would be *hyperbole* in the event that the indicator shows that it is one-quarter full; in this case, the speaker is indicating that the level of gas in the tank is too low for comfort. Perhaps the speaker is in a desert and far away from the civilization (for experimental work, see Deamer, 2013). Finally, EMPTY can be transformed to EMPTY* to describe someone, as in (10.7), but this too would call for context. It could be a sad statement about John's character, a nonce description of his place in a crowded scene or perhaps that he is inviting. In each of these cases, the addition of the asterisk amounts to an *ad hoc* meaning that reflects a temporary transformation of the prototype.

So, one can see that the role of context is capital for Relevance Theory right down to lexical meanings. As far as metaphor is concerned, a term takes on temporary *ad hoc* meanings and in the service of figuring out the speaker's intention. Consider a scenario in which a swimming instructor who – while giving a parent-infant class in a pool – says encouragingly to a young father, "your son is a tadpole!" The instructor's utterance effectively conveys, in a compact way, just how well she thinks the baby takes to water. The word *tadpole*, which refers to a young amphibian, is transformed into TADPOLE*, to refer to the son. The implicature would be along the lines of "Your son is a young creature who is comfortable in water." Now, consider another case, in which the same metaphoric remark were made in response to a question such as "Can I swim across the lake?" from a young swimmer in a beginner class in a summer camp. Here, the transformation to TADPOLE* occurs as well but one could draw a different set of assumptions which is consistent with the intention –"You are too young to stray so far." Here, we see the same remark in two slightly different contexts, each drawing the listener's attention to singular aspects of the speaker's intentional state. Inference about the speaker's intentions is called on in each case in order to understand the remark and aspects of the same concept can be transformed in unconventional ways.

The approach from Relevance Theory is buttressed by classic psychological work. I'll mention two contributions, in particular. The first comes from Barsalou (1983), who famously showed just how flexible our category-making skills are. While the study of categorization had been primarily concerned with the way participants list exemplars for "common" categories, such as *birds* or *furniture* (or, vice versa, how participants profit from exemplars to come up with a "common" category), Barsalou showed that *ad hoc* categories share many of the same features. For example, if a participant is asked to name *things to save in a fire*, participants come up with lists that have many of the same features one finds in their common category lists. There will be items that have higher salience than others (just as *robin* is more typical than *penguin* in the category *bird*, *pets* will likely predominate over *suitcase* in the case of *things to save in a fire*) and there will be items that are on the fringes (just like *radio* is on the fringe for the category *furniture, trophy* would arguably be on the fringe of *items to save in a fire*). His highly cited work showed that objects and actions are practically as categorizable based on *ad hoc* contexts as robins and pigeons are classifiable as birds.

Other inspiration comes from Gregory Murphy, who points to the flexibility offered by prototype concepts when an adjective modifies a noun. In Murphy and Andrew (1993; also see Murphy, 2002), participants were asked to provide antonyms and synonyms to both single adjectives and to adjective-noun combinations. For example, they asked participants to provide the antonym to the word *fresh* alone and to the same word when it is part of a combination (consider *fresh fish*). The dependent variable was the consistency in responses. Alone, the word *fresh* might provide the antonym *stale*, let's say. When part of a combination, participants' choices change. The most cited opposite of *fresh shirt* was *dirty* and the most cited opposite of *fresh fish* was *frozen*. The same held for synonyms. The word *fresh* in *fresh bread* and *fresh water* do not yield similar synonyms either. As Murphy (2002, p. 417) put it, "The adjective *fresh* seems to take on somewhat more specific meanings depending on the noun it modifies."

Relevance Theory's approach is unlike those in the previous section in at least two ways. First, while the two accounts that respond to the psycholinguistic question view metaphor, irony, idioms, indirect requests, and so on, collectively as a category deserving one overarching explanation, Relevance Theory treats each of these individually. It is only after careful reconsideration, did Relevance Theory place metaphor on a particular dimension (with *approximation* and *hyperbole*). Second, the Relevance account is not entirely focused on the role played by the literal meaning of the metaphor vehicle, however interesting that might be. Relevance Theory emphasizes the role played by the speaker's intention and how intentions affect a word's lexical meaning. So the source of slowdowns could be due to factors other than the listener's access to features associated with the lexical meaning of the word. This could explain why one can discern a rare discord among Relevance theorists. Sperber and Wilson (2008) indicate that a metaphor's literal reading ought to have no influence on discerning the metaphor's intended meaning (in line with the Direct Access view). While Wilson claims that metaphor is due to broadening, Carston (2012) claims that metaphor is due to broadening and narrowing (because the listener promotes the concept's peripheral properties). Carston's approach also intimates that literal readings should leave some sort of lingering effect. As will be seen immediately below, experimental data are in line with the more recent position.

Relevance Theory Inspires Investigations on Metaphor

Noveck et al. (2001) adopted Gibbs's metaphoric reference study, summarized in (10.1–4) above, in order to reinvestigate the way children and adults carry out the metaphoric-reference task. Other than the inclusion of children, the only real difference between our task and Gibbs's was that we did not include

Table 10.1. *Reading times in milliseconds of metaphoric versus synonymic referential utterances from Noveck et al.'s (2001) developmental study: while the gap closes with age, it is not bridged; and, in parentheses, rates of correct responses to comprehension questions*

| Age | N | Reference type | |
		Metaphoric	Synonymic
9-year-olds	50	7,908 (74%)	5,586 (82%)
11-year-olds	48	4,510 (73%)	3,842 (77%)
14-year-olds	51	3,609 (86%)	2,967 (87%)
Adults	40	2,851 (90%)	2,321 (83%)

nonsequitor controls (cases like 10.4), we carried it out in French, we avoided conventional metaphors and we added a concluding line that followed the critical metaphoric (or synonymic) line. To give a flavor of one of our stimuli, one story was about second-graders who went to a swimming pool and, after a few exercises, heard the lifeguard say, "All toads to the side of the pool" or "All students to the side of the pool." The final line said that the children then returned to their lockers.

We showed, through reading times of the critical line of text, that utterances, which contain metaphoric references (e.g., 10.2), do take longer to read than literal controls (10.3), and across all ages (see Table 10.1). We also considered responses to comprehension questions (e.g., "Were the pupils the ones who went to the side of the pool?"). We showed that, while children's rates of correct responses appeared to suffer (just) slightly when the story turned to the metaphoric reference (as in 10.2), as opposed to a synonymic reference (as in 10.3), adults actually benefited slightly from concept loosening.[1] The two columns in Table 10.1– under *Metaphoric* and *Synonymic*– show two sets of results (from Noveck et al., 2001, Experiment 2), the reading time of the utterance and (in parentheses) the rate of correct responses to the follow-up question as a function of age.

Our study showed that adults took significantly longer to read the sentences with metaphoric readings when compared to synonymic ones. These reading time differences are even more evident among the younger participants. Additionally, there appears to be a growing competence in answering the comprehension question that develops with age in the metaphoric stories (and remains more or less static for responses in the synonymic condition). This can be taken to indicate that the metaphor arguably comes with a cost for younger participants but that, with age, it provides positive effects that a synonymic reference does not (see Almor et al., 2007 for a replication; also see Winer et al., 2001). Arguably, the *ad hoc* transformation of a word calls for a pragmatic enrichment (in this case, in the form of broadening and narrowing). Sophisticated listeners, unlike unsophisticated ones, have more resources available to derive nonliteral meanings, suggesting that pragmatic enrichments of all sorts are costly.

A second study I will highlight here comes from Rubio-Fernández (2007), who contends that the enhancement of the relevant properties of the metaphor, and suppression of those that are irrelevant for the figurative interpretation, is a necessary process in metaphor comprehension. To support her claims, she carried out a cross-modal lexical priming study in which she aurally presented 20 two-sentence-long vignettes whose second sentence concluded with a metaphor. For example, participants would read sentences such as (10.8):

(10.8) Nobody wanted to run against John at school. John was a cheetah.

At the end of the vignette, a probe word appeared on a screen either immediately (0 ms), 400 ms later, or 1,000 ms later. These probes were part of a lexical-decision task, which requires participants to determine whether the probe word was a word of English or not; in these cases, a "yes" (it is a word in English) provides a measure of just how well the stimulus word is linked to the concept in the probe at the time of decision. The probes were of three sorts, one that was *categorically* associated with the critical term, one that was unrelated, and one that referred to the intended property. The categorical (i.e. superordinate) probe for the word "cheetah" in (10.8) was *cat*, the unrelated probe was *plant* (a superordinate from another vignette), and the "distinctive-property" (i.e., the relevant) probe was *fast*. Analyses were based on the difference between either the superordinate and the unrelated one, or else between the distinctive property and some other unrelated property. The *immediate* reactions to the three types of probes (viz. 0 ms from the time the critical term appeared) revealed that the unrelated meaning is significantly slower than both the metaphor's literal superordinate meaning *and* the metaphor's intended meaning. So, participants' immediate reactions indicate that the manipulation worked in that both the literal and metaphoric readings are distinguishable from the control condition, but neither of them individually appear preferred.

The interesting data arise later. As far as the literal meaning is concerned, the decision latencies for the probes showed that listeners maintained their preference for processing the superordinate probe over the unrelated one at 400 ms (644 vs. 698 ms, respectively), but that this preference disappeared at 1,000 ms (791 vs. 799 ms, respectively). One can see that the categorical information in the critical word had lost its impact on the listener by the time a second had passed. In contrast, the decision latencies also showed that listeners had a preference for processing the distinctive-property probe over the unrelated one at 400 ms (658 vs. 710 ms, respectively) and that the preference remained at

1,000 ms (598 vs. 651 ms, respectively). As Rubio-Fernández (2007) wrote, results supported the notion that "metaphor interpretation involves enhancing relevant properties of the metaphor vehicle" (p. 345). She also argues that the categorical (superordinate) associations get actively suppressed.

Overall, experimental investigations inspired by Relevance Theory's approach show that metaphoric readings emerge at a cost. Noveck et al.'s (2001) study showed that processing is slower across all ages when an original metaphor, as opposed to a synonym, refers to a previously mentioned entity. Rubio-Fernández's (2007) study showed that while a metaphor can give rise to many associated concepts, including one linked with a word's prototypical meaning, only a small subset of these will be relevant to working out the speaker's informative intention. The concept that emerges as a result appears to linger longest and to provide an enriching comprehension. While Relevance Theorists can appear less concerned about processing costs in metaphor comprehension (Sperber and Wilson, 2008) or even divided about it (see Carston, 2010), it does appear that, contra Gibbs, one cannot readily claim that metaphor arises directly and that it is costfree. The Graded salience approach might argue that there is an effect of (un)familiarity, but it would not consider distinctive properties of a word as selected and highly accessible.

Recent Experiments

The traditional psycholinguistic literature has not really gotten beyond the Direct versus Indirect access debate. On the one hand, this is unfortunate because there are other interesting issues to consider, such as the role of Theory of Mind in metaphor comprehension (which has been largely the reserve of Autism studies, see Chapter 12, and to a lesser extent schizophrenia studies). On the other hand, this debate continues to generate increasingly innovative investigations. In this section, I review the findings from a clever design from Petra Schumacher and Valentina Bambini.

Metaphor and Masked Priming

After each gave a talk at one of the early experimental pragmatic conferences which took place in Lyon, 2009, Valentina Bambini and Petra Schumacher realized that they were in a position to launch an adversarial collaboration. While Valentina was inclined toward the direct access view to metaphors based on the Relevance-theoretical approach (e.g., see Bambini and Resta, 2012), Petra was favorable toward the indirect accounts based mostly on her prior findings on metonymy (see Chapter 13). This ultimately led to a very fruitful collaboration, including Weiland et al.'s (2014) EEG study, which I summarize here.

They began their cleverly conceived study by first presenting sentences resembling those of Pynte et al. (1996) or McElree and Nordlie (1999). More concretely, participants were asked to listen to a phrase, such as (10.9) in German:

(10.9) Those lobbyists are hyenas, if you believe the kindergarten teacher.

Of course, the critical phrase is the first one. The second phrase ("if you believe ...") is there to make the out-of-the-blue nature of the metaphor less jarring. As is the case with several prior studies, Weiland et al. were keen to determine whether one would find an N400. When participants were presented utterances (aurally), such as (10.9) above, they indeed report finding N400s and P600s when compared to sentences such as (10.10):

(10.10) Those carnivores are hyenas, if you believe the Kindergarten teacher.

This provides a baseline for the next phase of their study. In their next experiment, Weiland et al. tested for literal processing by placing a masked-prime *before* the metaphor appeared.

What is a masked prime? In such studies, participants are presented a prime (a word) that appears at a key moment. In this case, the prime is visually presented just prior to hearing the word *hyenas* and so quickly (for just 67 ms) that participants are usually not even sure they saw it (in Weiland et al., participants were able to report them on around 60 percent of the trials in a brief supplementary experiment). What are these primes? The primes are words whose meanings are related to the literal (and not the metaphorical) reading of the phrase. In the case of (10.9), the experimenters presented the word "furry" visually and (to repeat) very briefly just before the participants heard the word "hyenas."

The thinking behind the experiment went as follows. If listeners have direct access to the metaphoric reading of the phrase then the literal prime should hamper processing – and potentially enhance the N400 component – because it would help prompt a clash between the literally-linked prime (*furry*, in our example) and the metaphoric reading for *hyenas*, which expresses properties such as *aggressive* or *ferocious*. On the other hand, if listeners *indirectly* construct a metaphoric reading, then the prime should have no [negative] effect on processing the metaphoric term; in fact, the literal prime should facilitate computation of both literal and metaphoric conditions (i.e., the prime should make the metaphor seem more neutral at onset than an unprimed metaphor). That is because, in the early going, the critical term (*hyenas*) is not necessarily treated metaphorically so adding information that feeds the linguistically encoded meaning could even be salutary.

What did they find? They reported that the primes did indeed have a strong effect on the processing of both the metaphoric and literal uses of the same word. That is, upon seeing a word, such as *furry*, very briefly before hearing the test word *hyenas*, it suppressed the N400 effects for the critical word in both conditions when compared to unprimed cases. They took this to mean that the prime enhances the literal reading of the metaphor and without immediately creating a clash within the sentence, indicating that the metaphoric reading is not engaged directly. They did note a late positivity (a later occurring P600) remained in both the primed and unprimed conditions, pointing to late processing step in which the listener builds up the speaker's meaning via inference.

Concluding Remarks about Metaphor

Work on metaphor captures just how far Gricean notions have traveled. According to Grice's seminal proposal, metaphor is expressed through a word whose literal meaning becomes part of *what is said*; nonliteral interpretations follow from flouting a maxim that rejects the literal meaning as the listener determines *what is meant*. In such an account words have set meanings. While for some current theorists (e.g., Borg, 2010), words have conventional meanings that are rich in conceptual structure, for others (e.g., Bosch, 2007; Carston, 2010) a word represents a minimal frame that could be modulated in order to determine the speaker's intended meaning.[2] Of these two opposing modern accounts, experimental work plays a critical role in supporting the latter. This also underlines how the area of *lexical pragmatics* (Wilson & Cartson, 2007) can address lingering questions from the traditional psycholinguistic literature.

Notes

1. In another off-line experiment in the same paper (Noveck et al., 2001) and with the same materials, 230 children between the ages of 8 and 12 were measured for their answers to the comprehension question and we found that metaphoric reference versions consistently prompted rates of correct responses that were slightly lower than the synonymic ones (between 3 and 7 percent) for each age.
2. According to Lepore and Stone (2015), some words do come with set meanings that optimize communication, whereas other terms call on our imaginations.

11   Irony

Shifting Attention and Reading Intentions

> At a time like this, scorching irony, not convincing argument, is needed.
>
> Frederick Douglass

Deirdre Wilson, one of the world's leading authorities on irony, once remarked to me that despite her obvious interest in this topic (not to mention the fact that she describes herself as "ironically inclined" and British, which implies a culturally ingrained sense of irony), she could be caught unaware from time to time whenever an ironic remark came her way. In an email exchange with me, she wrote:

I do have a clear memory of being caught out ... when I went into a small baker's shop in London with lots of loaves and a few pastries on display and, when the server turned to me before I'd quite decided what I wanted, I asked "Do you sell cakes?" She replied, deadpan, conversational and not moving a muscle, "No, we don't sell cakes." I was about to point out to her that she actually had quite a lot of cakes on display when I realised she was being ironical.

I took solace when Deirdre shared that story with me because I am often unprepared for irony myself (whether in the United Kingdom or elsewhere), even though I am always ready for a pun or a good joke. As we will see later in the chapter, it is also the case that research supports a claim that says detecting irony is not fluid. It is a phenomenon that is highly dependent on context and that calls on turning one's attention toward something specific in the speaker's perspective. It helps to be prepared for irony in order to appreciate it.

Deirdre Wilson's anecdote highlights two features of irony. One is that irony clearly calls on non-linguistic processes. As Deirdre's reaction to the server made clear, there are cognitive resources other than linguistic encoding that need to be engaged in order to comprehend an ironical utterance. Given that these resources – shifts of attention and intention-reading – are crucial to irony comprehension, one can anticipate that Theory of Mind (ToM) is going to be called upon. A second feature to notice here is that appreciating irony relies on comprehending an entire utterance in context. One would be hard-pressed to isolate a single word and reduce all of the pragmatic processing to it – as many researchers do for logical terms, for reference, or for metaphors.[1] Taking both of these features together, irony is a paragon of pragmatic processing. In what follows, I will briefly describe how Grice viewed irony before turning to each of the two lines of research that he has indirectly generated.

Grice's Maxims and Attitude

Grice, it will be remembered, lumped irony with other tropes such as metaphor, meiosis, and hyperbole by explaining that they all arise in the wake of a violation of the "maxim of Quality." It should be noted that his remarks on irony did not end there. He pointed out that irony is nevertheless distinctive from the others because "irony is intimately connected with the expression of a feeling, attitude, or evaluation. I cannot say something ironically unless what I say is intended to reflect a hostile or derogatory judgment or a feeling such as indignation or contempt" (Grice, 1989, pp. 53–4). However, he did not expand on this remark. He also indicated that he did not think that there was a prosody specifically designed for irony but that it would be a tone "connected with one or more particular feelings or attitudes." While his observations indicated that he was moving away from the standard notion (that irony is a "remark to be taken in reverse"), his reflections on irony moved the ball forward somewhat. Whether or not one agreed with him, his approach to irony laid the tracks for two lines of irony research that have since dominated the experimental literature.

Echoic Mention Theory

Sperber and Wilson (1981) radically reconceptualized irony by fully weaving attitude-ascription into irony understanding. As Wilson (2009, p. 197) wrote, "the point of irony is not to commit the speaker to the truth of the proposition expressed but, on the contrary, to express a certain type of derisory or dissociative attitude to a thought with a similar content." In the interest of being more thorough, let me show how Sperber and Wilson's account goes deeper still.

Sperber and Wilson begin their analysis of irony through a distinction between two types of utterances – *descriptive* and *attributive*. Descriptive uses are about a state of affairs and attributive uses ascribe a thought to someone else. A subtype of attributive uses is the *echoic* use, which occurs when the message that the speaker wants to convey is not the content of the attributed thought but rather her own attitude or reaction to it. To make these three uses – descriptive, attributive, and echoic – clear, consider two different attributive responses, in (11.2) and (11.2'), to a run-of-the-mill descriptive use in (11.1):

(11.1) Nivian: US citizens can now visit Cuba.

(11.2) Nivian's father: "My daughter thinks US citizens can now visit Cuba"
(Nivian's father has awoken from a coma and is informing someone
about what Nivian just said).

(11.2') Nivian's father: "My daughter thinks US citizens can now visit Cuba!"
(Nivian's father is aghast that Nivian would consider it acceptable
for US citizens to visit Cuba).

While (11.1) is an ordinary *descriptive* use of language with which Nivian
describes a state of affairs, (11.2) is an *attributive* use of language because the
father's utterance does not refer directly to the state of affairs but to her thought.
More germane to our discussion on irony, (11.2') is an *echoic* use of language
because the content of the sentence is used to convey her father's reaction to
Nivian's utterance. Verbal irony is a subtype of echoic use in which the utterance conveys a skeptical, mocking attitude about a thought that is attributed to
someone else. At the heart of irony, then, is a speaker who is not expressing her
own thoughts, but is *echoing* a thought – making reference to a thought – that
can be attributed to some real or prototypical speaker. The *thought referred to*
could emanate from someone else or from the speaker herself.[2] Irony arises
while expressing a dissociative (mocking, skeptical, or contemptuous) attitude
to that echoed thought. To bring this notion home, consider this example (from
Wilson, 2006, p. 1724), which concerns Mary who, after a difficult meeting,
says, *That went well*.

Mary might use "That went well" to communicate that it was ridiculous of her to think
that the meeting would go well, stupid of her friends to assure her that it would go well,
naïve of her to believe their assurances, and so on. Mary echoes a thought or utterance
with a similar content to the one expressed in her utterance, in order to express a critical
or mocking attitude to it.

Aside from being an original account that dates back at least three decades, the
echoic mention account came with seminal empirical support as well.

Jorgensen, Miller, and Sperber (1984) presented six stories to participants,
each ending with a potentially innocuous remark. In the experimental condition, the story-ending remark echoed back to someone else's thought; in the
control condition that previously uttered thought was removed. To make this
clear, let us consider one story whose final remark was "Tedious, wasn't it?"
In the experimental condition, the story-ending remark was uttered by Harry
to classmate Anne about an entertaining lecture that they had just attended;
the remark was full of ironic potential because Anne had complained earlier
about going to that particular lecture by saying "How tedious!" The control
condition presented the very same story but without the prior encounter with
Anne (Harry only ran into Anne after the lecture). Jorgensen et al. (1984)

straightforwardly measured the perceived irony of stories by asking participants "why did the speaker say [the concluding remark]" and by determining
whether the participant responded by saying that the "speaker intended to be
ironic, sarcastic or facetious" (p. 117). The number of participants who cited
irony (or its synonyms) in their responses was nearly three times higher in the
experimental condition compared to those in the control condition. Again, this
occurred as a function of the presence of raised expectations that were made
explicit earlier in the story.

The echoic mention account is not the only proposal to give pride of place
to the detection of a speaker's attitude. Clark and Gerrig (1984), in response to
the Echoic Mention account, presented their own account: the Pretense Theory
of irony. Following up on Grice (1989, p. 54), who had written "to be ironical
is, among other things, to pretend (as the etymology suggests)," Clark and
Gerrig proposed that the speaker of an ironical utterance is only *pretending* to
perform a speech act in order to convey a mocking, skeptical, or contemptuous attitude. This proposal generated some heated discussions with the echoic
mention camp (e.g., see Wilson, 2006). However, the debate has not produced
comparative studies.

All told, it can be seen that, from early on in the Gricean and post-Gricean
cognitive literature, there have been proposals, debates, and empirical studies
on irony that focus on attitude ascription and its link to irony. They all share
the fundamental idea that the communication of the speaker's attitude is the
hallmark of irony. They also generated several follow-up studies that incorporated these ideas – Gibbs (1986) investigated the echoic-mention theory,
and Kreuz and Glucksberg (1989) considered how irony calls on normative
situations (i.e., on negative situations in which the ironic remark appears positive), much like the "that went well" example mentioned previously, more than
non-normative ones (i.e., where an ironic remark is negatively valenced in a
positive situation). Nevertheless, as we will see, the importance of attitude in
irony would not remain a permanent fixture of irony debates.

Is It Effortful or Not?

The Blessed SPM

Despite these early, thoughtful, and empirically supported attitude-rich
accounts, these approaches got largely eclipsed, and to an extent forgotten,
by psycholinguistically oriented researchers who were preoccupied with the
role of literal meaning. This second line of Grice-inspired research ought to
be familiar from issues throughout the book (from the discussion of scalar
inferences and metaphors) and starts with the so-called Standard Pragmatic
Model (SPM), which was attributed to Grice and Searle. According to those

who treat the SPM as a processing model for irony, generating the intended meaning ought to be a time-consuming affair, say, compared to understanding the very same utterance expressed literally; after all, the ironic meaning, unlike the literal one, calls on the listener to go through several steps – rejecting the literal reading and making inferences – before getting at the intended meaning.

As should be clear by now, this irony-is-effortful claim struck some as implausible, and it was Ray Gibbs who argued most strenuously in favor of the idea that listeners access ironic interpretations *directly*. As we saw in the last chapter, his approach is known as the Direct Access view, and he applied it to irony (as well as to indirect requests, metaphors, and idioms among other figures of speech). So, it follows that Gibbs (1986) would be interested in determining whether a sentence with an ironic reading is more arduous than the same sentence with a literal reading. He thus investigated sarcasm (a form of irony), and he did so by having participants read seven sentence-long vignettes that provided context for a target sentence, such as in (11.3):

(11.3)   You're a big help.

In the ironic version, the remark in (11.3) was uttered by a character to his brother after the latter did not show up on time to help build a house. In the literal story, (11.3) was uttered by a speaker who was sincerely thankful for the math tutoring he had received from his roommate. Critically, both lines were read at equivalent speeds, thus undermining the claim that irony requires processing that goes above and beyond the literal (sincere) reading.

The upshot is that findings showing fast figurative interpretations have made it easy for critics to rail against the SPM and, in so doing, the entire Gricean approach. That said, Gibbs's data did not put the issue to rest. As we will see, at least one alternative view claims that irony is time-consuming and put in motion an everlasting debate.

Graded Salience

As should be familiar from the previous chapter, the Direct Access view provided a contrast with another proposal: Rachel Giora's (1997) Graded Salience hypothesis. Giora argues that ironies (and other figurative utterances) generate both literal and figurative meanings, but that the non-literal meaning can essentially compete for the most salient status with the literal one. Again, the extent to which a figurative meaning emerges varies as a function of different features, such as familiarity, conventionality, frequency, and prototypicality, of a critical word in the utterance. Much of the original work from the Graded Salience view focuses on irony and to a lesser extent on idioms (Giora, 1997; Giora, Fein, & Schwartz, 1998; Giora & Fein, 1999; Filik & Moxey, 2010).

What does this evidence look like? To give one example with respect to irony, Giora, Fein, and Schwartz (1998) presented participants with a lexical decision task (*is this a word?*) with the probe word related either to the literal or ironic reading of an utterance. In (11.4a), for example, the context sets up an ironic reading of (11.5) while (11.4b) sets up a literal reading for it:

(11.4) a. Anna is a great student, but she is very absentminded. One day, while I was well through my lecture, she suddenly showed up in the classroom. I said to her:
        b. Anna is a great student and very responsible. One day she called to tell me, she did not know when she would be able to show up for my lecture. However, just as I was starting, she entered the classroom; I said to her:

(11.5) "You are just in time."

One of two probe words, "late" and "punctual," was prepared for this story and presented after the critical phrase in (11.5). The former is compatible with the ironic reading of (11.5) and the latter with a literal reading. Giora et al. (1998) showed that after delays of 150 and 1,000 ms, reaction times to probe words related to the literal interpretation were significantly faster than those related to the ironic interpretation (whether or not they were compatible with the context). However, this difference disappeared at 2,000 ms. Given sufficient time, irony-related probes can be read off as quickly as the literal ones. This suggests that the ironic interpretation becomes salient with time. Importantly their first experiment also established that reading times for target sentences (such as in 11.5) in the irony-biasing context (following 11.4a) were longer than those in the literal-biasing contexts (following 11.4b).

As this brief review of the Direct Access and Graded Salience accounts of irony shows, the two accounts provide diametrically opposing predictions. Gibbs, by dismissing the importance of the linguistically encoded meanings and by emphasizing context, predicts that ironic readings prompt responses that are similar to literal readings. Graded Salience emphasizes that – at least at some level – addressees need to consider the linguistically encoded meaning of a critical word in a figurative utterance. This debate has ushered in a series of studies that either defended the notion that irony was effortful (Schwoebel et al., 2000; Filik & Moxey, 2010) or showed that irony was not effortful (e.g., Ivanko & Pexman, 2003).[3] Given that each side provided experimental support, it has left the literature at an impasse.

Doing Experimental Pragmatics on Irony

In order to correct for the literature's lasting oversight and to potentially get beyond the "is irony-processing time-consuming?" impasse, Nicola Spotorno and I led a group of our colleagues on a series of investigations designed to show the extent to which irony depends on attitude ascription. One advantage of the long pause (between the time that the attitude-rich accounts first came out in the 1980s and our own recent efforts) is that we were able to take advantage of techniques, such as neuroimaging, that did not exist when the first attitudinal accounts of irony appeared. That is, by the end of 2010 or so, the neuroscience literature had – through the development of dozens of clever tasks – localized brain regions associated with understanding other minds (i.e., ToM areas). These regions are the right and left temporal–parietal junctions (rTPJ and lTPJ), the medial prefrontal cortex (MPFC), and the precuneus (PC) (see Saxe & Kanwisher, 2003; Frith & Frith, 2006; for meta-analyses, see Van Overwalle, 2009; Van Overwalle & Baetens, 2009). In Chapter 4, I described one of these studies in which Rebecca Saxe and colleagues had participants watch a scene of an actor simply walking toward and behind a bookcase and, after a brief pause, stepping out from behind it; the pause led to intention-reading – specifically, in the right TPJ. We reasoned that if irony relied on capturing the attitude of one's interlocutor, it should similarly engage deeper mind-reading activity, or what neuroscience calls *mentalizing*, when compared to a literal reading of that same utterance (Spotorno et al., 2012). This amounted to a unique prediction for the neuroscience literature.

We thus prepared stories, modeled on Gibbs (1986), that included a line that could be interpreted as either ironical or literal (as a function of slight changes in context). To make the paradigm concrete, imagine reading a quote "We went to see a wonderful film," under one of two slightly different conditions as in (11.6):

(11.6) a. Clara and Isabelle must decide which film to see at the cinema.
  b. They see a poster for a film outside.
  c. They aren't familiar with it, but they decide to go see it.
  d. The two friends buy tickets and popcorn.
  e. The film turns out to be banal and very boring, so Clara says to Isabelle:
  f. "We went to see a wonderful film."
  g. They leave the theater and buy an ice cream.

The critical utterance is intended to be ironic (after all, the story's two characters see a mediocre film); in another case, (11.6e) is replaced by (11.6e'), which describes the film positively, and allows (11.6f) to be understood literally:

(11.6) e'. The film turns out to be exciting and surprising, so Clara says to Isabelle:

Assuming that the ironic reading calls for increased ToM processing when compared to the literal control, the neural imaging work ought to predict that irony processing specifically calls on the ToM areas (Spotorno et al., 2012).[4]

Let me point out three other features of the paradigm in order to highlight the experimental care that is required for investigating irony. First of all, participants do not see both versions of the same story (of course), but rather a random collection of either a literal or an ironic version of any one of twenty stories (with the constraint that half of the stories will be read in their ironical version). Second, the utterances in the sixth line are all roughly the same in length (ranging from 10 to 12 syllables in French) so that the time required to read the critical line is equivalent across all conditions. Third, there are two sorts of "filler" stories other than these experimental (ironic and literal) items; some of these, called *decoys*, purposely provide a negatively themed scenario (e.g., ordering a tea that turns out to be too bitter) that was *not* followed by an ironic remark. The purpose of including the decoys was to prevent participants from establishing a link between a negatively themed story and the expectation of an irony.

Now let me turn to two of the main findings from that fMRI study. Again, we made a very specific prediction that said that *Ironic* target sentences, when compared to their *Literal* controls, will elicit differences in regions known to be associated with the ToM processing that were identified *a priori* based on an extensive meta-analysis of the literature on ToM. That is exactly what we found in this first finding. Whole brain analyses (i.e., investigations into brain activity that occurred without focusing our interest on relevant regions in advance) showed that understanding verbal irony engages a network of brain regions typically associated with ToM – the rTPJ and lTPJ, the MPFC, and the PC. The same held when we analyzed the data from these four Regions of Interest. Second, analyses known as Psycho-physiological Interaction analyses revealed an increase in functional *connectivity* between ToM and language networks, i.e., the signal in the ventral part of the MPFC (vMPFC) and in the left Inferior Frontal Gyrus (IFG) increases together when participants read a target sentence in the *Ironic* condition as opposed to one in the *Literal* condition. Given that the vMPFC is crucial for ToM processing (e.g., Ma et al., 2011) and that the left IFG is strongly involved in the integration process in language (e.g., Hagoort, 2005), it is highly plausible that this represents an exchange of information or integration precisely between these two regions (Figure 11.1).

Two follow-up studies aimed to better capture how mindreading interacts with processing. In one EEG study, our group (Spotorno et al., 2013) used the same paradigm, except that the target sentence was presented word by word, and we collected measures from its last word. This work was designed to investigate event-related brain potentials (ERPs) (and specifically the P600 component, which is a recurring index of pragmatic phenomena) and to apply a Time Frequency Analysis (TFA), which can capture more subtle distinctions. As expected, we found an increase in the amplitude of the P600, in the *Ironic* condition when compared to the *Literal* one. We also observed an increase of

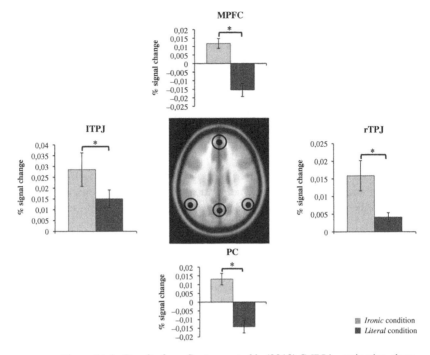

Figure 11.1. Results from Spotorno et al.'s (2012) fMRI investigation showing the four main regions of interest (rTPJ, lTPJ, MPFC, and PC) with respect
to ToM and the relative activations that result from ironic versus literal interpretations of critical sentences such as the one in (11.6f)

power in the gamma band for the *Ironic > Literal* contrast. This is an intriguing
finding because it takes place in the 280–400 ms time window. This could indicate that integration operations during irony processing start well before the
latency associated with the P600 and that the integration between the linguistic
code and the contextual information is *not* obligatorily a late Gricean step in
the comprehension of an utterance. That said, let me point out again that these
studies are accompanied by a late-going process that is expressed through a
noticeable P600.

The last follow-up study (Spotorno & Noveck, 2014) used the same paradigm to carry out three experiments. In some ways that research paper was
more traditional (because it used reading times), but it was also a bit more
involved because we made manipulations to the environment surrounding the
ironic utterances in order to better understand how one can facilitate or delay

irony understanding over the course of an experimental session. For example, in Experiment 1, we showed that the presence of our *decoys* among the filler items prompted readers to take longer to read the genuinely ironic utterances when compared to their literal controls and *throughout* the experimental session.

In contrast, when we removed decoys in Experiment 2, we still found a significant irony-related slowdown. However, it was limited to the first half of the experiment so that by the time participants got to the second half, the reading times of ironic utterances were comparable to those of literal controls. We referred to this as an *Early–Late* effect. A second relevant finding was that we had collected scores on a version of Baron-Cohen et al.'s Autism Quotient (AQ) for each participant and found that not all participants reacted similarly. There were individual differences such that we found a positive correlation between one subscale of the AQ (the Social Skill subscale, which included ToM-related questions) and an individual's Ironic-minus-Literal reading time difference in the second half of the experiment. Those who scored higher on the AQ (a higher score is associated with approaching the autistic spectrum) were more likely than those who scored lower on the AQ to continue processing ironies at a relatively slower pace even into the second half of the session. In other words, those who we described as *socially disinclined* were more likely than those who we described as *socially inclined* to continually react differently to the ironical utterances (compared to the literal controls) throughout the task. This indicated that – under conditions that encouraged readers to anticipate ironies – socially inclined people were able to practically predict ironic utterances as the experiment wore on. These correlations are supportive of our hypothesis that ToM abilities have a role to play in irony processing.

Experiment 3 returned to the technique first used by Jorgensen et al. (1984) thirty years earlier. We again presented our stories in a decoy-free manner and this time added what we referred to as *antecedents* that could be echoed later. To accomplish this, we added a little kicker to the third sentence of each story. To see how this worked, let us return to the "wonderful film" story we saw in (11.6). Now, (11.6c) appears as (11.6c'), i.e., with an additional sentence announcing Isabelle's positive expectations:

(11.6) c'. They aren't familiar with it, but they decide to go see it. Isabelle says: "This should be a good movie."

This way, when Clara later says, "We went to see a wonderful film," it is echoing Isabelle's earlier remark. The results again revealed an Early–Late effect in that ironical-utterance reading times decrease over the course of the experiment so as to become similar to the literal-utterance reading times. Outwardly, this could be interpreted as indicating that the *to-be-echoed antecedent* had no additional effect on the comprehension of irony. However, this is not the case. This time the results showed a *negative* correlation between the Social Skill subscale and the (Irony-minus-Literal) reading time difference. In digging deeper into the data, we saw that the socially disinclined read the ironic and the literal statements with comparable speeds from the beginning to the end of the experimental session. This creates a negative correlation because the more socially inclined continue to distinguish between ironic and literal readings uniquely in the first half of the session as in Experiment 2. The reading times among the socially inclined were not terribly affected by the antecedents while the reading times for the socially disinclined were.

We concluded that paper by suggesting that of the two cues to ToM investi- gated — (a) the reliable link between negative events and irony across stories (by removing decoys), and (b) the role of echoic mention – the former can be viewed as representative of a second level of ToM. Arguably, those who are more socially inclined are seeking to better understand the structure of the task (as presented by an absentee experimenter) and are looking for ToM-related cues. However, mind-reading abilities need time to tune into irony, which accounts for the slow processing times only at the beginning of the experiment.

Overall, the neuroimaging studies and the classical behavioral studies allowed us to draw three conclusions. The main one is that this work allowed us to re-establish that attitude ascription is indeed a hallmark of irony under- standing as originally claimed by prominent pragmatists. Second, while there is no definitive evidence indicating that ironic utterances are generally harder or more effortful to process (intervening factors can make critical ironic utter- ances appear as easy as their literal controls), it is fair to say that unexpected uses of irony (especially early uses in an experiment) do consistently prompt slowdowns (as Deirdre Wilson's anecdote at the top of the Chapter reminds us). Finally, certain experimental conditions and individual inclinations can make at least some participants anticipate irony. These last two facts could help address why both the Direct Access and the Graded Salience views were each able to muster supporting evidence in support of its own side.

From the point of view of ostensive-inferential approaches, it is also appar- ent that one should not paint irony with the same brush as metaphor for the two have little in common. While both irony and metaphor are figures of speech and while both are *usually* viewed as literally false utterances, mechanisms behind the two phenomena are rather different.[5] Metaphor comprehension is a process of enrichment through the adjustment of concepts conveyed by a critical word such as "cheetah" in "John is a cheetah." In contrast, the hall- mark of irony comprehension is the addressee's access to the speaker's attitude while she is echoing a previously intimated (or explicitly stated) proposition. The distinction between the two has been made clearly through experimental pragmatics.

Notes

1. Thanks to Valentina Bambini for pointing out that even though irony is not local, it could be expressed through a one-word utterance.

2. Echoing, according to Sperber and Wilson, is "expressing the speaker's attitude to views she tacitly attributes to someone else." So, if you were to say, "That James Bond film was fantastic," and your interlocutor were to respond "Fantastic?" the speaker is echoing your original remark while also conveying an attitude (in this case, wonder at how you could find that film fantastic). That someone else could also be yourself (e.g., in reference to a remark made in the past).

3. A compelling model that tries to find a middle ground between the Direct Access view and the Graded Salience Hypothesis is the *Parallel constraint satisfaction account* (e.g., Katz, 2005; Pexman, 2008). According to this account, various cues – such as expectations about the speaker's style of communication, the familiarity or conventionality of the ironic utterance and paralinguistic cues (e.g., prosody) – are used in parallel during the processing of the utterance.

4. Our irony stories, like most in the literature, present positive utterances in the context of a negatively valenced situation (seeing a bad film, singing off-key, making a bad investment, etc.). This reflects the normative bias mentioned earlier (see Kreuz & Glucksberg, 1989). From personal experience, I can attest that setting up concise vignettes non-normatively, in which an ironic remark occurs in the context of a positive situation, is very challenging for experimental purposes.

5. I say usually because irony need not be false. Imagine walking into a rainstorm and saying "I love sunny days." While ironic, it is probably true.

12   Pragmatic Abilities among Those with Autism

It's not about being right, it's about getting it right.

Liz Spelke[1]

Lorna Wing was the psychiatrist who coined the term "Asperger's Syndrome" to refer to the relatively mild form of Autism Spectrum Disorder (ASD). She was crediting the Austrian psychiatrist, Hans Asperger, who first described the cluster of traits that are now familiar to scientists and non-scientists alike. Part of her motivation was to better categorize this milder version of autistic behavior while removing some of the inaccurate terminological baggage (such as *psychopathy* or *schizophrenia*), that had become associated with prior descriptions. She also aimed to underline that Asperger's is not purely a childhood disorder in the way envisioned by Leo Kanner, who is the other person recognized as being among the first to have documented autism (Kanner coined *that* term). Wing's seminal article (1981, see also Wing and Gould, 1979), presented a "clinical picture" of Asperger's. Allow me to describe this picture.

Wing wrote that autism is much more common in boys than in girls (as had been noticed by Asperger), that autistic behavior is marked by repetitive activities such as "spinning objects" (or, as others have noticed, collecting, and stacking), and that those with Asperger's have intellectual skills that are characterized by "excellent rote memories" and also by a pedantic interest or two, such as astronomy, geology, or bus timetables that dominate their thinking "to the exclusion of all else." There are three other features of autism that she describes in her (1981) article concerning social interaction, speech, and non-verbal communication.[2] Wing described Asperger's social interaction as "naïve and peculiar," writing that they do not know how to "adapt their approaches and responses to fit in with the needs and personalities of others." With respect to speech, she noted that their pedantic side can end up dominating a conversation, that they might substitute the "second or third person for the first-person forms," and that they might not get "subtle verbal jokes." According to Wing's description, non-verbal communication is generally impaired and clumsy.[3]

It is these last three traits that are of interest to experimental pragmatists. As far as experimentation goes, it is only natural to want to home in on distinctive autistic behavior through carefully controlled investigations in order to bring some consistency and order to what are, after all, clinical observations. As far as pragmatics is concerned, these three features ultimately involve communication. Experimental pragmatic work, then, can be vital in substantiating many of the claims about communication that are related to autism or to come up with, perhaps, more fine-tuned distinctions and, eventually, alternative diagnoses. Understanding traits among people with autism can also shed light on the way more typical communication works.

For the purposes of this chapter, I will remain focused on the pragmatic phenomena that have been covered in the book so far. That is, while styles of conversation (perseveration and conversational dominance) among people with autism might be interesting from a sociolinguistic point of view, it would be more relevant to our current enterprise to know how they react to pragmatically rich utterances and also to determine the tasks that generate differences in performance between them and typically developing participants. So, we will revisit topics such as scalar inference, metaphor, irony, and conditionals. Given the importance of Theory of Mind reasoning, we will review tasks that address intention attribution. But before we get to that point, let us briefly review how researchers approached concerns about autism from the time that diagnoses such as Wing's appeared. This will provide the setting in which we can better appreciate how the study of pragmatics has influenced, and can continue to impact, our understanding of autism.

How Autism Became a Topic for Experimental Pragmatics

In Chapter 4, I reviewed some of the findings substantiating the existence of a Theory of Mind capacity, one of the most consequential contributions to arise out of the cognitive sciences. Essentially, that literature – initiated by Premack and Woodruff (1978) on non-human primates and then brought to the cognitive literature through studies based on the False Belief task (by a multitude of researchers) – was extended to autism. It was Simon Baron-Cohen, who most notably proposed that autism disorder is marked by "mindblindness," a categorical lack of awareness with respect to other people's minds.[4] Support for his claim came from the way children with autism would have great difficulty with the Sally-Anne task (Baron-Cohen, Leslie, & Frith, 1985). While neurotypical children would succeed at the task (after four years of age), most children with autism failed (see Baron-Cohen, 2001). One concern for this work was that there was still a sizeable percentage (around 20 percent) of children with autism who would resolve the Sally-Anne task, indicating that autistic participants were not completely mindblind. This led Baron-Cohen to adopt another task (from Josef Perner) that called for second-order mind reading, one in which a participant needed to recognize that a character in a story would make the wrong assumption about another character.

In Baron-Cohen's (1989) ice-cream van story, two friends, John and Mary, are at their local park. At some point, John wants to buy ice cream from an ice-cream van but realizes that he doesn't have enough money, and so he goes home to get some. During John's absence, the ice-cream van driver decides to try his luck at a second venue, the local church, and he announces this to Mary. On his way to the church, the ice-cream van driver runs into John and tells him where he's going, so John heads to the church. Later, Mary looks for John at his house only to discover that he is not home, and so she asks John's mother where can he be found. John's mother says that he went to get an ice cream. The question for participants is, Where would Mary go? If Mary knew that John knew that the truck had moved to the church, then she would go there. On the other hand, Mary had no way to know that John was informed about the move, so she should assume that John went to the park. Given Mary's state of knowledge, the "right" answer is to go back to the park. Whereas, nine out of ten neurotypical seven-year-olds succeeded, none of the children with autism (also out of ten) did. This is a demonstration that individuals with autism have difficulty with *levels* of metarepresentation.

If this sort of progressive mindblindness gets more impaired with more demanding levels of metarepresentation, it follows that it ought to be revealed as a range of *disabilities* in communication among autistic participants. Francesca Happé (1993) proposed that such myopia should have effects on language:

This impairment should have serious consequences for communication, if, as Sperber and Wilson (1987, p. 699) claim, "communication exploits the well-known ability of humans to attribute intentions to each other." For people with autism, then, ostensive-inferential communication – which requires the recognition of intentions – may be an unattainable goal. What might be available, however, even to an individual with "mind-blindness," would be coded communication.

This led Happé to investigate autistic participants' comprehension of similes, metaphor, and irony in order to test some unique claims about their communicative abilities. The logic behind Happé's (1993) study goes as follows.'

Similes can be most readily understood by neurotypicals and autistic participants alike because they are literally true and do not need to rely on Theory of Mind processes (or at least do not need to rely excessively on ToM). If one were to say to an autistic participant that "Mary dances like a butterfly," this is hardly problematic because there is no reason to doubt its truthfulness. Compare that simile, however, to "Mary is a butterfly," and one can begin to appreciate the presence of intention-reading. That is because one has to recognize that the utterance is speaking loosely and that Mary is not literally a butterfly. According to Happé, this will require some amount of Theory of Mind work in order to determine the speaker's intention. Specifically, it will require a single order of metarepresentation; i.e., the listener needs to understand what the speaker meant specifically through the metaphoric expression. Finally, if one says (ironically), "Mary is definitely graceful," after she trips over her own two feet, this requires an even higher level of intention-reading, a second-order metarepresentation (a thought about a thought), because the speaker is expressing an attitude *about* a thought (see Chapter 11).

It should be pointed out that there is nothing in Relevance Theory (one of Happé's inspirations for her seminal work) that says metaphors require one level of metarepresentation that goes above and beyond similes. Nevertheless, Happé's continuum of Theory-of-Mind engagement ought to correlate with comprehension of everyday pragmatic phenomena – with similes requiring a minimal amount of ToM and irony being representative of a maximal end. This added nuance to the notion of mindblindness because, instead of assuming a general *in*ability to read intentions, she was proposing different levels of ability that correlate with the extent to which one is able to metarepresent. This is why she had participants carry out different False Belief tasks that could indicate the extent to which they employ Theory of Mind successfully and determine whether Theory of Mind abilities correlate with increasing levels of pragmatic comprehension.

To test her hypothesis, she had participants with and without autism complete a battery of Theory of Mind tasks whose success depended on the amount of metarepresentation required (zero level of metarepresenation, one level, or two). Happé then divided participants into three groups. The lowest group was made up of those who could not succeed on First-order Theory of Mind tasks (i.e., Sally-Anne types of tasks); the members of this group were called No-ToM. The middle group was made up of those who successfully answered First-order tasks but not Second-order tasks; the members of this group were considered to have First-Order ToM. Finally, the highest group was made up of those who could successfully resolve Second-order tasks (those akin to the John-Mary task above). When presented with stories that relied on similes, metaphors, and irony, there was a strong correlation with ToM abilities. To give a taste of one ToM-rich task, here is an example of a story followed by an ironic statement:

David is helping his mother make a cake. She leaves him to add the eggs to the flour and sugar. But silly David doesn't break the eggs first – he just puts them in the bowl, shells and all! What a silly thing to do! Just then father comes in. He sees what David has done and says, "What a clever boy you are, David!"

Participants would then be asked, "What does David's father mean? Does he mean David is clever or silly?" It turns out that in both the autism group (whose mean age was seventeen years of age), and the control group (whose mean age was around five), those who passed second-order ToM tests scored significantly higher on the irony task than their peers who failed to make it into this most sophisticated group (who were considered part of the first-order ToM group).

This is the approach that generated much of the experimental pragmatic work that followed. The question was, to what extent does mindblindness map onto linguistic-pragmatic phenomena? Can those with autism carry out scalar inferences to the same extent as neurotypicals; are they less prone to turn conditionals into biconditionals? As we will see, much follow-up work showed that participants with autism are, at best, only subtly different than control participants with respect to linguistic-pragmatic phenomena. Thanks in part to these experimental pragmatic studies it has become clear that early claims linking autistic behavior and pragmatic inference appeared too strong. I will start with work that emanated out of our own lab in order to show how experimental pragmatic data helped modify an initial view on ASDs and how it opened the door to entirely new proposals.

A Universal Deficit?

Coralie Chevallier defended her thesis in Lyon in 2009, but she carried out her studies in London where, at the time, ASD diagnoses were more reliable. One of her first studies was a straightforward scalar-inference study in which participants were shown two objects – for example, a star with a monkey – and were required to respond "right" or "wrong" (by hitting a key on a computer's keyboard) as a function of an auditorily presented utterance. A control item would appear as "There is a star and a monkey," and an underinformative version (one that has the potential to engage a scalar inference) would be "There is a star or a monkey." What did she find? Participants with autism and the controls were practically identical in terms of both their rates of "right" and "wrong" responses and in terms of their reaction times (Chevallier et al., 2010).

In other words, she was finding no differences in behavior across these two groups of participants. This did not make sense to either of us because there was a consensus in the literature at the time that said that autistic participants are supposed to be generally incapable of pragmatic inference and scalars are standard pragmatic inferences. Combined with the categorical syllogism below, one should find that individuals with autism are less pragmatic than neurotypical participants when carrying out a classic scalar-inference task:

Theory of Mind deficits should include difficulty with pragmatic inference.
All scalar inferences are pragmatic inferences.
Anyone with a Theory of Mind deficit should have difficulty with scalar inference.

This was supposed to be Coralie's first study on autism, and things were not going as planned.

As it turns out, Coralie's experience was not so surprising. That paper (Chevallier et al., 2010) ended up joining others that drew a similar conclusion (as I indicate later, we would soon discover that Judith Pijnacker and colleagues had run a similar study with *some*). In fact, a small cottage industry arose showing just how capable participants with autism were at the kind of linguistic-pragmatic tasks that they were supposed to have difficulty with. For example, Coralie would go on to show that teenagers with autism are able to process a range of prosodic cues, including complex ones that call on mind-reading skills (see the section on prosody in Chapter 13). It follows that individuals with autism, or at least some of them, are able to mindread and to use mindreading skills for communicative purposes. Mikhail Kissine and colleagues (Kissine et al., 2015) would go on to show how children with autism would perform better than neurotypicals on an indirect speech act (e.g., a participant who is playing with a Mr. Potato Head would hear indirectly from a speaker "Oh! He has no hat on!" and would typically add that accessory). This is consistent with fMRI work showing that, in fact, there are no detectable differences between participants with and without autism on False-Belief-tasks (Dufour et al., 2013).

One need not rely on experimental studies alone. As Coralie is wont to show, one can refer to anecdotal evidence showing that people with high-functioning autism spontaneously use irony and make jokes, as well as write books about these intention-heavy speech acts. Consider the irony from this neurodiversity blog, as Coralie cited in her dissertation:

Aspies did not exist yet, and autistics, as everyone knew, were children who did not speak and certainly did not make appearances in the hallways of "regular" schools.

In short, the reporting of null effects is not entirely bad news. Rather than assume a blanket pragmatic inability among those with ASD, the data show that accounts need to be much more nuanced. It is entirely possible that people with autism are unexceptional with respect to some linguistic-pragmatic phenomena and exceptional with respect to others. It is also conceivable that since autism rests on a spectrum, performance will differ as a function of autism severity.

Consider a set of papers by Judith Pijnacker and colleagues (2009a, b) in which they compared neurotypical adults to those with autism on a small range of linguistic-pragmatic tasks, including the scalar task in which participants are required to answer true or false to underinformative items, such as *Some cats are mammals*. To cut to the chase, the opening line of their conclusion in their (2009b) paper on scalars went as follows: "Contrary to our expectations, our results demonstrate that on the whole, high-functioning adults with ASD are rather good at deriving implicatures," meaning that the rates of false responses to the underinformative items were generally comparable across the two groups (with roughly 70 percent saying false to the underinformative items in each). However, this is not the end of the story. Those with autism were further subdivided into (a) those who were diagnosed with Asperger's (at the time, Asperger's was a proper label), and (b) those who were more severely affected by autism and considered High-Functioning adults with Autism (HFA). The authors found that the two groups of autistic participants differed slightly in their reactions. Those diagnosed with Asperger's were actually slightly more likely than the neurotypicals to respond "false" to the underinformative items (roughly 90 percent of those in this group responded "false" compared to the 70 percent of neurotypicals mentioned earlier) while the High-Functioning adults with autism were closer to chance levels (at around 60 percent).

The other paper by Judith Pijnacker et al. (2009a) compared these same groups with respect to conditional inferences. As described in Chapter 8, this implies presenting simple syllogisms like those in (12.1) and (12.2):

(12.1) If Mary has an exam, she will study in the library.
        Mary has an exam.
        Will she study in the library?

(12.2) If Mary has an exam, she will study in the library.
        Mary will study in the library.
        Does she have an exam?

The syllogism in (12.1) puts participants in a position to endorse a standard Modus Ponens inference by saying, "Yes" and the one in (12.2) tests whether participants will endorse the Affirmation of the Consequent argument. If participants say, "Yes" (instead of "Maybe") to (12.2) it is tantamount to accepting the pragmatic invited inference. Pijnacker and her colleagues presented all four kinds of conditional syllogism: the two above, plus Modus Tollens, and Denial of the Antecedent (see Chapter 8). The answers from the participants in the Autism group indicated that they were less likely than those in the neurotypical control group to make the invited inferences (the "Affirmation of the Consequent" and the "Denial of the Antecedent" cases).[5] That is, the control group was more likely than the participants with autism to make the pragmatic inference. So, in this case, one does tend to find a difference between neurotypicals and those with autism.

When one takes the data collected as a whole, one can see that the initial view was too stark. One cannot simply make a blanket statement saying that autism is linked with a total lack of pragmatic inference making. However, there are enough subtle differences so that one can conclude that participants with autism are not equivalent to neurotypical controls. Instead of mindblindness, it pays to think of their deficits as mind-*myopic*.

Alternative Accounts

Given that one can remove from consideration the universal-pragmatic-deficit hypothesis that was initially attached to autism, what does distinguish those with autism from neurotypicals? While people with ASD themselves would say that they are not as apt as neurotypicals at conversation and at making pragmatic inferences, it is hard to find radically different responses in a laboratory setting. What gives? Let me mention briefly two alternatives that come from linguistic-pragmatic researchers that aim to account for this more nuanced picture.

One comes from Coralie and her colleagues who are skeptical that those with autism have universal social-cognitive deficits or impairments with respect to Theory of Mind. Chevallier and colleagues (2012) propose that reported deficits are better viewed as deficits in *social motivation*. This framework underlines the range of motivations that are necessary to deal with our conspecifics and how "each of these can vary across individuals or be selectively impaired ... [so we] argue that ASD is characterized by a fairly specific disruption of motivation for social affiliation" (Chevallier et al., 2012, p. 234). One prediction that follows from this framework is that socially related actions, which naturally attract the attention of neurotypicals, do not hold intrinsic interest among those with ASD to the same degree. They point to a wide range of autism studies in order to support their claims:

In the auditory modality, children with ASD do not exhibit a preference for socially salient sounds over non-social control noise (Klin, 1991; Kuhl et al., 2005) and display attention deficits for speech but not for non-speech sounds (Ceponiene et al., 2003; Gervais et al., 2004). These differences in social attention are among the first manifestations of ASD (Elsabbagh et al., 2012) and preference for non-social patterns in toddlers has recently been identified as a robust predictor of ASD (Pierce et al., 2011).

The social motivation approach has also provided the autism literature with original findings.

Consider a task that compares neurotypical participants to those with ASD as they carry out a pictorial completion task (see Chevallier et al., 2014, who adopted a study from Brunet et al., 2003). In this task, a series of vignette-telling pictures are presented, and the test phase involves choosing a picture (out of three options) that would make for a highly reasonable follow-up. There are three kinds of picture-series. One kind involves a physical situation concerning objects (for example, one series depicts a crane picking up, badly, a mat containing a pile of bricks). Another kind depicts a cause-effect situation involving people (e.g., wind forcing a sailor's hat to fly off). Finally, there are pictures that call on reading intentions (e.g., a parent preparing a bath ultimately for her baby). Critically, the participants carried out this task either with an experimenter or with direction from a computer program. While performance was generally comparable across the two populations for the physical and cause-effect picture-series, there was – interestingly – one exceptional outcome when it came to the intention-reading condition. There, only the neurotypical controls improved dramatically when the task was presented by a human (meaning, the participants' performance was not as strong when the task was conducted by a computer program). Meanwhile, the participants with autism remained unaffected by a personal administration of the materials. This is evidence indicating that human–human interaction affects neurotypical participants more than those with autism.

A second alternative that aims to account for performance deficits among those with autism comes from Mikhail Kissine, who argues that it is not Theory of Mind per se that is at the source of autism spectrum disorders, but limitations in cognitive flexibility. As Kissine (2012, p. 3) writes "false-belief tasks require the participant to be able to shift from one perspective to another – which is an executive skill that is deficient in ASD." This would explain why ASDs have difficulty "cancelling rules they acquired and conclusions that they have already drawn (Russell, 2002)" as well as why "Hughes and Russell (1993) report that children with autism (having a mental age of around six years and five months) experience difficulties to disengage from a habitual motor sequence and to conform to an arbitrary motor rule, like throwing a switch before reaching for a marble" (p. 6). How does a lack of cognitive flexibility affect language comprehension and language use? The lack becomes important when an utterance requires appreciating a speaker's perspective, which could be different than one's own. While ASD's can rely on context to interpret utterances, they will be limited to their own perceived contexts and partly because they cannot readily switch out from their own perspective.

Concluding Remarks

Advances in autism research have relied to a great extent on behavioral and language-related measures. Given the nature of the difficulties associated with autism, pragmatics has figured prominently into the development of these studies. It is not surprising then that the literature is populated with interventions and diagnostics aimed at identifying and improving autistic language abilities. I think it fair to say that no one would have guessed that a Gricean approach to utterance understanding would have had practical benefits, but, clearly, it has brought light to our understanding of this distinctive cognitive profile.

Notes

1. From the *New York Times* (Angiers, 2012).
2. As Chapter 13 describes, atypical prosody was considered part of an Autism Spectrum Diagnosis.
3. In 2013, the American Psychiatric Association folded the diagnostic expression "Asperger's Syndrome" into a more general *Autism Spectrum Disorders* (see *Diagnostic and Statistical Manual of Mental Disorders*, fifth edition, or *DSM-5*, 2013, which periodically updates its classification of mental disorders). For that reason, I will be using the expression Autism or Autism Spectrum Disorder for those previously considered *Asperger's*.
4. Baron-Cohen (2002) followed up on Asperger's observation (as well as Kanner's and Wing's) by claiming that male predominance of autism is the expression of an "extreme male brain."
5. The difference between the two groups was marginally significant when each (AC and DA) are treated separately. However, Judith Pijnacker informed me that if the two invited inference conditions are treated as a group the Autism versus Control differences are indeed significant. That said, the participants in the autism group were overall more likely to respond "maybe," even to the logical inference forms, *Modus Ponens* and *Modus Tollens*.

13 More Topics for Experimental Pragmatics

An All-You-Can-Eat Buffet

One can't be forever dwelling on what might have been.

Kazuo Ishiguro

One of the book's goals is to give an overview of the topics addressed by experimental pragmatics and, to a large extent, I think we have done that. Nevertheless, there are many topics that remain, and we now turn our attention to these. They might not have received as much attention as those having their own chapters, but they are equally exciting. The topics here are listed in alphabetical order so as not to play favorites.

Logical Metonymy

Logical metonymy (Pustejovsky, 1995) refers to utterances, such as those in (13.1), whose underdetermined nature compels the listener to develop a richer meaning:

(13.1) The author started the book.

The verb *started* can indicate the beginning of many possible actions. While it is arguably most plausible here that the author started *writing* the book, it is also plausible that she started reading it. But the list does not end there. It is also possible that the author started editing, reviewing, downloading, or even burning the book. Of course, there are preferred readings and dispreferred ones (what this literature calls *contextually biased* and *contextually unbiased interpretations*, respectively); the context is recognized as determinative. So when the noun phrase becomes *The student* (13.2), the most plausible interpretation for *started the book* is arguably *started reading the book*.

(13.2) The student started the book.

Of course, these interpretational ambiguities can be eliminated with a clearer verb, such as *wrote* (13.3):

(13.3) The author wrote the book.

In an original paradigm from McElree et al. (2001), participants are asked to read sentences like those in (13.1), and (13.3), as well as (13.4):

(13.4) The author read the book.

Results generally show a reading slowdown following the verb in sentences like (13.1) when compared to post-verbal words in controls like (13.3), or (13.4) (also see Traxler et al., 2002; McElree et al., 2006), and the verbs themselves are associated with signature effects in ERP studies (e.g., Kuperberg et al., 2010) and MEG investigations (e.g., Pylkkanen & McElree, 2007). The question for this largely semantic literature has been, What accounts for these effects? One argument is that verbs such as *start* semantically select for certain types of activities–specifically, events. So that when a speaker uses *started*, one expects it to be followed by an event like running. When the listener is confronted by an *entity* instead (as in *book* here), the listener needs to make adjustments. Logical metonymy is sometimes referred to as a *type-shift* because it involves changing the type of the argument from entity to event (Pustejovsky, 1995; McElree et al., 2001). Interestingly, the literature also includes a pragmatic position (de Almeida and colleagues). According to de Almeida's group (de Almeida, 2004; de Almeida & Riven, 2012), the structure of sentences such as those in (13.1) are indeterminate (the VP contains an empty slot that needs to be filled) and engages pragmatic mechanisms that are post-semantic. In other words, de Almeida places a focus on pragmatic processes instead of relying uniquely on syntactic-semantic ones.

Metonymy

While covering metaphor in Chapter 10, I wrote about the (very friendly) adversarial collaboration between two colleagues: Petra Schumacher and Valentina Bambini. Here, I describe their work on metonymy. Their interest was to determine how generalizable their metaphor data were. In fact, Weiland et al. (2014), whose masked-priming technique was described in Chapter 10, went on to investigate metonymy in the second half of the paper. But before getting to that, it pays to present some background.

Metonymy is a topic, like metaphor, that has attracted the attention of psycholinguists well before anyone even heard of experimental pragmatics. Consider one seminal paper, from Frisson and Pickering (1999), who investigated place-for-institution (*these applicants consulted with the university*) and event-for-place (*A lot of Americans protested during Vietnam*) metonymies. The authors employed eye-tracking techniques (e.g., they measured the total time readers spent on, as well as returning looks [*regressions*] to, critical sections) as they compared metonymic uses with more literal ones (*A lot of sightseers stopped at the university*, and *I hitchhiked around Vietnam* for the two examples above). Frisson and Pickering's data indicated that metonymic uses are no more difficult to process than literal uses, leading them to conclude that both senses emanate from one underspecified representation.

Metonymy is not a one-size-fits-all phenomenon. Metonymy can be expressed in myriad ways and participants' reactions vary as a function of the sort being used. As Schumacher (2013) showed, "container-for-content alternations" (*goblet* in "What did Heinz drink hastily? He drank the goblet hastily") prompt EEG profiles with Late Positivities (including a P600) while "content-for-container alternations" (the *magic potion* in "What did Asterix fasten to his belt? He fastened the magic potion to his belt") do not.

Findings from both of these cases differ from the ham-sandwich types of metonymy (as in Nunberg's "The ham sandwich is sitting at Table 20," which was presented back in Chapter 1). In order to appreciate how, let us briefly walk through one of Schumacher's earlier experiments. Compare the two kinds of scenarios in (13.5). The second sentence in (13.5a), can be completed either with a metonymy or a literal expression (see the two in italics) and are presented without (much) supporting context from the first sentence. The second sentence in (13.5b), drawn from Schumacher (2011) is similar, but it does provide (more) supporting context through mentions of *doctor* and *assistant* in its first sentence:

(13.5) a. Thomas asks Claudia again who had called that early. Claudia responds that *the hepatitis/the therapist* had called that early.
        b. The doctor asks his assistant again who had called that early. The assistant responds that *the hepatitis/the therapist* had called that early.

In these cases, one finds differences as a function of provided background (Schumacher 2014). Without supporting context, as in (13.5a), ham-sandwich metonymies prompt N400s and late positivities (components similar to P600's); with supporting context, as in (13.5b), one finds just late positivities (most similar to the "container-for-content metonymies").[1]

To return to the Weiland et al. (2014) study, the authors first had participants listen (without primes) to producer-for-product metonymies, such as the one in (13.6a) which refers to *reading Böll*, and compared these to control items, such as (13.6b):

(13.6) a. At that time the student read Böll during an assembly.
        b. At that time the student met Böll during a protest.

Under these conditions, the metonymy exemplified by (13.6a) prompts N400s. They then ran the same study with masked-priming with these metonymies (see Chapter 10). The primes were adjectives that concerned human or biographical details, such as *lively* or *divorced*. Lo and behold, with primes, the N400s effects were no longer in evidence either. Studies on metonymy thus provide the gamut of ERP profiles, and they appear to be extremely sensitive to context while lexical meanings appear to remain active.

I would be remiss if I did not shine a light on the small but growing literature on metonymic acquisition (Rundblad & Annaz, 2010; Van Herwegen et al., 2013; Falkum et al., 2016) before concluding this section. Let me present one example from Falkum and her colleagues' recent (2016) work, in which children listen to a vignette as they look at a picture. In one trial, a photo shows two people talking next to a bicycle (with one of the interlocutors wearing a helmet); this photo is presented as participants listen to the vignette that concludes with "the helmet gets on her bike." At this point, the participants are asked to choose one of three photos that corresponds to the final sentence. Falkum and colleagues (2016) reported that three-year-olds tend to interpret the metonymic sentence as intended and at rates that are higher than those found among five-year-olds; i.e., 60 percent of the three-year-olds appropriately choose a photo showing the woman-with-a-helmet on the bike (as opposed to a photo of the helmet literally on the bike) while 40 percent of five-year-olds do. It is as if the children become more metalinguistically aware of the literal meaning as they get older. That said, adults in the same study do choose the metonymically-appropriate picture at a 100 percent rate indicating that, at some point in development, addressees bounce back to their younger selves and with conviction.

Negation

Negation has been a regular, though not routinely investigated, topic for experimentalists and from very early on in the cognitive revolution. Notably, Wason (1961; Wason & Jones, 1963) aimed to better understand why negation consistently slows down sentence processing. It was his opening sentence (Wason, 1965) that underlined the importance of "pragmatic factors" in negation as he introduced the expression "plausible denial" to describe the importance of felicity when employing negation. Consider the utterance "a whale is not a fish," which appears to be a felicitous use of negation because it renders salient the idea that whales could plausibly be misclassified as fish; on the other hand, "a robin is not a vehicle" is integrated with greater difficulty because no one would have considered a robin a bicycle or some other vehicle. To support his claim, he investigated the way an abstract item – which is either a member of a majority group or else exceptional – is classified affirmatively or negatively. An exemplary trial would be one in which eight circles are presented, of which seven are blue and one is red, followed by a test sentence that asks participants to describe the single dissimilar item (let us suppose that it was labeled as "Circle number 4") as in (13.7) or (13.8):

(13.7) Circle no. 4 is ...

(13.8) Circle no. 4 is not ...

It was the participant's job to complete the sentence by hitting either a button labeled *red* or a button labeled *blue*. Whereas *dissimilar affirmative* items (to indicate that Circle 4 is red) were completed most quickly, *dissimilar negative* items (to indicate that Circle 4 is not blue) typically took longer, but not as long as *similar negative* items (which refer to negative sentences whose completion describes a circle that resembles those in the overwhelming majority, as in "Circle number 7 is not red"). While plausible denial facilitates the comprehension of a negation, a sentence containing a negation is still linked with a slowdown when compared to an affirmative. That negation can affect comprehension across a variety of tasks has been confirmed through other classic work in the psycholinguistic literature (e.g., Just & Carpenter, 1971; Trabasso et al., 1971; Clark & Chase, 1972). Many in this early literature proposed that negations first prompt a step in which a negative utterance is processed as an affirmative (without negation) before it gets negated.

As the above sort of finding indicates, it is a bit effortful to come up with an alternative when cued by a negation. However, this does not tell us what negations are lexically meant to do. One exemplary debate about negation asks "Does negation simply deny or does it assert alternatives?" When a door is said to be *not open*, does it deny being opened or does the negation prompt the notion that it is closed? The field of reasoning has been implicated in this line of research and by extension experimental pragmatics. One school of thought is that *not* narrowly focuses on what is denied and goes no further. As described by Evans and colleagues (1996), "the negation's function is 'to deny propositions rather than assert information' ... If someone tells you that they did not watch the football game last night, the topic of their discourse is clearly the [game] ... They are not asking you to think about any of the many things they may have done instead" (p. 394). The football game in the Evans et al. quote is exemplary in highlighting how the listener is not supposed to go beyond the object mentioned in the sentence. I will call this the "narrow" view.

The other school of thought is that negation processing can also be viewed more widely, as a guide to making a negation the basis for a search for alternatives, i.e., "the many things" that the denied proposition can be. According to this reading, participants detect that, e.g., the not-H and the not-6 in "If there is not an H, then there is not a 6" are the basis of further processing that will lead a reasoner to find non-H's and eventually non-6's. According to this account, participants' failures are presumably due to computational errors linked to the processing of negations. Oaksford (2002) made this argument by saying that a negation leads a listener to construct a contrast class and that this is done "with greater or lesser success." One can call this the *search-for-alternatives* view of negation.

Jerome Prado and I (Prado & Noveck, 2006) investigated cases in which either the antecedent or the consequent of the conditional was negated. We focused most specifically on the case having an affirmative antecedent and a negated consequent, which we called AN (e.g., *If there is an H, then there is not a square*), in a task that would present such a rule and then a figure that showed a *letter-in-a-form*. According to a narrow reading of *not*, the conditional puts the focus on "square" and (initially, at least) goes no further; the participant ought to be prepared for the square and little else. If that is the case, the appearance of an H-in-a-square in a verification task (*does the letter-in-a-form conform to the rule?*) ought to be correctly rejected with relative ease when compared to a Hit (*H-in-a-circle*), which affirms the rule. In other words, a narrow reading should translate into higher rates of correct responses or faster reaction times for the Correct Rejection of AN cases when compared to the Hit. According to the search-for-alternatives approach, one should be prompted to search for an H-in-a-non-square (e.g., an *H-in-a-circle* or an *H-in-a-triangle*). If that is the case, the appearance of an *H-in-a-square* in a verification task (for the AN case) ought to be surprising. It follows that a Correct Rejection of this item (e.g., an *H-in-a-square*), ought to trigger more errors and take more time than an item such as *H-in-a-circle* (a Hit). Experiment 1 revealed higher rates of Correct Rejections than Hits for AN cases, which is in-line with a narrow-reading view on negations.

This narrow-reading view of negations conforms with semantic insights, such as the fact that denials readily entail other denied propositions, i.e., from sets to subsets. When a speaker says, e.g., "I did not eat ice cream," it entails that she did not eat chocolate ice cream, strawberry ice cream, or pistachio ice cream, etc. If the primary role of negation were to point to things I ate, instead, it would be hard to envision how negations could license such monotonic inferences so readily. Prado and Noveck further argued that the narrowed-reading account and the search-for-alternative account are compatible. In order to know what the speaker has in mind by saying *not-p*, one indeed needs to know something about the object being negated – *p*. An initial reading of a negation can be narrow, and in some scenarios, this might be good enough. However, an interlocutor (a participant) can further process the negation (especially if the ongoing task calls for it), leading to an analysis of alternatives.

Another set of studies on negation assumes that language is processed through simulations, and that negation is processed with a "two-step simulation," in which the affirmative information (in a negative utterance) is first simulated and then rejected. To support this claim, Kaup and colleagues (2007) required participants to determine, as quickly as possible, whether the object in a sentence, e.g., the eagle in "The eagle is not in the sky," appeared in an image that followed (250 ms later). The main manipulation concerned the way an eagle was portrayed, which was either as flying (with stretched wings and viewed from below) or sitting. When the image shows an eagle in the sky, "yes" responses (meaning an eagle does appear in the image) are faster when compared to cases of sitting. When the same manipulation was carried out, but with a 1,500-ms delay, the effect disappeared (Kaup et al., 2005).

This account has led to two skeptical responses among experimental pragmatists. In one, Nieuwland and Kuperberg (2008) used EEGs to demonstrate that there are cases that escape this general description. They reasoned that any two-step theory of negation processing assumes that listeners initially disregard the negation, and, if that is the case, one should then predict a larger N400 (on a critical word) in a negative true statement (see *dangerous* in (13.9)), when compared to (a critical word in a) negative false statement (see *safe* in (13.10)):

(13.9)   Bulletproof vests aren't very *dangerous* and used worldwide for security (true).

(13.10)   Bulletproof vests aren't very *safe* and used worldwide for security (false).

To appreciate this claim, read the sentences as if they did not contain the negation (i.e., *Bulletproof vests are very dangerous* versus *Bulletproof vests are very safe*).

In fact, Nieuwland and Kuperberg find support for the two-step approach, i.e., the critical word in sentences like the one in (13.9), which I italicized, prompted larger N400s than the critical word (which I italicized) in sentences akin to (13.10). However, when sentences "pragmatically license" negations, one no longer finds this effect; in fact, it prompts the opposite. To appreciate how this could have occurred, consider the processing of the critical words that I have italicized in the negative true sentence and the negative false sentence in (13.11) and (13.12), respectively:

(13.11)   With proper equipment, scuba-diving isn't very *dangerous* and often good fun (true).

(13.12)   With proper equipment, scuba-diving isn't very *safe* and often good fun (false).

This sort of reversal follows from the authors' pragmatic account, according to which all terms – including negations – are incorporated on-line during sentence comprehension as the listener works out the intended meaning. Again, this account predicts a larger N400 for the critical word in the false negative, as in (13.12), when compared to the critical word in the true negative case (13.11), and this is what they report. Pragmatic influences can easily intervene in the on-line processing of negative statements.

A second study that challenges the two-step approach comes from Tian et al. (2010). They used the Kaup et al. (2007) paradigm but manipulated the sentence form. To start, consider the declarative sentence in (13.13). Participants were presented two types of pictures: one showing spaghetti in its box (the "matched" case) and another showing cooked spaghetti on a plate (the "mismatched" case).

(13.13) Jane didn't cook the spaghetti.

When participants needed to respond to (13.13) (with a "yes," to indicate that there was spaghetti in the picture), reaction times with respect to the "matched" picture (with uncooked spaghetti) were substantially longer than reaction times to the "mismatched" picture (the plate of cooked spaghetti). In other words, Kaup et al.'s finding was replicated. Participants' immediate reaction appeared to privilege the affirmative version of the negative sentence. However, when the sentence structure was clefted, which is a presupposition trigger, the outcomes were inverted:

(13.14) It was Jane who didn't cook the spaghetti.

That is, with sentences such as (13.14), participants now respond (by indicating "yes") more quickly to the "matched" picture as opposed to the mismatched one. Tian et al. (2010; also see Tian et al., 2016) reasoned that a clefted sentence prompts a presupposition of the sort *someone did not cook the spaghetti* and an assertion of the sort *It was Jane*.[2] By slightly changing the nature of the communicative intention behind the utterance, one can bypass the claim that negative processing involves asserting the affirmative version of the utterance and then negating it.

Presupposition

Presupposition is a well-known linguistic-pragmatic phenomenon in which an expression prompts a double-barreled proposition containing asserted content as well as presupposed content. Consider the examples in (13.15–13.19) and the way that each can be divided into two as the result of a "trigger":

(13.15) Marshall continues to run away.
     a. Marshall runs away.
     b. Marshall has run away in the past.

(13.16) Carley regrets that he did not see Claire.
     a. Carley did not see Claire.
     b. Carley feels bad about not seeing Claire.

(13.17) I want to go to the cinema, too.
     a. I want to go to the cinema.
     b. Someone else wants to go to the cinema.

(13.18) It is the butler who murdered the heiress.
a. The butler murdered the heiress.
b. Someone murdered the heiress.

(13.19) The French Co-Prince of Andorra is not popular.
a. One of the Co-Princes of Andorra is not popular.
b. There is a Co-Prince of Andorra who is French.[3]

The nature of the trigger varies across a wide range of structures. Here, we only considered five: an aspectual verb in (13.15), a factive in (13.16), an iterative adverb in (13.17), a cleft sentence in (13.18) and a definite description in (13.19). There are at least a dozen presupposition triggers according to some counts (see Geurts & Beaver, 2007). They all generate two kinds of information: an assertion, expressed as (a) in the above examples, and a presupposition that may or may not have been made part of public knowledge previously, expressed as (b). This wide variety of triggers actually presents a challenge for those who study presuppositions because they are not uniform in nature nor are they all equally frequent. For example, a corpus study (Spenader, 2002, as cited by Schwarz, 2007) shows that the presupposition of *too* has an antecedent in the text much more often than factives do (96 percent versus 20 percent).

Presupposition has long preoccupied semanticists and pragmatists, and this short entry about it will not do justice to the serious exchanges that can be found in the literature. Suffice it to say that it has prompted intense discussions among prominent theorists as far back as Frege and then Russell, and it took a more pragmatic turn after Grice. Deirdre Wilson did her thesis on presuppositions (with Noam Chomsky as her adviser), and Robert Stalnaker (1973) has been a prominent investigator of presuppositions too. Both of these theorists insist on the idea that presuppositions cannot be explained based on the content of sentences but with respect to intentions and beliefs, or what Wilson (1973) called "preferred interpretations" (also see Simons, 2013).

It was also a topic of developmental studies in the 1970s soon after Grice's famous William James lectures. One natural assumption to make – in light of what we know now on scalar inference – would be that accessing presupposed content is extra pragmatic work and that this should be harder to produce than the asserted content. In line with this, consider work from Brian Ackerman (1978), who was essentially a lone pioneer of developmental linguistic-pragmatics during the 1970s (see Note 11 in Chapter 5). While placing factive sentences into read-aloud stories, he found that five-year-olds were weaker than their older cohorts (eight-year-olds) as well as adults at drawing out presupposed information. For example, he strategically placed the sentence *Billy continued to shine his shoes* into a story about a missing jacket; when the participants were asked, "Was Billy polishing his shoes when his mother asked about the jacket?" they showed clear developmental progress – from random

responding among the youngest participants to more competent "accommo-
dation" with age (see also Kail, 1978). In the meanwhile, questions whose
answers call for rote memory or explicit information lead to a much stronger
performance among all three age groups.

Presupposition has recently re-emerged as an object of experimental pragmatic studies. As far as developmental studies are concerned, researchers are
wont to show that children need not wait until they are eight to show greater
competence with presuppositions. Using *too* and *again* in German, Berger,
and Hohle (2012) show that three-year-olds can be quite competent, even as
performance improves with age. Other work has aimed to better categorize
the unwieldy set of presuppositions in terms of their pragmatic potential. For
example, Domaneschi and colleagues (2014) had participants listen to a story
that contains five different kinds of triggers about which they would be asked
questions. The researchers wanted to determine whether some triggers called
for more effortful processing than others, which partly explains why they also
had participants carry out their listening task under one of two memory loads
(an easy one or a harder one). They indeed found differences. For the five
triggers investigated, they concluded that Definite Descriptions (see 13.19),
Factive Verbs (see 13.16) and Focus-Sensitive Particles (e.g., *even*) seem to
be less cognitively demanding categories of triggers compared to Iteratives
(13.17) and Change of State Verbs (e.g., *bloom*).

Semanticists, in particular, are taken by the way presuppositions are maintained in grammatical environments such as questions or negations. So, to take
one example, consider (13.15) and turn it into the sentence (13.15'):

(13.15') Marshall did not continue to run away.

Here, one can now assert that Marshall did not run away while the presupposed
information (13.15) persists – Marshall used to run away. This persistence is
known as *projection* or the *projection problem* (because there is no generally
accepted account for the way it works). It will be recalled that in the case of
scalars, one often finds the absence of pragmatic enrichments under negation
and in question forms. The ability for triggers to project into these particular
linguistic environments is therefore intriguing. I will mention two studies that
aim to take this on.

One comes from Chemla and Bott (2014) who use the Bott and Noveck
(2004) paradigm in order to study sentences such as "Zoologists [visit-
ing from another planet] do not realize that elephants are birds," which can
lead to two interpretations. It could be false because it could be read off –
"globally" according to the authors – as "Elephants are birds, and it is not the
case that Zoologists [visiting from another planet] believe so." In other words,
the assertion escapes negation. Another interpretation could lead to a true
response because it could be read off – "locally" according to the authors – as

"It is not the case that (elephants are birds and zoologists believe so)." This account assumes a standard lexical entry for negation, which does not distinguish between the presuppositional content and the asserted content. Their evidence supported the global account. Another important study on presuppositions and projections comes from Florian Schwarz and colleagues who have investigated triggers across different environments in on-line sentence processing tasks. For example, Schwarz and Tiemann (2017) find processing delays among German speakers immediately after they read the expression "wieder nicht" (i.e., *again not*, as in *Tina again did not go ice-skating*) when prior context indicated that she had indeed gone ice-skating a week before. In other words, *again not* did not have any negative event to refer back to prior to the test sentence, leading to an infelicity that is captured on-line. Remarkably, though, when a similarly infelicitous presupposition is used when the trigger is embedded under negation (imagine reading that Tina did not go ice-skating again [*nicht wieder Schlittschuhlaufen*] when prior context indicated that she had tried but failed to go ice-skating a week earlier), this combination of words does not spur processing delays. While this last result could be due to extra processing, brought on by a negation that subverts the presupposition processing, Schwarz and Tiemann argue that these data suggest that global interpretations are favored by participants.

Prosody

Prosody is an enormous topic that technically concerns (acoustic and) auditory features of a speaker's voice, such as intonation, stress, rhythm, duration, and intensity. It is obviously involved in linguistic processing (consider how prosody distinguishes between the verbal and nominal meaning of *record*), and it has an inestimable potential to influence intentional meaning as well, so it is implicated in everything linguistic-pragmatic. Prosody can be divided into categories that make sense to pragmatists, such as prosody related to decoding versus inference-making as well as prosody that is revealed accidentally versus intentionally (Wilson & Wharton, 2006). For instance, an utterance punctuated by shivering will reveal that the speaker is cold but not intentionally while a tired voice could be revealed by the speaker either accidentally or purposely. In the rest of this section, I will show different ways in which prosody has been used in experimental pragmatic research.[4]

Prosody and Scalar Inferences

In the scalar literature, one of the early studies to show how prosody affects performance in a unidirectional manner concerned the stress put on the disjunction *or*. Chevallier et al. (2008) presented disjunctive sentences such as

"There is an A or a B," which were stated to describe (as True or False) five-letter words such as TABLE or non-word strings such as POJET. In the case like TABLE, the disjunctive utterance above has two true elements (making it part of the true-true condition) and can be considered true based on the lexical meaning of *or*, but it can be false through a pragmatically driven exclusive reading. When the disjunctive sentence was presented in a written form, rates of *True* responses were quite high (81 percent), and when the disjunction was stressed (by capitalizing and underlining, as in OR), and only in the case where both disjuncts were true, rates of *True* responses dropped to 57 percent. The effect was even stronger when the sentences were veritable utterances. When the speaker presented *or* in an unstressed manner, rates of true responses were 77 percent, and when the speaker's voice carried a focalization accent in the *true-true or* condition, rates of true responses dropped to 27 percent. Otherwise, rates of correct responses remained high with respect to the other disjunctive sentences (e.g., saying true to cases in which only one disjunct was present as in "There is an R or an M" after the string JAMIS) as well as to other control conjunctive sentences (e.g., saying true to "There is an O and a B" after seeing the string RSOUB). This was one of many different kinds of studies supporting the notion that enrichment goes in one direction (see Chapter 6) while many others view scalar inferences as either a default reading or as ambiguous.

Prosody and Autism Spectrum Disorders

Prosody became a relevant feature to study among those with ASD because, from the start, atypical prosody was considered part of an ASD diagnosis (Kanner, 1943; Asperger, 1944). That ASD participants have prosody-related difficulties was later validated (e.g., Rutherford et al., 2002). Prosody has obvious links to pragmatics because it can help determine a speaker's intention, e.g., in detecting irony in the voice (Wang et al., 2001, 2006, 2007). This encouraged my own lab to take a closer look.

In the last chapter, I described (surprising) results showing how adolescent participants with ASD are similar to typically developing participants with respect to scalar inferences (Chevallier et al., 2010). Coralie would go on and widen her skeptical net by comparing these groups in two further studies with respect to prosody. I'll review one here. In a paper entitled "What's in a voice?" Coralie (Chevallier et al., 2011) set up an original design in which participants (those with ASD as well as neurotypical controls) listened to a man (who was Tim Wharton) say something relatively banal but with prosodically unique characteristics. For example, a participant would hear "Ben" say in a whisper, "I want to watch television", and participants would have to decide whether it was spoken as a whisper or as a scream. The idea behind this work was to provide prosodic cues that are increasingly dependent on Theory of

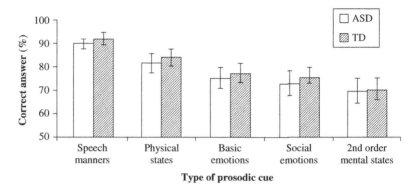

Figure 13.1. The summary from Chevallier et al. (2011) shows how accuracy in choosing between two kinds of voice-related attributes declines – among neurotypical participants and those with autism – as the prosodic category in question becomes increasingly dependent on metarepresenting.

Mind. The example above comes from the Speech Manners condition, which requires little intention-reading. On the higher, more ToM-dependent end, one would want to see whether participants detect Second Order Mental States, such as irony (as opposed to admiration). In between were three other categories that were hypothesized to rely on increasing degrees of Theory of Mind: Physical States – in which participants needed to distinguish between a voice that was, for example, tired or in pain; Basic Emotions – in which participants needed to distinguish between a voice that was, for example, angry or sad; and Social Emotions – where participants needed to distinguish between, say, pride and guilt. The focus was the difference between those with autism and neurotypicals, and the paper reported no differences. This is not what Coralie expected to find, but "data are data" and these forced her to reconsider the way researchers viewed ToM deficits among those with ASD. Another feature of the data that has garnered less attention is worth pointing out here. As one can see (Figure 13.1), all participants become less accurate at making prosodically based judgments as the category becomes increasingly metarepresentational. So, while participants with autism are comparable to neurotypicals, all participants have greater difficulty making fine distinctions between two states as the task relies to a greater extent on Theory of Mind attributions.

Prosody and Irony

Whenever I present the work that Nicola and I carried out (Spotorno et al., 2012; Spotorno and Noveck, 2014), I almost invariably get a question on prosody that goes something like this: "Obviously, there are no prosodic cues when reading a line of text, so what would happen if the utterance were presented auditorially? In other words, wouldn't participants figure out the irony from prosodic cues if given the chance?" In order to investigate this, Santiago González-Fuente, Pilar Prieto, and I ran an interesting study in France to investigate the extent to which prosody reveals an ironic intent (González-Fuente, Prieto, & Noveck, 2016). Fortunately, Santi and Pilar are experts on prosody and it allowed us to come up with a two-step design.

The first step was to model French speakers' natural prosodic profiles when reading ironic utterances. In order to accomplish this, Santi invited ten French speakers from Lyon (all were women in order to minimize variability) to vocalize the concluding (ironic or literal) utterances from (very slightly modified) stories from Spotorno and Noveck (2014). In this way, he was in a position to capture the pitch, duration, and intensity of an ironic reading of a sentence, such as "Nous sommes allées voir un film formidable" (We went to see a wonderful film), when meant ironically or literally. Santi then looked at participants' acoustic features on both the entire sentence and the last word (*formidable*) and found that acoustic correlates varied in expected ways (based on the prior literature). For example, the average fundamental frequency (f0), duration, and f0 variability were higher in ironic utterances compared to literal utterances for the final word (which provided contrasts with literal readings that were even stronger than what we found with whole-sentence analyses).

The next step provided us with a test. We surmised that if participants are able to read off prosody from (the final word of) an utterance, then it ought to be the case that participants could induce the completion of a story, even if a key background feature had been rendered ambiguous. That is, participants were visually presented the first five lines of a story with one word obscured (as in 13.20):

(13.20) Cynthia and Léa sing together in the same opera group.
         On the night of the premiere, they meet at the theater.
         The show begins exactly on time.
         Their performance ends up being ########.
         After the show, Cynthia says to Lea:

The final line of the story (13.21) was delivered auditorily, and it was manipulated synthetically so that its final word came across as ironic or literal (based on the prior modeling of the ten women speakers). This explains why I put the last word in (13.21) in bold:

(13.21) "Our performance was **majestic**."

The dependent measure, which was collected through a crowdsourcing site (SurveyGizmo), was based on the participants' coming up with the most appropriate word to fill the blank at the end of the fourth line.[5] For example, one would expect a word such as *miserable* (in place of the ###) if their reading of **majestic** in (13.21) had been ironic, and one would expect a word such as *beautiful* if the participants' reading had been literal. The experiment included five conditions. One condition presented lines like (13.21) with all three acoustic features (intensity, duration, and pitch) that are associated with irony; a second condition was a control, which included none of the enhancing acoustic features; and the remaining three condition provided just one of the three ironic-acoustic features. We made two discoveries. The first is that we needed to inform participants that "some, all, or none" of the stories might have an ironic reading, because piloting showed that the participants' choice was generally consistent with a literal reading when we gave no specific forewarning (this is in itself was revealing of participants' limited readiness for irony). Once forewarned, the next goal was to determine whether one needed one or all three prosodic features in order to encourage an ironic reading through prosody. It turns out that, in order to get participants to detect irony consistently, one needs to include all the acoustic features linked to irony (this leads to an 80 percent rate of ironic readings). Importantly, the control condition (which, again, had no acoustic clues to irony) also encouraged participants to import irony 20 percent of the time. When modifying just one of the enhancing features, participants provide ironic readings about 40 percent of the time (on average), with (prolonged) duration being the strongest of the three prosodic cues.

Concluding Remarks

I do not want to leave the impression that these five topics exhaust a list of up-and-coming topics. One could easily imagine investigating linguistic stalwarts such as anaphora (see Klin et al., 2004), or any of the other figures of speech not discussed, such as alliteration (e.g., see Lea et al., 2008), or hyperbole (mentioned briefly in Chapter 10). One could also anticipate work on speech acts, as set out by the late Josie Bernicot and her collaborator Virginie Laval (2004) in the first volume on Experimental Pragmatics. It is difficult to predict how scientific areas evolve, but the ones summarized here have attracted notice from experimental pragmatists, and they have engaged more than one group.

Notes

1. While citing a theoretical distinction between "regular" and "creative" metonymy, Ingrid Falkum (p.c.) suggests that "content-for-container" metonyms are based on frequently occurring, conventional patterns, while *the ham sandwich* type is less conventional.
2. The authors invoke the notion of Questions Under Discussion (QUD), as advocated by Ginzburg (2012).

. Other presuppositions are available, such as the following: Andorra has a non-traditional government.
4. This section is strongly influenced by papers with Coralie Chevallier, who introduced prosody into our lab, and by a paper from Wilson and Wharton (2006), who provided theoretical context to issues about prosody and pragmatics.
5. I took a little liberty in translating this one line into English, which in French was *La représentation est ###* .

14   Opinionated Conclusions and
        Considerations for the Future

From breadth through depth to perspective
Foundational motto of Harpur College (Binghamton University)

In 2013, while on my hands and knees for a single day in the one archeological dig I would ever participate in, I learned from the chief archeologist of the site (and colleague at the time), Fanny Bocquentin, that there are essentially two approaches to an archeological excavation. One approach, which was revolutionized by a French ethnologist-cum-archeologist, André Leroi-Gourhan, is to gain a wide spatial view of a site so as to reconstruct the way the people used objects and organized their space. This can provide (not just artifacts but) anthropological information about the way our ancestors interacted. This described the dig I was at (investigating prehistoric Beisamoun in the Jordan Valley) and explains why I was placed at one sub-site while other volunteers were digging at two others 10 to 20 m away. She went on to explain that the other way, the Wheeler-Kenyon method, is focused on a stratigraphic approach (more geology than anthropology) and thus on piercing through time. While focused on collecting ancient materials, its shortcoming is that one does not see the material in a human context. It is more focused on artifacts and discovering successive changes over time.[1]

Hearing this, I instantly drew a parallel with experimental pragmatics. As this volume makes clear, many scholars take a wide view of pragmatics in that they want to gain an understanding of a large set of phenomena across language and, to an important extent, to better understand how human beings operate in conversational space. As findings accrue, pragmatic accounts become more informed as they aim to see how the wide-ranging data fit together. While Aristotle and Grice might have considered figurative language as a category, this interpretation of the data falls to the side as one digs wider and deeper. Thanks in part to experimental work, one can reconfigure "figurative language" into something else. For example, Deirdre Wilson and Robyn Carston put two figures on a spectrum – metaphor and hyperbole – along with approximation, but they do not feel obliged to have an account for figurative language generally. Sam Glucksberg considered a metaphor such as "Some lawyers are sharks" as simply a (novel) categorical assertion, making it no different than literal language. Viewing pragmatic phenomena as a part of human communication is key to this approach.

The other (stratigraphic) approach is to focus on a narrower area while assuming that underneath lies a deep structure that will reveal the workings of pragmatics. This is an approach that describes those researchers who focus on singular phenomena, e.g., on scalar utterances or presuppositions. Many, especially formally minded, researchers dig with the expectation that the work will unearth the existence of something more primitive (and typically linguistic) hidden deep under the soil. This approach is less concerned with the larger human context but rather with exposing underlying rules, which often amount to making predictions about what other treasures they suspect should be found deep underground. These anticipated findings are designed to justify the existence of the single (albeit fascinating) finding discovered closer to the surface.[2]

Ever since that fateful day, I have distinguished researchers as coming from the wide-excavation (Leroi-Gourhan) school or as coming from the stratigraphic (Wheeler-Kenyon) school. This book is an example of an approach from the former and the grammatically oriented semanticists are examples of those coming from the latter. This a modern distinction for experimental pragmatics that mirrors the positions of the Ordinary vs Ideal Language schools described in the opening chapter. This is just analogical, but it is, I think, a useful way to view the current experimental pragmatic research and to better understand what it is we, as part of a research community, are trying to do.

With this analogy in mind, this chapter takes stock of the work summarized in the book by doing three things. First, by considering emerging patterns, I will argue for a distinction between two kinds of pragmatic inference in action. Second, I will go over a few current issues related to implicatures while defending a position that Dan Sperber and I argued for over ten years ago. Third, I want to consider some other emerging findings coming from different sub-sites at the wide experimental pragmatic excavation and consider what it might suggest for future work.

Two Kinds of Pragmatic Inference?

Linguistic-pragmatics advances by making fine distinctions. Grice began his project by distinguishing between natural vs non-natural meaning. Sperber and Wilson profited from the philosophical distinction between *use* and *mention*, to provide a view on irony (as echoic mention). Levinson distinguished between implicatures based on heuristics that were inspired by Grice's maxims and so did Horn. This very book is essentially based on the Gricean distinction between the linguistically encoded meaning of an utterance and its intended meaning. In nearly all the above cases, the distinction began as theoretical and empirical evidence would come, for the most part, from examples. As time wore on, experiments have been integrated, laying these distinctions bare.

Before getting to a distinction I would like to propose, first consider what pragmatic inferences have in common when the analysis starts from a spoken sentence: a narrowing down from what a speaker said. This narrowing can be appreciated by considering Wilson and Carston's (2007) lexical pragmatics program, which describes a variety of different lexical pragmatic phenomena that are assumed to result from a single interpretive process. Their list includes lexical narrowing (e.g., "drink" used to mean ALCOHOLIC DRINK), approximation (e.g., "flat" used to mean RELATIVELY FLAT), metaphorical extension (e.g., "bulldozer" used to mean FORCEFUL PERSON), and hyperbole (e.g., "raw" to mean UNDERCOOKED). Their approach entails viewing a listener as creating "an ad hoc concept, or occasion-specific sense, based on interaction among encoded concepts, contextual information, and pragmatic expectations, or principles" (p. 230). In all these cases, the listener is taking a linguistic stimulus, which could prompt a number of readings, in order to come up with a more precise reading. Generally speaking, there is a form of narrowing in each case. "Drink" covers a wide array of beverages and ALCOHOLIC DRINK, a very specific subpart. "Bulldozer" initially generates many associative features, but in the right context, it could refer to a specific type of person. "Raw" has many overlapping meanings and uses, but one of them could refer to uncooked or undercooked meat.

It is no surprise that the two most investigated experimental pragmatic phenomena, scalar inference and metaphor, figure into this list and, superficially, the two have one experimental finding in common. Both provide developmental effects in which younger children have a greater tendency to adopt a literal meaning (cf. Noveck et al., 2001; Noveck, 2001). A more careful look at the data, however, reveals that these two phenomena are far from comparable. For example, children seem more ready to interpret metaphoric terms than they are to enrich the quantifier *some*. Similarly, whereas there is a preponderance of data that shows that the pragmatic enrichment of scalars is costly for adults, the data on metaphors is more of a mixed bag. Trying to determine the nature of pragmatic effects with respect to metaphor is more difficult than it is with scalars. The distinctions between the two sorts of pragmatic phenomena prompted Nicola Spotorno and me to modestly propose that there are two kinds of pragmatic inference (Noveck & Spotorno, 2013).

In that paper, we argued for two distinctive psychological processes that drive pragmatic narrowing. The first of our two sorts we labeled *voluntary*, which refers to cases in which the linguistically encoded meaning can provide an interpretation that is good enough, but that can also lead with extra effort, and if the listener so chooses, to a more informative reading. Importantly, the more informative reading in these cases entails the (uttered) weaker, linguistically encoded one. This would account for the routine examples of scalars. A linguistically encoded reading is often good enough for providing the listener with an adequate interpretation, and, moreover, the pragmatic reading entails it. So, to take one seminal example from Bott and Noveck (2004), *Some cats are mammals* is trivially true with a linguistically encoded reading and false (and harder to process) with an enriched reading.

With the adequate linguistically encoded meaning in hand, one can appreciate the voluntary narrowing in other uses, e.g. when describing the conjunction of two events (*Monica had a baby and got married*). The sentence does not in itself imply an order, but an implied *and then* would render the interpretation more informative because, with this pragmatically enriched reading, it allows the listener to adopt one reading (*first baby then marriage*) and to incidentally remove the inverted order (*first marriage and then baby*) from consideration. Developmental work (Noveck & Chevaux, 2002; Noveck et al., 2009) points to effects that resemble those found with scalars. Here, too, the enriched reading entails the uttered one.

Adjectival modification, covered in Chapter 9, is an example of voluntary narrowing too. To investigate the role of adjectives for informativity, cases like (14.1) were presented to participants when they were required to choose an object from an array of three or four objects:

(14.1) Pick up the tall glass.

The statement has a linguistically encoded reading that provides enough information to make *a choice* in an experiment because all the utterance is indicating is that there exists a singular glass that is tall. Note that the description could be informative enough as is. For example, imagine a participant who simply looks over a set of glasses and takes the first one in his sight that appears tall to him. Under certain conditions, there is no need to further investigate a potentially noisy background. However, there is a deeper, narrower reading that one can apply to the sentence in these scenarios. Namely, the word "tall" in (14.1) can help a listener determine that there is one *relatively* tall glass that is to be distinguished from a smaller glass, providing for an enriched reading that can be glossed as (14.2):

(14.2) Pick up the tall glass and not a shorter one.

This enriched reading eliminates another, hitherto unnoticed, member of the collection. The added value of the enriched reading explains the results from Kronmüller et al. (2014). Those data showed that younger participants do not benefit at all from the added information provided by the adjective in (14.1) while their older cohorts do; these data conform with those from the classic scalar developmental effect. Without the pragmatic enrichment, one can have a reading that is sufficiently satisfying; with it, one can have a sharper description of the problem space.

We called the second of our two sorts of narrowing *imposed*, which refers to cases in which a speaker practically requires the addressee to enrich an aspect of an utterance in order to provide an approximation of the speaker's intended meaning. This sort of narrowing is not more informative on a *logical* scale (which can be captured by entailment relationships, for example) or a *probabilistic* one (in which an intended reading captures a more refined probabilistic space); nevertheless, the procedure indirectly prompts the consideration of possibilities that get reduced. In the case of a (novel) metaphor, an intended reading is one of several possible meanings, including the linguistically encoded meaning, to be derived from a non-conventional vehicle. When a runner is described as a "cheetah" (which can independently generate a range of associated features, including say, *cat, spotted, slender, mustached,* and *fast*), only a subset (or probably one feature) will be adopted in a way that is sensitive to the context. If anything, the linguistically encoded meaning (related to being a cat) is arguably suppressed as the listener adopts the more informative one (see Rubio-Fernández, 2007). Critically, in the imposed sort, there is no obvious entailment relation between an uninformative linguistically encoded meaning and its intended one.

Another (slightly more complex) example of imposed narrowing can be detected in conditional sentences. But it is less obvious. As described in Chapter 8, many linguistic scholars (e.g., Geis and Zwicky, 1971) had observed that the pragmatic enrichment of conditionals can resemble a biconditional. After all, many conditionals (e.g., *If the light is on, then the switch is up*) seem to invite a biconditional interpretation. With the double-barreled definition described earlier, this would make conditionals appear to be a voluntary narrowing process. However, as described in Chapter 8, this is a ruse, which becomes clear when the steps of a conditional are broken down (for example, when participants carry out and even accept the conclusion from an Affirmation of the Consequent argument), as in (14.3):

(14.3) If it's raining then the streets are wet.
         The streets are wet.
         Therefore, it's raining.

Again, many had assumed that an AC conclusion falls out naturally because *if* is narrowed to mean *if and only if*. However, all the data (behavioral and ERP) we collected indicate that the very step of affirming the consequent in the minor premise appears unexpected to all participants (it produces slowdowns compared to Modus Ponens and prompts ERP's indicating surprise, even when it is repeated nearly thirty times in the same paradigm). So, when the inference is analyzed more minutely, this pragmatic inference (for those who accept the conclusion) does not appear to result from a voluntary effort to narrow the meaning of *if* (to *if and only if*) earlier in the syllogism; according to a view developed in Noveck et al. (2011), those who accept AC arguments as pragmatically valid are doing work to make sense post hoc of the speaker's assertion (the minor premise). Typically, when participants are presented a conditional, it raises expectations that only further information about the antecedent will do (see Bonnefond et al., 2012), so, in light of a conditional, the listener would not be expecting the conditional's consequent as a minor premise. When the consequent appears (e.g., in the AC argument), it puts the listener in the position to make a pragmatic reading that is imposed by the speaker. Those participants who ultimately reject AC arguments stubbornly maintain their initial expectation. Those who do not or cannot are more likely to allow logically illicit conclusions to impose themselves through post hoc justifications. The minor premise (and its accepted conclusion) is imposed upon a generous or lax listener as they suppress the expectation for a minor premise justifying Modus Ponens, but the listener need not accept it.

Critical to the *voluntary* versus *imposed* distinction is the role played by a sentence's linguistically encoded meaning. My radical pragmatic allies might consider this heretical, but it is hard to ignore the data (specifically those that rely on the out-of-the-blue sentences) that indicate that readings generated by the linguistically encoded meaning do have (perhaps a limited) role to play. That a semantic reading for scalars is often considered acceptable, and that the literal reading of metaphors appears to at least linger (Carston & Wearing, 2015), are indications that linguistically encoded readings crop up when processing a sentence and that they could even become useful. This does not make the interpretational process any less pragmatic. Nor does it mean that a listener must fully consider the linguistically encoded reading and reject it *in order to* generate an enriched reading (à la Grice). It simply means that the utterance, which serves as an indication of the speaker's meaning, leaves a linguistically encoded trace. A linguistically encoded reading arguably results from a parallel process, one that is more or less accessible, regardless of the listener's success in attaining the speaker's intended meaning.

Unlike pragmatic theories that consider what a speaker could have said, but did not, this account remains within the bounds (of generated narrowings and associates) that emerge from the utterance. Thus, there is no need to consider how the use of *some* in "Some of the congresswomen are wearing white" would have been more informative if the quantifier had been All nor is there a need to reject these imaginary alternatives. That said, further relevant context may obviate the need to count on, or attend to, the linguistically encoded reading.

This psychological distinction is designed to apply across regularly occurring pragmatic inferences but without remaining beholden to linguistic categories. While the flagship examples – scalars for *voluntary* and metaphor for *imposed* – provide guideposts for what is normally part of the ad hoc instances of pragmatic processing, it is not expected that the two types of narrowing will be determined uniquely by their linguistic descriptions. For example, one could imagine cases where metaphoric uses do not fall exclusively into the *imposed* category. If I say "Kate is a princess" to mean that Catherine Middleton is a lovely person, it could be cited as evidence that not all metaphors are imposed, since this example fits better as a member of the other category. Given the particularized nature of pragmatic inferences, the voluntary/imposed distinction is to be applied to individual pragmatic enrichments on a case-by-case basis. With this distinction in hand, one can review many pragmatic phenomena and better appraise findings.

Here I turn to three sets of data that can be better appreciated by having this distinction in hand. First, the voluntary/imposed distinction can explain several ERP findings. For instance, ERP eccentricities are relatively difficult to find with scalar terms (see Noveck & Posada, 2003) unless more contextual information is added (see Nieuwland et al., 2010) while it is the opposite with novel metaphors. That is, out-of-the-blue novel metaphors appear to produce N400s, but with just a little-added context, they are harder to come by (Pynte, 1996). Given that the literal import of the two differs, context modulates them quite differently. ERP results with metonymies can be better appreciated based on this distinction, too. Arguably, content-for-container metonymies (*potion* in *Helga fastened her potion to her belt*) call on voluntary processes because all the essentials are there for a more literal reading whose added information (that the potion is in a bottle or flask) is essentially a feature that is optional. In contrast, container-for-content metonymies (*goblet* in *Heinz drank the goblet hastily*) prompt EEG profiles with Late Positivities because the pragmatic process is imposed. Without a pragmatic narrowing (that the goblet contained a potion, beverage, or something else), the listener would not be able to understand the speaker's intended meaning.

Second, the voluntary/imposed distinction can add light to difficult cases. In the last chapter, I referred to two observations on negations. On the one hand, *Larry is not eating ice cream* can be narrowed further to *Larry is not eating chocolate ice cream*. One might be tempted to consider the semantic entailment as voluntary because (with little effort) one can take *no ice cream* and narrow it to *no chocolate ice cream* if the listener thinks it serves some purpose. However, a narrowed reading from a negation does not entail the uttered one (*Larry is not eating chocolate ice cream* does not entail that *Larry is not eating ice cream*). So, one of the conditions for a voluntary description is not met. The other observation made about negations is that it can be used to point the listener elsewhere. If *Larry is not eating ice cream* were part of a disjunction elimination argument (*Larry is eating cake or ice cream; he is not eating ice cream*), the negation in this particular context is imposed on the listener so that he rebounds to an alternative. This makes negation in disjunction eliminations a source of imposed effort[3] (and could explain why one logical rule, disjunction elimination, is slightly more effort-demanding than another, Modus Ponens, see Reverberi et al., 2007).

Third, another difficult case concerns participants with autism. Participants with autism are largely competent with pragmatic processing and much more so than originally assumed. That said, there remain many reported cases of differences between neurotypical participants and participants with autism with respect to pragmatic processes. One avenue to explore (based on Pijnacker et al., 2009b) is that participants with autism reveal more atypical behavior when an interlocutor imposes a pragmatic process on them. Thus, when differences are found, they are typically related to imposed sorts of pragmatic inference such as metaphor or irony (Happé, 1993). Time will tell whether this distinction can hold under more severe testing conditions.[4]

Revisiting Scalar Inferences

The Wide-Excavation Approach

In Noveck and Sperber (2007), we defended a rather straightforward view on scalars that distinguished itself from Levinson's default account and laid out an approach that accounted for all the data that my colleagues and I had gathered until then. Here is one money quote (with credit to Dan Sperber):

From a relevance-theoretic pragmatic point of view, the use of an expression of the form "some of the Xs," just as that of any linguistic expression, serves not to encode the speaker's meaning, but to indicate it. In particular, the denotation of the concept indicated by a given use of "some of the Xs" may be an ad hoc concept SOME OF THE Xs* with a denotation different from that of the literal SOME OF THE Xs. Rather than ranging over all subsets of Xs between 2 and the total number of the Xs, the extension of SOME OF THE Xs* may be narrowed down at either end, or it may be extended so as to include subsets of one.

The paper essentially contrasted the Relevance Theory point of view and Levinson's GCI account as had been done in Bott and Noveck (2004) and several other papers at that time. As we wrote,

In the absence of contextual factors that make an enriched interpretation of an utterance easier to arrive at, relevance theory predicts that a literal interpretation – which involves just the attribution to the speaker of a meaning already provided by linguistic decoding – should involve shallower processing and take less time than an enriched one – which involves a process of meaning construction.

As Chapters 6 and 7 make clear, this opening debate on scalars, which we had thought had been resolved, was just heating up. In what follows, I present two accounts that challenge our straightforward view: one inspired by a fellow wide-excavator and another from a series of stratigraphic investigators.

Scalars Enrichments in Politeness Situations

Bonnefon et al. (2009) aimed to show that there are contexts in which utterances using the quantifier *some* prompt semantically comparable readings while appearing to require *more* effort than pragmatic readings and specifically in certain politeness situations. To make their point, Bonnefon et al. (2009) address participants in the second-person and ask that they put themselves in the shoes of a character navigating a public encounter, for example, as someone who has just given a speech to a small group of people. A fictional character then provides feedback about the speech while using the quantifier *some* (while referring to the audience members). The participant is eventually asked a metalinguistic question – what Mazzarella et al. (2018) call the *semantic compatibility question–* about the feedback. To make this concrete, here is a version of one task in three parts: the background information (14.4), the scalar utterance (14.5), and the semantic compatibility question (14.6):

(14.4)   Imagine you gave a speech at a small political rally. You are discussing your speech with Denise, who was in the audience. You are considering whether to give this same speech to another audience.

(14.5)   Hearing this, Denise tells you: "Some people hated your speech."

(14.6)   Given what Denise tells you, do you think that it is possible that everybody hated your speech?

Given concerns about politeness, it was expected that participants would react differently to the semantic compatibility question when the scalar utterance had contained the verb *hated* as opposed to *loved* (with its semantic compatibility question becoming "Do you think that it is possible that everybody loved your speech?"). This prediction has been supported: Participants are much more likely to say "Yes" to the semantic compatibility question in the face-threatening context (when the verb is *hated*) than in the face-boosting one (when the verb is *loved*). In the earliest published experiment (using a different theme concerning a poetry reading), 42 percent said, "Yes" to the semantic-compatibility question in the face-threatening situation, and 17 percent said "Yes" in the face-boosting situation. According to the authors, rendering *some* as compatible with *everybody* ought to be effortful (and harder than the pragmatic, *Some and not all*, interpretations) in order to be polite (to produce "affective effects"). A reading time experiment (Bonnefon et al., 2011) appears to reinforce their claims because those who say, "Yes" to the semantic compatibility question take longest in the face-threatening (the *Some people hated your speech*) case, i.e., longer than those who said, "Yes" in the face-boosting (the *Some people loved your speech*) case and longer than all the rest who said, "No" (in either condition).

Upon looking over these claims, Diana Mazzarella (2015) had a different interpretation for their reported effects. She argued that what actually happens in these tasks is, not that participants slowly adopt a broad (semantic-like) interpretation of *some* but, that participants prompt a pragmatic enrichment so that the utterance is indeed enriched to *Some but not all people hated your speech*; however, participants go on to reconsider this enrichment. Essentially, Bonnefon and colleagues conflate the interpretation of *some* with a second mechanism, one in which a participant decides whether or not to *accept* a speaker's intended meaning. Her analysis was inspired by a proposal from Sperber et al. (2010) that describes how listeners police comprehended-information through a capacity known as *epistemic vigilance*, which enables hearers to avoid being accidentally or intentionally misinformed. According to the epistemic vigilance hypothesis, there are two main factors affecting the believability of a piece of communicated information: the reliability of its source and the believability of its content. As far as Bonnefon et al.'s data are concerned, Mazzarella suspects that epistemic vigilance towards the source may affect the believability of scalar inferences in face-threatening contexts.

Moreover, Mazzarella et al. (2018) point out how Bonnefon et al.'s (2011) data are based on a confound, i.e., claims about the interpretation of (14.5) are based on the joint presentation of (14.5) and (14.6), so it is difficult to attribute slowdowns uniquely to the existential utterance. In that paper, we carried out a crowdsourcing task that presented (14.5) and (14.6) successively in two separate steps while registering reaction times in order to isolate the source of slowdowns. In line with Mazzarella's hypothesis, according to which the slowdown is due to the participant's effort to epistemically evaluate the piece of incoming information and particularly in the face-threatening contexts, delayed reaction times are actually linked to answering the semantic compatibility question in (14.6) and not to the scalar utterance in (14.5). It is the *Yes* responses to the face-threatening situation that are associated with the slowdowns, indicating that participants are essentially enriching the scalar utterance and then rejecting it because they understand what the speaker wants to imply, but they also understand the implications of politeness. While the ultimate interpretation aligns with a semantic interpretation because the addressee understands that *Some and perhaps all hated the speech*, he also understands that the speaker intended to soften the blow by implying a narrowed *some but not all* interpretation.

The Stratigraphic Approach to Scalars

To recap (from Chapter 7), semantically oriented *conventionalists* have pursued a line according to which scalar inferences are to be viewed as *non*-pragmatic. By taking issue with one of Grice's claims – that implicatures operate globally

over entire sentences (and by mostly focusing on *some*) – conventionalists propose that a covert operator is ready to be applied at just about any juncture in
a sentence in order to enrich a scalar term. So, rather than consider that the
lexical reading can suffice, the stipulation sets up situations in which enriched
readings are always potentially likely. This is a default approach placed in
the grammar. As Geurts (2010) points out, this leads to some untenable conclusions. As he puts it, "having been designed specifically for dealing with
'embedded implicatures' [conventionalist theories] are committed to the view
that upper-bounded interpretations systematically occur in embedded positions. Consequently, by their very nature, conventionalist theories are prone to
overgenerate readings." As Geurts and van Tiel (2013) add, "truth-conditional
narrowing applies across the board, and therefore we should expect to observe
Upper-Bounded Construals (local implicatures) all over the place, regardless
of whether scalar expressions are embedded or not" (also, see Ippolito, 2010).
Of course, as the data in Chapter 6 lay out (about which I expand below), scalar
inferences are not at all ubiquitous.[5]

When one considers the experimental data that conventionalists have
inspired, evidence in its favor is rather limited, and so is, in my view, its impact
on the experimental pragmatic literature. Let me point to three reasons for
saying that. First, investigations from across the scalar literature (which is populated mostly with unembedded cases) have prompted several pieces of reliable data, one of which shows that often participants do *not* enrich at all and
that, when they do enrich, it is accompanied by a cost. As described in detail
in Chapter 6, children famously do not enrich as often as adults, and there are
individual differences showing that some adults will not enrich scalar utterances while others will. In these cases, a semantic reading is generally easier
to access than a pragmatic one. That is, one would think that a conventionalist
position would claim that the making of a local *only some* reading is relatively
effortless because the semantic and enriched readings are considered ambiguous. That would be in line with the definition – and cognitive behavior – of
an ambiguous term (Onifer & Swinney, 1971). However, the data indicate –
overwhelmingly – that this is likely not the case. There are also two corpus
studies showing that uses of "some" are not homogeneously linked with upper-
bounded meanings that could be cancelled (Larrivée & Duffley, 2014; Degen,
2015). So it seems odd to attribute to a covert operator a function that fails to
engage in a large proportion of target utterances (let alone, a majority of them).
Second, embedded cases are exceptional, so to base an entire approach on
them seems precarious. Third, the strongest data, the ones that make the local
implicatures appear commonplace (Potts et al., 2016), are limited to what are
mostly reasoning-type studies. These kinds of studies are useful for demonstrating proof-of-concept perhaps (like the early Grice-inspired developmental scalar studies), but notice how strenuous it was to get to a point where

embedded scalar implicatures emerged (as I discuss later, it called for major modifications to Geurts and Pouscoulous's 2009 study, which was described in Chapter 7). Besides, as I describe directly below, one should not be so quick to attribute results showing the facilitation of embedded implicatures to anything that is necessarily grammatical. Let us take a closer look under the hood of Potts et al.'s (2016) study.

As a reminder, Potts et al. (2016) asked participants to make a (true or false) response with respect to a complex doubly quantified statement (with an embedded quantifier) concerning three players (each of whom could have made all, none, or half their attempted basketball shots). For example, in one trial the study showed that when the statement is *Exactly one player hit some of his shots* along with images of three basketball players (two whose pile of green balls indicated that they hit all and a third whose piles indicated that he hit half), a large percentage make the judgment "true" which can only be justified when *some* is locally enriched to further mean *not all*. From categorical data like these, the authors assume that this is sufficient for supporting the conventionalist claim. When one turns to the results, one can point to three reasons to be circumspect about such specific claims.

One reason why I am circumspect is that in the slightly different (and arguably more complex) tasks, Geurts and Pouscoulous's (2009) found little or no evidence of local implicatures (see Chapter 7, Figure 7.1). This does not mean that local implicatures are impossible to construe, but it does indicate that upper-boundedness is rather permeable in more complex tasks or that the alleged covert operator has difficulty taking root when there are other complex task features to attend to. The *here-in-simpler-tasks-and-not-in-complex-tasks* effect is reminiscent of the earliest failed attempts to establish the existence of scalars; Newstead (1995) concluded that scalar inferences did not exist based on a study using fully fledged Aristotelian syllogisms before I (Noveck, 2001) and others began to make the case that they appear more readily, in certain more user-friendly contexts, when they were accessible and pragmatic concerns call for them. The *here-in-simpler-tasks-and-not-in-complex-tasks* effect is a pattern that has been repeated in the cognitive literature throughout its history. The task that most famously made this clear is Wason's (1965) Selection Task, whose correct responses are facilitated when the task's content is more social or relevant (Johnson-Laird, Legrenzi, & Legrenzi, 1972; Cosmides, 1989; Cheng & Holyoak, 1985; Sperber, Cara, & Girotto, 1995). Agreed, something is changing as one makes a task more accessible, but it is a leap to attribute increased facility to an alleged grammatical rule.[6] The second reason that I am circumspect about conventionalist claims emanating from Potts et al. is that other data in the same study (using cases like *None of the players hit some of the shots* or *Every player hit some of his shots*) show that the evidence of local implicatures is variable. Whereas the *Exactly one player hit some of his shots* sentence appears to generate a "local implicature" about half the time (evidenced by rates of true responses), other sentences such as *No player hit some of his shots* (presented with two players who always succeeded and a third who never succeeded) prompt "true" responses less reliably. Recent work (van Tiel et al., in press) addresses these issues and shows the extent to which "upper-bounded construals" (local implicatures) depend on features of the task (such as the quantifier phrase that embeds *some*). The third reason is that Potts et al. (2016) also assume, without procuring new data, that scalar implicatures are ubiquitous in *un*embedded cases. When new ubiquity claims are made about scalar enrichments that look past *years* of robust results (that often point to the lack of such enrichments), it is difficult to validate its claims about exceptional embedded cases.

All told, these reasoning studies reflect just one small part of the experimental pragmatic arsenal.[7] When the conventionalist account can make the kind of predictions that a plethora of Gricean-inspired on-line studies have made, they will then be in a stronger position. At the moment, I am aware of only one processing study that investigates the time course of embedded scalar inferences (Chemla, Cummins, & Singh, 2016), and that one, too, does not conform with the proposal that a local *only some* reading is ambiguous and relatively effortless to produce. Chemla et al.'s (2016) reading time findings suggest that local enrichments, like in the standard cases, are relatively time-consuming. If one does not assume that the two readings are equally available, it means one is more effortful, and when it is the enriched case, it is more in line with the classic pragmatic processing accounts for unembedded cases.

Even though conventionalists' strong claims rely on (what are essentially) debatable findings that center on an exceptional case, some defenders of the grammatical program (e.g., Chemla & Singh, 2014) dismiss Relevance Theory as a competing account for scalar inferences because its advocates (e.g., Noveck & Sperber, 2007) do not argue for a separate *theory* of scalars. Again, Relevance Theory, which prompted the earliest falsifiable (and counterintuitive) predictions about the pragmatic enrichment of *some* on scalar tasks (Bott & Noveck, 2004), views such pragmatic enrichments as a minor adjustment (an explicature) that a listener makes on occasion to better understand a speaker's intention in a specific circumstance. Whether one defends a highly technical grammatical model (whose processing is ultimately as, or more, inexplicit), or a highly detailed descriptive pragmatic model, one needs to adjust (or eventually reject) theories in light of empirical facts. The grammatical approach presents itself as immune to data as it is based essentially on a stipulation (Russell, 2006) or fiat (Geurts, 2010). Such an approach makes the conventionalist program susceptible to a confirmation bias. That is, if experimentally drawn facts are ignored (e.g., spontaneous enriched readings are nearly always effort-demanding in ceteris paribus conditions), then the grammatical approach makes itself appear non-falsifiable. This puts the conventionalist account in a weak position with respect to the Gricean approaches.

The Wide-Excavation Approach: Current and Future Work

It should be clear by now that the Grice-inspired wide-excavation approach to experimental pragmatics is concerned with, not only the role of sentences in communication, but with the understanding of a speaker's intention. There are two ways to investigate the way intentions play a role. One way is to determine how intention-reading interdigitates with sentence processing as some work in this volume has shown. For example, when describing fMRI studies on irony, we showed how brain regions associated with Theory of Mind are more intensively activated when the same sentence is understood ironically as opposed to literally (Spotorno et al., 2012). In reviewing the work from Mazzarella on scalars and politeness in this chapter, too, one can see how enrichments are part and parcel of a listener's effort to understand the speaker's intention. In the example in (14.5), the speaker's (Denise's) intention concerns sharing an opinion about whether the listener (the participant) ought to give the same speech again. So, if a listener hears that "Some people hated your speech," it is in the context of answering a larger question. The speaker's informative intention can be understood as "having non-unanimous support for the speech is a good reason not to give it again." If the listener hears "Some people loved your speech," it is not clear how to interpret the speaker's informative intention. When the listener hears "Some people hated your speech," the informative intention is likely unchanged by knowing whether *some* needs to be enriched or not. The effort to enrich the existential quantifier will depend ultimately on what the listener deems is the speaker's intention.

A second way to appreciate how intentions are elemental to communication is to consider very young non-verbal human beings (under, say, two years of age) and their understanding of pointing. As described in Chapter 9 (on referring), infants' pre-verbal communication shows the extent to which they rely on non-verbal information. In that chapter, I described how babies are sensitive to ostensive cues that make them follow the gaze of the speaker (also see Chapter 2, Note 23) and that they use pointing as a way to communicate. These young, pre-verbal participants are fundamental to investigating underlying pragmatic principles without considering the words they need to process. Comprehension depends on a listener having a ready awareness that the speaker wants to communicate something. This implies that the very basis of utterance comprehension has an underlying layer of intention-reading that babies exploit in order to make pragmatic inferences.

This investigation of fundamental pragmatic assumptions is now emerging in the literature. For example, Mascaro and Kovacs (in preparation, discussed in Mascaro and Sperber, 2016) investigate how very young children, between the ages of 15 and 24 months, will increasingly rely on an experimenter's point when searching for a toy under one of two buckets, i.e., older participants will choose a bucket that was the object of a point from an experimenter even if they had just seen it was empty. That said, participants do not give blanket endorsements of the "speaker" because this work also shows that young children could ignore the point if the bucket is transparent (and that they can see for themselves the sought toy). So, the young participants will increasingly trust their interlocutor under conditions where they are unsure, indicating that they readily use a communicator's intention to make decisions. This is in line with a range of data showing how very young children choose messages based on the extent to which a speaker is reliable. For example, when eight-month-olds are shown a screen that could have one of four boxes illuminated with an animation (a trial begins with four empty boxes and one of two friendly faces in the middle), Tummelsthammer et al. (2014) show the infants will inspect the animated box longer when it is preceded by a speaker who reliably looks (100 percent of the time) in the correct corner that will show the animation (imagine the speaker looks in the direction of one of four corners and says, "Wow") as opposed to a speaker who looks in the correct corner (before the animation) just 25 percent of the time. These precocious pragmatic abilities (to notice informative features linked to speakers) are at the very heart of communicative competence and can serve as the basis on which language learning and language comprehension take place.

How Did We Get Here? Do We Conclude?

Experimental Pragmatics has come into being through the interplay of Gricean and post-Gricean debates, and the input from experimental investigations. The book aimed to provide a broad overview of the state of play while considering a wide variety of phenomena and the experiments they inspired. This book has been subtitled *The making of a cognitive science* because influential accounts come, not just from linguistics but, from many other allied disciplines, including psychology, neuroscience, and philosophy.

Experimentation provides the forum in which the exchange of ideas can be rigorously tested. Once engaged in the same forum, researchers can agree on the contours and contrasts that they see in a phenomenon. It would be surprising if all of, or even a large minority of, my fellow experimental-pragmatic colleagues were to agree with my approach, my take on a phenomenon or with my conclusions. This is par for the course. Experimental work is essentially a conversation. However, by being in the same conversation, we can avoid introspection and agree (or come to agree) about objective facts. These facts (the best of which are surprising) come about through rigorous and replicable third-person techniques. Certain practices, such as adversarial collaborations, can facilitate the clarity of these conversations. All of these features – the debates, the experiments, and the reliable data these produce – are essential for the science to advance.

Notes

1. Here is what Fanny wrote me (in February 2017) when I asked her for a confirmation of the conclusions I had drawn from our conversation (which took place in 2013). "Il y a la méthode Wheeler (britannique) qui est focalisée sur la stratigraphie et donc sur la succession des événements, l'évolution des assemblages au cours du temps. Elle est appliquée dans beaucoup de pays et notamment en Israël. Elle a le défaut de ne pas permettre d'avoir une approche spatiale large. C'est cette dernière approche qui est privilégiée en France sous l'impulsion d'A. Leroi-Gourhan un ethnologue reconvertit et pour qui ça n'est pas les objets qui compte mais bien la relation spatiale qu'ils entretiennent entre eux afin de pouvoir reconstruire la façon dont les hommes les manipulaient et comment ils s'organisaient dans l'espace. Cette technique de décapage n'est toutefois pas adaptée à tous les contextes mais elle peut apporter des informations vraiment d'ordre ethnologique sur des sites bien conservés (exposition des sols d'habitat tels qu'ils ont été abandonnés par les hommes préhistoriques)."

2. The probabilistic pragmatic modeling work from Frank and Goodman (2014, 2016) and their associates as well as from Michael Franke (2011) and his associates (and, it should be noted, that Judith Degen intersects with both groups) arguably represents a hybrid of the two archeological approaches. That is, these Grice-inspired accounts apply a Bayesian approach in order to account for behavior with respect to a wide range of pragmatic phenomena, including word learning (Frank & Goodman, 2014), hyperbole (Kao et al., 2014), irony (Kao & Goodman, 2015), reference resolution (Frank & Goodman, 2009; Franke & Degen, 2016), and embedded implicatures (Potts et al., 2016; Franke et al., 2016). Rather than boring underground, however, in order to discover something new or surprising about pragmatic phenomena or in order to investigate a feature of a phenomenon that distinguishes between competing theoretical accounts, it would be fairer to say that these approaches gather the evidence found closer to the surface in order to account for them through comprehensive probabilistic models. These models operate at Marr's computational level. When such computational approaches to communication employ experiments, they are typically (though not always) designed to determine how well a model accounts for, what are often, existing data. So, it represents an approach that is complementary to experimental pragmatics (Franke & Jager, 2016). That said, there is modeling work that aims to account for individual differences (Franke & Degen, 2016) or that compares models in order to test whether literal interpretations play a role in embedded implicatures (Franke & Bergen, in preparation).

3. This could explain why disjunction elimination is slightly more effort-demanding than Modus Ponens, even though the two are both valid logical inferences that are used interchangeably in studies on logical processing, e.g., see Reverberi et al. (2007).

4. Lauer (2013) subtly distinguishes between two quantity-related Gricean implicatures. The optional one refers to standard Gricean quantity violations (akin to the scalar case) and mandatory implicatures refer to cases in which a listener ("needs a reason") for a pragmatic inference to go through, otherwise the utterance would be infelicitous. His main example of a mandatory implicature concerns the so-called ignorance implicature (drawing out "I don't know where John is exactly" from "John is in Paris or London").

5. As my colleague Bob van Tiel pointed out to me, conventionalists differ from each other with respect to the extent of this ubiquity. While Chierchia et al. (2012) say "that SIs can occur systematically and freely in arbitrarily embedded positions," they also argue that enriched readings occur whenever it results in a stronger interpretation. Chemla and Spector (2011) go further and say that "there is an overall preference for deriving SIs, independently of considerations of logical strength" (also see Magri, 2011). In more recent work Dieuleveut et al. seem to suggest that people generate all possible readings and that pragmatics decides which one to use.

6. Echoing advocates of the conventionalist account, I investigated the Wason Selection Task (Noveck & O'Brien, 1996) with the intention of demonstrating that at the heart of successful performance is a participant's discovery of a mental logical rule. In light of our data, which pointed to a host of non-logical features (e.g., making negative information explicit) as the source of facilitated performance, I essentially abandoned that approach.

7. Interestingly, the literature has gone full circle. The opening round of scalar studies was based on a reasoning study before widely expanding to a full range of psycholinguistic tasks. The main support for local implicatures comes mostly from tasks that are arguably reasoning tasks.

Bibliography

Ackerman, B. P. (1978). Children's comprehension of presupposed information: Logical and pragmatic inferences to speaker belief. *Journal of Experimental Child Psychology*, 26(1), 92–114.

(1979). Children's understanding of definite descriptions: Pragmatic inferences to the speaker's intent. *Journal of Experimental Child Psychology*, 28(1), 1–15.

(1982a). On comprehending idioms: Do children get the picture? *Journal of Experimental Child Psychology*, 33(3), 439–54.

(1982b). Contextual integration and utterance interpretation: The ability of children and adults to interpret sarcastic utterances. *Child Development*, 53: 1075–83.

(1983). Form and function in children's understanding of ironic utterances. *Journal of Experimental Child Psychology*, 35(3), 487–508.

Ackerman, B. P., Szymanski, J., & Silver, D. (1990). Children's use of the common ground in interpreting ambiguous referential utterances. *Developmental Psychology*, 26(2), 234.

Almor, A., Arunachalam, S., & Strickland, B. (2007). When the creampuff beat the boxer: Working memory, cost, and function in reading metaphoric reference. *Metaphor and Symbol*, 22(2), 169–93.

Altmann, G. T. (1998). Ambiguity in sentence processing. *Trends in Cognitive Sciences*, 2(4), 146–52.

Altmann, G. T., & Kamide, Y. (1999). Incremental interpretation at verbs: Restricting the domain of subsequent reference. *Cognition*, 73(3), 247–64.

Altmann, G. T., van Nice, K. Y., Garnham, A., & Henstra, J. A. (1998). Late closure in context. *Journal of Memory and Language*, 38(4), 459–84.

American Psychiatric Association. (2013). *Diagnostic and Statistical Manual of Mental Disorders (DSM-5)*. American Psychiatric Publishing, Arlington, VA.

Angier, N. (2012, May 1). From the minds of babes. *The New York Times*. Retrieved from www.nytimes.com.

Asperger, H. (1944). Die "Autistischen Psychopathen" im Kindesalter. *European Archives of Psychiatry and Clinical Neuroscience*, 117(1), 76–136.

Austin, J. L. (1956a). Ifs and cans. *Proceedings of the British Academy*, 42, 232. Philosophical Papers (1961).

(1956b). Ifs and cans. *Proceedings of the British Academy*, 42, 109–32. Reprinted in Austin (1979): 205–32.

(1975). *How To Do Things with Words*. Oxford University Press.

(1979). *Philosophical Papers*, 3rd edn. Clarendon Press, Oxford.

Bach, K. (1994). Conversational impliciture. *Mind and Language*, 9(2), 124–62.

Bambini, V., & Resta, D. (2012). Metaphor and experimental pragmatics: When theory meets empirical investigation. *Humana Mente – Journal of Philosophical Studies*, 23, 37–60.

Baratgin, J., Douven, I., Evans, J. S. B., et al. (2015). The new paradigm and mental models. *Trends in Cognitive Sciences*, 19(10), 547–8.

Bar-Hillel, Y., & Carnap, R. (1953). Semantic information. *The British Journal for the Philosophy of Science*, 4(14), 147–57.

Barner, D., Brooks, N., & Bale, A. (2011). Accessing the unsaid: The role of scalar alternatives in children's pragmatic inference. *Cognition*, 118(1), 84–93.

Baron-Cohen, S. (1989). The autistic child's theory of mind: A case of specific developmental delay. *Journal of Child Psychology and Psychiatry*, 30(2), 285–97.

  (2001). Theory of mind in normal development and autism. *Prisme*, 34(1), 74–183.

  (2002). The extreme male brain theory of autism. *Trends in Cognitive Sciences*, 6(6), 248–54.

Baron-Cohen, S., Leslie, A. M., & Frith, U. (1985). Does the autistic child have a "theory of mind"? *Cognition*, 21(1), 37–46.

Baron-Cohen, S., Wheelwright, S., Skinner, R., Martin, J., & Clubley, E. (2001). The autism-spectrum quotient (AQ): Evidence from Asperger syndrome/high-functioning autism, males and females, scientists and mathematicians. *Journal of Autism and Developmental Disorders*, 31(1), 5–17.

Barrouillet, P., Grosset, N., & Lecas, J. F. (2000). Conditional reasoning by mental models: Chronometric and developmental evidence. *Cognition*, 75(3), 237–66.

Barr, D. J., & Keysar, B. (2002). Anchoring comprehension in linguistic precedents. *Journal of Memory and Language*, 46(2), 391–418.

Barsalou, L. W. (1983). Ad hoc categories. *Memory & Cognition*, 11(3), 211–27.

Bach, K. (1987). On Communicative Intentions: A Reply to Recanti. *Mind & Language*, 2(2), 141–54.

Bates, E., Camaioni, L., & Volterra, V. (1975). The acquisition of performatives prior to speech. *Merrill-Palmer Quarterly of Behavior and Development*, 21(3), 205–26.

Bennett, D. J. (2004). *Logic Made Easy: How to Know When Language Deceives You*. W.W. Norton & Company.

Berger, F., & Höhle, B. (2012). Restrictions on addition: Children's interpretation of the focus particles auch 'also' and nur 'only' in German. *Journal of Child Language*, 39(02), 383–410.

Bernicot, J., & Laval, V. (2004). Speech acts in children: The example of promises. In I. Noveck & D. Sperber (eds.), *Experimental Pragmatics* (pp. 207–27). Palgrave Macmillan, UK.

Bonnefon, J. F., De Neys, W., & Feeney, A. (2011). Processing scalar inferences in face-threatening contexts. In Carlson, L., C. Hölscher, & T. Shipley (eds.), Proceedings of the 33rd Annual Conference of the Cognitive Science Society. Cognitive Science Society, Austin, TX.

Bonnefon, J. F., Feeney, A., & Villejoubert, G. (2009). When some is actually all: Scalar inferences in face-threatening contexts. *Cognition*, 112(2), 249–58.

Bonnefond, M., Van der Henst, J. B., Gougain, M., et al. (2012). How pragmatic interpretations arise from conditionals: Profiling the affirmation of the consequent argument with reaction time and EEG measures. *Journal of Memory and Language*, 67(4), 468–85.

Bonnefond, M., & Van der Henst, J. B. (2009). What's behind an inference? An EEG study with conditional arguments. *Neuropsychologia*, 47(14), 3125–33.

Borg, E. (2010). Semantics and the place of psychological evidence. In *New Waves in Philosophy of Language* (pp. 24–40). Palgrave Macmillan, UK.

Bosch, P. (2007). Productivity, polysemy, and predicate indexicality. In Balder ten Cate & Henk Zeevat (eds.), *Proceedings of the Sixth International Tbilisi Symposium on Language, Logic & Computation* (pp. 58–71). Springer, Berlin.

Bott, L., Bailey, T. M., & Grodner, D. (2012). Distinguishing speed from accuracy in scalar implicatures. *Journal of Memory and Language*, 66(1), 123–42.

Bott, L., & Noveck, I. A. (2004). Some utterances are underinformative: The onset and time course of scalar inferences. *Journal of Memory and Language*, 51(3), 437–57.

Braine, M. D., O'Brien, D. P., Noveck, I. A., et al. (1995). Predicting intermediate and multiple conclusions in propositional logic inference problems: Further evidence for a mental logic. *Journal of Experimental Psychology: General*, 124(3), 263.

Braine, M. D. and Rumain, B. (1981). Development of comprehension of "or": Evidence for a sequence of competencies. *Journal of Experimental Child Psychology*, 31(1): 46–70.

Bransford, J. D., & Johnson, M. K. (1972). Contextual prerequisites for understanding: Some investigations of comprehension and recall. *Journal of Verbal Learning and Verbal Behavior*, 11(6), 717–26.

Breheny, R. (2006). Communication and folk psychology. *Mind & Language*, 21(1), 74–107.

Breheny, R., Katsos, N., & Williams, J. (2006). Are generalised scalar implicatures generated by default? An on-line investigation into the role of context in generating pragmatic inferences. *Cognition*, 100(3), 434–63.

Breheny, R., Ferguson, H. J., & Katsos, N. (2013a). Taking the epistemic step: Toward a model of on-line access to conversational implicatures. *Cognition*, 126(3), 423–40.

(2013b). Investigating the time course of accessing conversational implicatures during incremental sentence interpretation. *Language and Cognitive Processes*, 28(4), 443–67.

Brennan, S. E., & Clark, H. H. (1996). Conceptual pacts and lexical choice in conversation. *Journal of Experimental Psychology: Learning, Memory, and Cognition*, 22(6), 1482–93.

Brennan, S. E., & Hanna, J. E. (2009). Partner-specific adaptation in dialog. *Topics in Cognitive Science*, 1(2), 274–91.

Brown-Schmidt, S. (2009). Partner-specific interpretation of maintained referential precedents during interactive dialog. *Journal of Memory and Language*, 61(2), 171–90.

Brunet, E., Sarfati, Y., & Hardy-Baylé, M. C. (2003). Reasoning about physical causality and other's intentions in schizophrenia. *Cognitive Neuropsychiatry*, 8(2), 129–39.

Byrne, R. M. (1989). Suppressing valid inferences with conditionals. *Cognition*, 31(1), 61–83.

Byrnes, J. P., & Duff, M. A. (1989). Young children's comprehension of modal expressions. *Cognitive Development*, 4(4), 369–87.

Carnap, R., & Bar-Hillel, Y. (1952). *An Outline of a Theory of Semantic Information.* Research Laboratory of Electronics, MIT, Cambridge, MA.

Carston, R. (1988). Implicature, explicature, and truth-theoretic semantics. In R. Kempson (ed.), *Mental Representations: The Interface Between Language and Reality* (pp. 155–81). Cambridge University Press, Cambridge.

(2002). *Thoughts and Utterances: The Pragmatics of Explicit Communication.* Blackwell, Oxford.

(2010). Metaphor: Ad hoc concepts, literal meaning and mental images. In *Proceedings of the Aristotelian Society* (Vol. 110, No. 3, pt 3, pp. 295–321). Oxford University Press, Oxford.

Carston, R., & Hall, A. (2012). 3. Implicature and explicature. *Cognitive Pragmatics*, 4, 47.

Carston, R., & Wearing, C. (2015). Hyperbolic language and its relation to metaphor and irony. *Journal of Pragmatics*, 79, 79–92.

Ceponiene R., Lepisto, T., Sheshtakova, A., et al. (2003). Speech-sound-selective auditory impairment in children with autism: They can perceive but do not attend. *Proceedings of the National Academy of Sciences of the USA*, 100, 5567–72.

Chedd, G. (2013). Brains on trial, brainsontrial.com. How does fMRI brain scanning work? Alan Alda and Dr. Nancy Kanwisher, MIT, www.youtube.com/watch?v=nvB9hAarzw4&t=49s

Chemla, E., & Bott, L. (2014). Processing inferences at the semantics/pragmatics frontier: Disjunctions and free choice. *Cognition*, 130(3), 380–396.

Chemla, E., & Singh, R. (2014). Remarks on the experimental turn in the study of scalar implicature. *Language and Linguistics Compass*, 8(9), 373–99.

Chemla, E., & Spector, B. (2011). Experimental evidence for embedded scalar implicatures. *Journal of Semantics*, ffq023.

Chemla, E., Cummins, C., & Singh, R. (2016). Training and timing local scalar enrichments under global pragmatic pressures. *Journal of Semantics*, 34(1), 107–126.

Cheng, P. W., & Holyoak, K. J. (1985). Pragmatic reasoning schemas. *Cognitive Psychology*, 17(4), 391–416.

Chevallier, C., Kohls, G., Troiani, V., Brodkin, E. S., & Schultz, R. T. (2012). The social motivation theory of autism. *Trends in Cognitive Sciences*, 16(4), 231–9.

Chevallier, C., Noveck, I., Happé, F., & Wilson, D. (2009). From acoustics to grammar: Perceiving and interpreting grammatical prosody in adolescents with Asperger syndrome. *Research in Autism Spectrum Disorders*, 3(2), 502–16.

Chevallier, C., Noveck, I., Happe, F., & Wilson, D. (2011). What's in a voice? Prosody as a test case for the Theory of Mind account of autism. *Neuropsychologia*, 49(3), 507–17.

Chevallier, C., Noveck, I. A., Nazir, T., et al. (2008). Making disjunctions exclusive. *The Quarterly Journal of Experimental Psychology*, 61(11), 1741–60.

Chevallier, C., Parish-Morris, J., Tonge, N., et al. (2014). Susceptibility to the audience effect explains performance gap between children with and without autism in a theory of mind task. *Journal of Experimental Psychology: General*, 143(3), 972.

Chevallier, C., Wilson, D., Happé, F., & Noveck, I. (2010). Scalar inferences in autism spectrum disorders. *Journal of Autism and Developmental Disorders*, 40(9), 1104–17.

Chierchia, G. (2004). Scalar implicatures, polarity phenomena, and the syntax/pragmatics interface. *Structures and Beyond*, 3, 39–103.

Chierchia, G., Fox, D., & Spector, B. (2012). The grammatical view of scalar implicatures and the relationship between semantics and pragmatics. In *Semantics: An International Handbook of Natural Language Meaning* (Vol. 3, pp. 2297–332). Mouton de Gruyter, Berlin.

Chomsky, N. (1959). A review of BF Skinner's verbal behavior. *Language*, 35(1), 26–58.

Clark, E. V. (1990). Speaker perspective in language acquisition. *Linguistics*, 28(6), 1201–20.

Clark, H. H. (1996). *Using Language*. Cambridge University Press, Cambridge, MA.

Clark, H. H., & Chase, W. G. (1972). On the process of comparing sentences against pictures. *Cognitive Psychology*, 3(3), 472–517.

Clark, H. H., & Gerrig, R. J. (1984). On the pretense theory of irony. *Journal of Experimental Psychology: General*, 113(1), 121–6.

Clark, H. H., & Lucy, P. (1975). Understanding what is meant from what is said: A study in conversationally conveyed requests. *Journal of Verbal Learning and Verbal Behavior*, 14(1), 56–72.

Clark, H. H., & Wilkes-Gibbs, D. (1986). Referring as a collaborative process. *Cognition*, 22(1), 1–39.

Cohen, L. J. (1971). Some remarks on Grice's views about the logical particles of natural language. In *Pragmatics of Natural Languages* (pp. 50–68). Springer, Dordrecht.

Coltheart, M. (1999). Modularity and cognition. *Trends in Cognitive Sciences*, 3(3), 115–20.

Cooney, J. W., & Gazzaniga, M. S. (2003). Neurological disorders and the structure of human consciousness. *Trends in Cognitive Sciences*, 7(4), 161–5.

Cooper, L. A., & Shepard, R. N. (1973). Chronometric studies of the rotation of mental images. In W. G. Chase (ed.), *Visual Information Processing*. Academic Press, New York, NY.

Cosmides, L. (1989). The logic of social exchange: Has natural selection shaped how humans reason? Studies with the Wason selection task. *Cognition*, 31(3), 187–276.

Coulson, S. (2004). Electrophysiology and pragmatic language comprehension. In *Experimental Pragmatics* (pp. 187–206). Palgrave Macmillan, UK.

Csibra, G. (2010). Recognizing communicative intentions in infancy. *Mind & Language*, 25(2), 141–68.

Csibra, G., & Gergely, G. (2009). Natural pedagogy. *Trends in Cognitive Sciences*, 13(4), 148–53.

Dale, R., & Duran, N. D. (2011). The cognitive dynamics of negated sentence verification. *Cognitive Science*, 35(5), 983–96.

Davidson, D. (1974). Belief and the basis of meaning. *Synthese*, 27(3–4), 309–23.

Davies, C., & Katsos, N. (2010). Over-informative children: Production/comprehension asymmetry or tolerance to pragmatic violations? *Lingua*, 120(8), 1956–72.

de Almeida, R. G. (2004). The effect of context on the processing of type-shifting verbs. *Brain and Language*, 90(1), 249–61.

de Almeida, R. G., & Riven, L. (2012). Indeterminacy and coercion effects: Minimal representations with pragmatic enrichment. In A. M. DiSciullo (ed.), *Towards a Biolinguistic Understanding of Grammar* (pp. 277–301). John Benjamins, Amsterdam.

Deamer, F. M. (2013). An investigation into the processes and mechanisms underlying the comprehension of metaphor and hyperbole (Doctoral dissertation, UCL (University College London)).

Degen, J. (2015). Investigating the distribution of some (but not all) implicatures using corpora and web-based methods. *Semantics and Pragmatics*, 8(11), 1–55.

Degen, J., & Tanenhaus, M. K. (2015). Processing scalar implicature: A constraint-based approach. *Cognitive Science*, 39(4), 667–710.

Dehaene, S., Naccache, L., Cohen, L., Le Bihan, D., Mangin, J. F., Poline, J. B., & Rivière, D. (2001). Cerebral mechanisms of word masking and unconscious repetition priming. *Nature Neuroscience*, 4(7), 752.

De Neys, W., Schaeken, W., & d'Ydewalle, G. (2005). Working memory and everyday conditional reasoning: Retrieval and inhibition of stored counterexamples. *Thinking & Reasoning*, 11(4), 349–81.

De Neys, W., & Schaeken, W. (2007). When people are more logical under cognitive load: Dual task impact on scalar implicature. *Experimental Psychology*, 54(2):128–33.

De Saussure, Ferdinand. (1993) *Third Course of Lectures on General Linguistics (1910–1911)*. Pergamon Press, New York, NY.

Denkel, A. (1985). What makes meaning non-natural? *The Southern Journal of Philosophy*, 23(4), 445–50.

Dennett, D. C. (1989). *The Intentional Stance*. MIT Press, Cambridge, MA.

De Renzi, E., & Vignolo, L. A. (1962). The token test: A sensitive test to detect receptive disturbances in aphasics. *Brain*, 85(4), 665–78.

Dokic, J. (2012) Indexicality. In A. Newen & R. van Riel (eds.), *Identity, Language, & Mind. An Introduction to the Philosophy of John Perry* (pp. 13–31). CSLI Publications, Stanford, CA.

Domaneschi, F., Carrea, E., Penco, C., & Greco, A. (2014). The cognitive load of presupposition triggers: Mandatory and optional repairs in presupposition failure. *Language, Cognition and Neuroscience*, 29(1), 136–46.

Donaldson, M. (1982). Conservation: What is the question? *British Journal of Psychology*, 73(2), 199–207.

Ducrot, O. (1972). *Dire et ne pas dire*. Hermann, Paris.

Dufour, N., Redcay, E., Young, L., et al. (2013). Similar brain activation during false belief tasks in a large sample of adults with and without autism. *PLoS One*, 8(9), e75468.

Duffley, P. J., & Larrivée, P. (2014) The emergence of implicit meaning: Scalar implicatures with some. *International Journal of Corpus Linguisitics*, 19, 526–44.

Dulany, D. E., & Hilton, D. J. (1991). Conversational implicature, conscious representation, and the conjunction fallacy. *Social Cognition*, 9(1), 85–110.

Eberhard, K. M., Spivey-Knowlton, M. J., Sedivy, J. C., & Tanenhaus, M. K. (1995). Eye movements as a window into real-time spoken language comprehension in natural contexts. *Journal of Psycholinguistic Research*, 24(6), 409–36.

Eimas, P. D., Siqueland, E. R., Jusczyk, P., & Vigorito, J. (1971). Speech perception in infants. *Science*, 171, 303–306.

Elsabbagh M., Mercure, E., Hudry, K., et al. (2012). Infant neural sensitivity to dynamic eye gaze is associated with later emerging autism. *Current Biology*, 22, 338–42.

Evans, J. S. B. (1993). The mental model theory of conditional reasoning: Critical appraisal and revision. *Cognition*, 48(1), 1–20.

 (1998). Matching bias in conditional reasoning: Do we understand it after 25 years? *Thinking & Reasoning*, 4(1), 45–110.

Evans, J. S. B., Clibbens, J., & Rood, B. (1996). The role of implicit and explicit negation in conditional reasoning bias. *Journal of Memory and Language*, 35(3), 392–409.

Evans, J. S. B., Handley, S. J., Neilens, H., & Over, D. (2008). Understanding causal conditionals: A study of individual differences. *The Quarterly Journal of Experimental Psychology*, 61(9), 1291–7.

Evans, J. S. B., Handley, S. J., & Bacon, A. M. (2009). Reasoning under time pressure: A study of causal conditional inference. *Experimental Psychology*, 56(2), 77–83.

Evans, J. S. B., Handley, S. J., Neilens, H., & Over, D. E. (2007). Thinking about conditionals: A study of individual differences. *Memory & Cognition*, 35(7), 1772–84.

Falkum, I. L., Recasens, M., Clark, E. V. (2017). "The moustache sits down first": On the acquisition of metonymy. *Journal of Child Language*, 44(7): 87–119.

Ferreira, F., Bailey, K. G., & Ferraro, V. (2002). Good-enough representations in language comprehension. *Current Directions in Psychological Science*, 11(1), 11–15.

Filik, R., & Moxey, L. M. (2010). The on-line processing of written irony. *Cognition*, 116(3), 421–36.

Flavell, J. H., Speer, J. R., Green, F. L., August, D. L., & Whitehurst, G. J. (1981). The development of comprehension monitoring and knowledge about communication. *Monographs of the Society for Research in Child Development*, 46(Serial No. 192).

Folstein, J. R., & Van Petten, C. (2008). Influence of cognitive control and mismatch on the N2 component of the ERP: A review. *Psychophysiology*, 45(1), 152–70.

Frank, M. C., & Goodman, N. D. (2012). Predicting pragmatic reasoning in language games. *Science*, 336(6084), 998.

    (2014). Inferring word meanings by assuming that speakers are informative. *Cognitive Psychology*, 75, 80–96.

Franke, M. (2011). Quantity implicatures, exhaustive interpretation, and rational conversation. *Semantics and Pragmatics*, 4, 1–1.

Franke, M., & Degen, J. (2016). Reasoning in reference games: Individual-vs. population-level probabilistic modeling. *PLoS One*, 11(5), e0154854.

Franke, M., & Jäger, G. (2016). Probabilistic pragmatics, or why Bayes' rule is probably important for pragmatics. *Zeitschrift für sprachwissenschaft*, 35(1), 3–44.

Franke, M., Schlotterbeck, F., & Augurzky, P. (2016). Embedded scalars, preferred readings and prosody: An experimental revisit. *Journal of Semantics*, 34(1), ffw007.

Frazier, L. (1979). *On Comprehending Sentences: Syntactic Parsing Strategies*. Indiana University Linguistics Club, Bloomington, IN.

Friederici, A. D., & Meyer, M. (2004). The brain knows the difference: Two types of grammatical violations. *Brain Research*, 1000(1), 72–7.

Friederici, A. D. (2002). Towards a neural basis of auditory sentence processing. *Trends in Cognitive Sciences*, 6(2), 78–84.

Frisson, S., & Pickering, M. J. (1999). The processing of metonymy: Evidence from eye movements. *Journal of Experimental Psychology: Learning, Memory, and Cognition*, 25(6), 1366.

Frith, C. D., & Frith, U. (2006). The neural basis of mentalizing. *Neuron*, 50(4), 531–4.

Garrod, S., & Anderson, A. (1987). Saying what you mean in dialog: A study in conceptual and semantic co-ordination. *Cognition*, 27, 181–218.

Gazdar, G. (1979). *Pragmatics: Implicature, Presupposition and Logical Form*. Academic Press, New York, NY.

Gazzaniga, M. S. (2003). The split brain revisited. *Scientific American–American Edition*, 287, 26–31.

Geis, M. L., & Zwicky, A. M. (1971). On invited inferences. *Linguistic Inquiry*, 2(4), 561–6.

Gergely, G., & Pléh, C. (1994). Lexical processing in an agglutinative language and the organization of the lexicon. *Folia Linguistica*, 28(1–2), 175–204.

Gerrig, R. J. (1989). The time course of sense creation. *Memory & Cognition*, 17(2), 194–207.

Gervais, H., Belin, P., Boddaert, N., et al. (2004). Abnormal cortical voice processing in autism. *Nature Neuroscience*, 7(8), 801–2.

Geurts, B. (2009). Scalar implicature and local pragmatics. *Mind & Language*, 24(1), 51–79.

    (2010). *Quantity Implicatures*. Cambridge University Press, Cambridge, MA.

Geurts, B., & Beaver, D. I. (2007). Discourse representation theory. *Stanford Online Encyclopedia*. In *The Stanford Encyclopedia of Philosophy*, ed. Edward N. Zalta. CSLI, Stanford University.

Geurts, B., & Pouscoulous, N. (2009). Embedded implicatures?!? *Semantics and Pragmatics*, 2(4), 1–34.

Geurts, B., & van Tiel, B. (2013). Embedded scalars. *Semantics and Pragmatics*, 6(9), 1–37.

Gibbs, R. W. (1980). Spilling the beans on understanding and memory for idioms in conversation. *Memory & Cognition*, 8(2), 149–56.

(1983). Do people always process the literal meanings of indirect requests? *Journal of Experimental Psychology: Learning, Memory, and Cognition*, 9(3), 524.

(1986). On the psycholinguistics of sarcasm. *Journal of Experimental Psychology: General*, 115(1), 3.

Jr. (1990). Comprehending figurative referential descriptions. *Journal of Experimental Psychology: Learning, Memory, and Cognition*, 16(1), 56.

(1992). Categorization and metaphor understanding. *Psychological Review*, 99(3), 572–7.

(1994). *The Poetics of Mind: Figurative Thought, Language, and Understanding*. Cambridge University Press, New York, NY.

Jr. (2002). A new look at literal meaning in understanding what is said and implicated. *Journal of Pragmatics*, 34(4), 457–86.

Gibbs, R. W., Jr., & Colston, H. L. (2012). *Interpreting Figurative Meaning*. Cambridge University Press, New York, NY.

Gildea, P., & Glucksberg, S. (1983). On understanding metaphor: The role of context. *Journal of Verbal Learning and Verbal Behavior*, 22(5), 577–90.

Giora, R. (1997). Understanding figurative and literal language: The graded salience hypothesis. *Cognitive Linguistics (includes Cognitive Linguistic Bibliography)*, 8(3), 183–206.

(1999). On the priority of salient meanings: Studies of literal and figurative language. *Journal of Pragmatics*, 31(7), 919–29.

(2002). Literal vs. figurative language: Different or equal? *Journal of Pragmatics*, 34(4), 487–506.

(2003). *On Our Mind: Salience, Context, and Figurative Language*. Oxford University Press, Oxford.

(2008). "Is metaphor unique." In R. W. Gibbs ed. *The Cambridge Handbook of Metaphor and Thought* (pp. 143–160). Cambridge University Press, Cambridge.

Giora, R., & Fein, O. (1999). Irony comprehension: The graded salience hypothesis. *Humour*, 12(4), 425–36.

Giora, R., Fein, O., & Schwartz, T. (1998). Irony: Grade salience and indirect negation. *Metaphor and Symbol*, 13(2), 83–101.

Ginzburg J. (2012) *The Interactive Stance: Meaning for Conversation*. Oxford University Press.

Girotto, V., Mazzocco, A., & Tasso, A. (1997). The effect of premise order in conditional reasoning: A test of the mental model theory. *Cognition*, 63(1), 1–28.

Glucksberg, S. (2003). The psycholinguistics of metaphor. *Trends in Cognitive Sciences*, 7(2), 92–6.

Glucksberg, S., Gildea, P., & Bookin, H. B. (1982). On understanding nonliteral speech: Can people ignore metaphors? *Journal of Verbal Learning and Verbal Behavior*, 21(1), 85–98.

González Fuente, S., Prieto Vives, P., & Noveck, I. A. (2016). A fine-grained analysis of the acoustic cues involved in verbal irony recognition in French. Barnes J, Brugos A, Shattuck-Hufnagel S, Veilleux N, eds. Speech Prosody 2016; 2016 May 31–June 3; Boston, United States of America. [place unknown]: International Speech Communication Association; 2016. p. 902–6. DOI: 10.21437/SpeechProsody. 2016-185.

Goodman, N. D., & Frank, M. C. (2016). Pragmatic language interpretation as probabilistic inference. *Trends in Cognitive Sciences*, 20(11), 818–29.

Grassmann, S., & Tomasello, M. (2010). Young children follow pointing over words in interpreting acts of reference. *Developmental Science*, 13(1), 252–63.

Grice, H. P. (1961). The causal theory of perception. *Proceedings of the Aristotelian Society*, 35, 121–52.

(1989). *Studies in the Way of Words*. Harvard University Press, Cambridge, MA.

(1967). *William James Lectures*. Harvard University Press, Cambridge, MA.

(1957). Meaning. *The Philosophical Review*, 66(3), 377–88.

(1975). *Logic and Conversation*. Academic Press, New York, NY, 41–58.

Grodner, D. J., Klein, N. M., Carbary, K. M., & Tanenhaus, M. K. (2010). "Some," and possibly all, scalar inferences are not delayed: Evidence for immediate pragmatic enrichment. *Cognition*, 116(1), 42–55.

Grodner, D., & Sedivy, J. (2011) The effect of speaker-specific information on pragmatic inferences. In E. Gibson & N. Pearlmutter (eds.), *The Processing and Acquisition of Reference* (Vol. 2327, pp. 239–72). MIT Press, Cambridge, MA.

Grossi, G. (2014). A module is a module is a module: Evolution of modularity in evolutionary psychology. *Dialectical Anthropology*, 38(3), 333–51.

Guasti, M. T., Chierchia, G., Crain, S., et al. (2005). Why children and adults sometimes (but not always) compute implicatures. *Language and Cognitive Processes*, 20(5), 667–96.

Hagoort, P. (2005). On Broca, brain, and binding: A new framework. *Trends in Cognitive Sciences*, 9(9), 416–23.

Happé, F. G. (1993). Communicative competence and theory of mind in autism: A test of relevance theory. *Cognition*, 48(2), 101–19.

Hare, B., & Tomasello, M. (2004). Chimpanzees are more skilful in competitive than in cooperative cognitive tasks. *Animal Behaviour*, 68(3), 571–81.

Hartshorne, J. K., Snedeker, J., Liem Azar, S. Y. M., & Kim, A. E. (2015). The neural computation of scalar implicature. *Language, Cognition and Neuroscience*, 30(5), 620–34.

Hartshorne, J. K., & Germine, L. T. (2015). When does cognitive functioning peak? The asynchronous rise and fall of different cognitive abilities across the life span. *Psychological Science*, 26(4), 433–43.

Haspelmath, M., & König, E. (1998). Concessive conditionals in the languages of Europe. In J. Van der Auwera & D. Ó. Baoill (eds.), *Adverbial Constructions in the Languages of Europe* (Vol. 3). Mouton, Berlin.

Hirst, W., & Weil, J. (1982). Acquisition of epistemic and deontic meaning of modals. *Journal of Child Language*, 9(03), 659–66.

Horn, L. R. (1972). On the semantic properties of logical operators in English. Doctoral dissertation, University of California, Los Angeles.

(1973). Greek Grice: A brief survey of proto-conversational rules in the history of logic. *CLS,* 9, 205–14.

(1984). Toward a new taxonomy for pragmatic inference: Q-based and R-based implicature. In D. Schiffrin (ed.), *Meaning, Form, and Use in Context: Linguistic Applications (GURT '84)* (pp. 11–42). Georgetown University Press, Washington, DC (Reprinted in Kasher (ed., 1998), vol. IV: 389–418.)

(1989). *A Natural History of Negation.* University of Chicago Press, Chicago, IL (Expanded reissue, Stanford, CA: CSLI, 2001).

(1992). *The Said and the Unsaid. Semantics and Linguistic Theory II* (pp. 163–92). Ohio State University Department of Linguistics, Columbus, OH.

(2000). From if to iff: Conditional perfection as pragmatic strengthening. *Journal of Pragmatics,* 32(3), 289–326.

(2006). The border wars: A neo-Gricean perspective. In K. von Heusinger and K. Turner (eds.), *Where Semantics Meets Pragmatics* (pp. 21–48). Elsevier, Amsterdam.

Huang, Y. T., & Snedeker, J. (2009a). Online interpretation of scalar quantifiers: Insight into the semantics–pragmatics interface. *Cognitive Psychology,* 58(3), 376–415.

(2009b). Semantic meaning and pragmatic interpretation in 5-year-olds: Evidence from real-time spoken language comprehension. *Developmental Psychology,* 45(6), 1723.

Hughes, C., & Russell, J. (1993). Autistic children's difficulty with mental disengagement from an object: Its implications for theories of autism. *Developmental Psychology,* 29, 498–510.

Inhoff, A. W., Lima, S. D., & Carroll, P. J. (1984). Contextual effects on metaphor comprehension in reading. *Memory & Cognition,* 12(6), 558–67.

Ippolito, M. (2010). Embedded implicatures? Remarks on the debate between globalist and localist theories. *Semantics and Pragmatics,* 3, 1–15.

Ironsmith, M., & Whitehurst, G. J. (1978). The development of listener abilities in communication: How children deal with ambiguous information. *Child Development,* 49(2), 348–52.

Ivanko, S. L., & Pexman, P. M. (2003). Context incongruity and irony processing. *Discourse Processes,* 35(3), 241–79.

Liszkowski, U., Carpenter, M., & Tomasello, M. (2007). Reference and attitude in infant pointing. *Journal of Child Language,* 34(1), 1–20.

Johansson, P., Hall, L., Sikström, S., & Olsson, A. (2005). Failure to detect mismatches between intention and outcome in a simple decision task. *Science (New York, N.Y.),* 310 (5745), 116–9. doi:10.1126/science.1111709

Johnson-Laird, P. N., & Byrne, R. M. (2002). Conditionals: A theory of meaning, pragmatics, and inference. *Psychological Review,* 109(4), 646.

Johnson-Laird, P. N., Legrenzi, P., & Legrenzi, M. S. (1972). Reasoning and a sense of reality. *British Journal of Psychology,* 63(3), 395–400.

Jorgensen, J., Miller, G. A., & Sperber, D. (1984). Test of the mention theory of irony. *Journal of Experimental Psychology: General,* 113(1), 112.

Just, M. A., & Carpenter, P. A. (1971). Comprehension of negation with quantification. *Journal of Verbal Learning and Verbal Behavior,* 10(3), 244–53.

Kahneman, D. (2011). *Thinking, Fast and Slow.* Macmillan.

Kahneman, D., & Tversky, A. (1982). On the study of statistical intuitions. *Cognition,* 11(2), 123–41.

Kail, M. (1978). La compréhension des présuppositions chez l'enfant. *L'année psychologique*, 78(2), 425–44.

Kanner, L. (1943). Autistic disturbances of affective contact. *Nervous Child*, 2, 217–50.

Kao, J. T., & Goodman, N. (2015). Let's talk (ironically) about the weather: Modeling verbal irony. In Noelle D. C. et al. (eds.), Proceedings of the 37th annual conference of the Cognitive Science Society (held 22–25 July 2015). Pasadena, CA, USA.

Kao, J. T., Wu, J. Y., Bergen, L., & Goodman, N. D. (2014). Nonliteral understanding of number words. *Proceedings of the National Academy of Sciences*, 111(33), 12002–7.

Katsos, N., Cummins, C., Ezeizabarrena, M. J., et al. (2016). Cross-linguistic patterns in the acquisition of quantifiers. *Proceedings of the National Academy of Sciences*, 113(33), 9244–9.

Katsos, N., & Bishop, D. V. (2011). Pragmatic tolerance: Implications for the acquisition of informativeness and implicature. *Cognition*, 120(1), 67–81.

Katz, A. N. (2005). Discourse and sociocultural factors in understanding nonliteral language. In H. Colston & A. N. Katz (eds.), *Figurative Language Comprehension: Social and Cultural Influences* (pp. 183–207). Erlbaum, Mahwah, NJ.

Kaup, B., Ludtke, J., & Zwaan, R. A. (2005, January). Effects of negation, truth value, and delay on picture recognition after reading affirmative and negative sentences. In Bara B. G., Barsalou L., Bucciarelli M., (eds.) Proceedings of the 27th Annual Conference of the Cognitive Science Society, (pp. 1114–1119). Lawrence Erlbaum, Mahwah, NJ.

Kaup, B., Yaxley, R. H., Madden, C. J., Zwaan, R. A., & Lüdtke, J. (2007). Experiential simulations of negated text information. *The Quarterly Journal of Experimental Psychology*, 60(7), 976–90.

Keysar, B., Barr, D. J., Balin, J. A., & Brauner, J. S. (2000). Taking perspective in conversation: The role of mutual knowledge in comprehension. *Psychological Science*, 11(1), 32–8.

Kintsch, W., & Van Dijk, T. A. (1978). Toward a model of text comprehension and production. *Psychological Review*, 85(5), 363–94.

Kissine, M. (2012). Pragmatics, cognitive flexibility and autism spectrum disorders. *Mind & Language*, 27(1), 1–28.

Kissine, M., Cano-Chervel, J., Carlier, S., et al. (2015). Children with autism understand indirect speech acts: Evidence from a semi-structured act-out task. *PLoS One*, 10(11), e0142191.

Klein, D. E., & Murphy, G. L. (2001). The representation of polysemous words. *Journal of Memory and Language*, 45(2), 259–82.

Klin A. (1991). Young autistic children's listening preferences in regard to speech: A possible characterization of the symptom of social withdrawal. *Journal of Autism and Developmental Disorders*, 21, 29–42.

Klin, C. M., Weingartner, K. M., Guzmán, A. E., & Levine, W. H. (2004). Readers' sensitivity to linguistic cues in narratives: How salience influences anaphor resolution. *Memory & Cognition*, 32(3), 511–22.

Korta, K. and Perry, J., "Pragmatics", The Stanford Encyclopedia of Philosophy (Winter 2015 Edition), Edward N. Zalta (ed.), https://plato.stanford.edu/archives/win2015/entries/pragmatics/

Kovács, Á. M., Tauzin, T., Téglás, E., Gergely, G., & Csibra, G. (2014). Pointing as epistemic request: 12-month-olds point to receive new information. *Infancy*, 19(6), 543–57.

Krauss, R. M., & Glucksberg, S. (1969). The development of communication: Competence as a function of age. *Child Development*, 40(1), 255–66.

Kreuz, R. J., & Glucksberg, S. (1989). How to be sarcastic: The echoic reminder theory of verbal irony. *Journal of Experimental Psychology: General*, 118(4), 374.

Kronmüller, E., & Barr, D. J. (2007). Perspective-free pragmatics: Broken precedents and the recovery-from-preemption hypothesis. *Journal of Memory and Language*, 56(3), 436–55.

  (2015). Referential precedents in spoken language comprehension: a review and meta-analysis. *Journal of Memory and Language*, 83, 1–19.

Kronmüller, E., Morisseau, T., & Noveck, I. A. (2014). Show me the pragmatic contribution: A developmental investigation of contrastive inference. *Journal of Child Language*, 41(5), 985–1014.

Kronmüller, E., Noveck, I., Rivera, N., Jaume-Guazzini, F., & Barr, D. (2017). The positive side of a negative reference: The delay between linguistic processing and common ground. *Royal Society Open Science*, 4(2), 160827.

Kuhl, P. K., Coffey-Corina, S., Padden, D., & Dawson, G. (2005). Links between social and linguistic processing of speech in preschool children with autism: Behavioral and electrophysiological measures. *Developmental Science*, 8(1), F1–12.

Kuperberg, G. R., Choi, A., Cohn, N., Paczynski, M., & Jackendoff, R. (2010). Electrophysiological correlates of complement coercion. *Journal of Cognitive Neuroscience*, 22(12), 2685–701.

Kutas, M. (1993). In the company of other words: Electrophysiological evidence for single-word and sentence context effects. *Language and Cognitive Processes*, 8(4), 533–72.

Kutas, M., & Hillyard, S. A. (1980a). Reading between the lines: Event-related brain potentials during natural sentence processing. *Brain and Language*, 11(2), 354–73.

  (1980b). Event-related brain potentials to semantically inappropriate and surprisingly large words. *Biological Psychology*, 11(2), 99–116.

  (1980c). Reading senseless sentences: Brain potentials reflect semantic incongruity. *Science*, 207(4427), 203–5.

  (1984). Brain potentials during reading reflect word expectancy and semantic association. *Nature*, 307(5947), 161–3.

Larrivee, P., & Duffley, P. (2014). The emergence of implicit meaning: Scalar implicatures with some. *International Journal of Corpus Linguistics*, 19(4), 530–47.

La Pointe, L. B., & Engle, R. W. (1990). Simple and complex word spans as measures of working memory capacity. *Journal of Experimental Psychology: Learning, Memory, and Cognition*, 16(6), 1118.

Lai, V. T., Curran, T., & Menn, L. (2009). Comprehending conventional and novel metaphors: An ERP study. *Brain Research*, 1284, 145–55.

Lauer, S. (2013). Towards a dynamic pragmatics (Doctoral dissertation, Stanford University).

Landman, F. (1998) Plurals and maximalization. In S. Rothstein (ed.), *Events and Grammar*. Kluwer, Dordrecht.

Lea, R. B. (1995). On-line evidence for elaborative logical inferences in text. *Journal of Experimental Psychology: Learning, Memory, and Cognition*, 21(6), 1469.

Lea, R. B., Rapp, D. N., Elfenbein, A., Mitchel, A. D., & Romine, R. S. (2008). Sweet silent thought alliteration and resonance in poetry comprehension. *Psychological Science*, 19(7), 709–16.

Lepore, E., & Stone, M. (2015). *Imagination and Convention: Distinguishing Grammar and Inference in Language*. Oxford University Press, Oxford.

Levelt, W. J. (1972). Some psychological aspects of linguistic data. *Linguistische Berichte*, 17, 18–30.

Levinson, S. C. (1980). Speech act theory: The state of the art. *Language Teaching*, 13(1–2), 5–24.

(1983). *Pragmatics*. Cambridge Textbooks in Linguistics, Cambridge, MA.

(2000). *Presumptive Meanings: The Theory of Generalized Conversational Implicature*. MIT Press, Cambridge, MA.

Lewis, D. (1989) *Convention*. Harvard University Press, Cambridge, MA.

Lewis, M. (2016) *The Undoing Project: A Friendship That Changed Our Minds*. W.W. Norton and Company, New York, NY.

Lichtenstein, S., Slovic, P., Fischhoff, B., Layman, M., & Combs, B. (1978). Judged frequency of lethal events. *Journal of Experimental Psychology: Human Learning and Memory*, 4(6), 551.

Liszkowski, U., Carpenter, M., Striano, T., & Tomasello, M. (2006). 12-and 18-month-olds point to provide information for others. *Journal of Cognition and Development*, 7(2), 173–87.

Ma, N., Vandekerckhove, M., Van Overwalle, F., Seurinck, R., & Fias, W. (2011). Spontaneous and intentional trait inferences recruit a common mentalizing network to a different degree: Spontaneous inferences activate only its core areas. *Social Neuroscience*, 6(2), 123–38.

MacLeod, C. M. (1992). The Stroop task: The "gold standard" of attentional measures. *Journal of Experimental Psychology: General*, 121(1), 12–14.

Magri, G. (2011). Another argument for embedded scalar implicatures based on oddness in downward entailing environments. *Semantics and Pragmatics*, 4, 1–51.

Marcus, S. L., & Rips, L. J. (1979). Conditional reasoning. *Journal of Verbal Learning and Verbal Behavior*, 18(2), 199–223.

Markman, E. M. (1978). Empirical versus logical solutions to part-whole comparison problems concerning classes and collections. *Child Development*, 49(1), 168–77.

Marr, D. (1982). *Vision*. Freeman, San Francisco.

Matsumoto, Y. (1995). The conversational condition on Horn scales. *Linguistics and Philosophy*, 18(1), 21–60.

Mazzarella, D. (2015). Politeness, relevance and scalar inferences. *Journal of Pragmatics*, 79, 93–106.

Mazzarella, D., Trouche, E., Mercier, H. & Noveck, I. A. (2018). Believing what you're told: Politeness and scalar inferences. Ms.

McElree, B., Frisson, S., & Pickering, M. J. (2006). Deferred interpretations: Why starting Dickens is taxing but reading Dickens isn't. *Cognitive Science*, 30(1), 181–92.

McElree, B., & Nordlie, J. (1999). Literal and figurative interpretations are computed in equal time. *Psychonomic Bulletin & Review*, 6(3), 486–94.

McElree, B., Traxler, M. J., Pickering, M. J., Seely, R. E., & Jackendoff, R. (2001). Reading time evidence for enriched composition. *Cognition*, 78(1), B17–25.

McGarrigle, J., & Donaldson, M. (1975). Conservation accidents. *Cognition*, 3(4), 341–50.

McGarrigle, J., Grieve, R., & Hughes, M. (1978). Interpreting inclusion: A contribution to the study of the child's cognitive and linguistic development. *Journal of Experimental Child Psychology*, 26(3), 528–50.

McGurk, H., & MacDonald, J. (1976). Hearing lips and seeing voices. *Nature*, 264, 746–8.

McKeon, G. (2014, April 29). Message in a bottle: 10 famous floating note discoveries. *ABC News Australia*. www.abc.net.au/news/2013-04-18/message-in-a-bottle-washes-up-after-28-years/4636320

Mellers, B., Hertwig, R., & Kahneman, D. (2001). Do frequency representations eliminate conjunction effects? An exercise in adversarial collaboration. *Psychological Science*, 12(4), 269–75.

Mercier, H., & Sperber, D. (2011). Why do humans reason? Arguments for an argumentative theory. *Behavioral and Brain Sciences*, 34(2), 57–74.

(2017). *The Enigma of Reason*. Harvard University Press, Cambridge, MA.

Metzing, C., & Brennan, S. E. (2003). When conceptual pacts are broken: Partner-specific effects on the comprehension of referring expressions. *Journal of Memory and Language*, 49(2), 201–13.

Miklósi, Á., & Soproni, K. (2006). A comparative analysis of animals' understanding of the human pointing gesture. *Animal Cognition*, 9(2), 81–93.

Monetta, L., Grindrod, C. M., & Pell, M. D. (2009). Irony comprehension and theory of mind deficits in patients with Parkinson's disease. *Cortex*, 45(8), 972–81.

Monti, M. M., Parsons, L. M., & Osherson, D. N. (2009). The boundaries of language and thought in deductive inference. *Proceedings of the National Academy of Sciences*, 106(30), 12554–9.

Morier, D. M., & Borgida, E. (1984). The conjunction fallacy: A task specific phenomenon? *Personality and Social Psychology Bulletin*, 10(2), 243–52.

Morisseau, T., Davies, C., & Matthews, D. (2013). How do 3-and 5-year-olds respond to under- and over-informative utterances? *Journal of Pragmatics*, 59, 26–39.

Murphy, G. L. (2002). *The Big Book of Concepts*. MIT Press, Cambridge, MA.

Murphy, G. L., & Andrew, J. M. (1993). The conceptual basis of antonymy and synonymy in adjectives. *Journal of Memory and Language*, 32(3), 301.

Neale, S. (1992). Paul Grice and the philosophy of language. *Linguistics and Philosophy*, 15(5), 509–59.

Newstead, S. E. (1995). Gricean implicatures and syllogistic reasoning. *Journal of Memory and Language*, 34(5), 644.

Nieuwland, M. S., Ditman, T., & Kuperberg, G. R. (2010). On the incrementality of pragmatic processing: An ERP investigation of informativeness and pragmatic abilities. *Journal of Memory and Language*, 63(3), 324–46.

Nieuwland, M. S., & Kuperberg, G. R. (2008). When the truth is not too hard to handle an event-related potential study on the pragmatics of negation. *Psychological Science*, 19(12), 1213–18.

Nisbett, R. E., & Ross, L. (1980). *Human Inference: Strategies and Shortcomings of Social Judgment*. Prentice-Hall, Englewood Cliffs, NJ.

Nisbett, R. E., & Wilson, T. D. (1977). Telling more than we can know: Verbal reports on mental processes. *Psychological Review*, 84(3), 231–59.

Noveck, I. A. (2001). When children are more logical than adults: Investigations of scalar implicature. *Cognition*, 78(2), 165–88.

Noveck, I., & Chevaux, F. (2002). The pragmatic development of and. In B. Skarabella (Ed.), Proceedings of the 26th Annual BUCLD (pp. 453–63). Cascadilla Press, Somerville, MA.

Noveck, I. A., & O'Brien, D. P. (1996). To what extent do pragmatic reasoning schemas affect performance on Wason's selection task?. *The Quarterly Journal of Experimental Psychology Section A*, 49(2), 463–489.

Noveck, I. A., Bianco, M., & Castry, A. (2001). The costs and benefits of metaphor. *Metaphor and Symbol*, 16(1–2), 109–21.

Noveck, I., Bonnefond, M., & Van der Henst, J. B. (2011). Squib: A deflationary account of invited inferences. *Belgian Journal of Linguistics*, 25(1), 195–208.

Noveck, I., Chevallier, C., Chevaux, F., Musolino, J., & Bott, L. (2009). Children's enrichments of conjunctive sentences in context (pp. 211–34). *Utterance Interpretation and Cognitive Models*. Emerald, Bingley.

Noveck, I. A., Chierchia, G., Chevaux, F., Guelminger, R., & Sylvestre, E. (2002). Linguistic-pragmatic factors in interpreting disjunctions. *Thinking & Reasoning*, 8(4), 297–326.

Noveck, I. A., Goel, V., & Smith, K. W. (2004). The neural basis of conditional reasoning with arbitrary content. *Cortex*, 40(4), 613–22.

Noveck, I. A., Ho, S., & Sera, M. (1996). Children's understanding of epistemic modals. *Journal of Child Language*, 23(3), 621–43.

Noveck, I. A., & Posada, A. (2003). Characterizing the time course of an implicature: An evoked potentials study. *Brain and Language*, 85, 203–10.

Noveck, I. A., & Reboul, A. (2008). Experimental pragmatics: A Gricean turn in the study of language. *Trends in Cognitive Sciences*, 12(11), 425–31.

Noveck, I. A., & Sperber, D. (2004) *Experimental Pragmatics*. Palgrave Macmillan, Basingstoke.

   (2007). The why and how of experimental pragmatics: The case of 'scalar inferences'. In N. Burton-Roberts (ed.), *Advances in Pragmatics*. Palgrave, Basingstoke.

Noveck, I.A., Spotorno, N. (2013). Narrowing. In L. Goldstein (ed.), *Brevity*. Oxford University Press, Oxford.

Nunberg, G. (1978). *The Pragmatics of Reference*. Indiana University Linguistics Club, Bloomington, IN.

Oaksford, M. (2002). Contrast classes and matching bias as explanations of the effects of negation on conditional reasoning. *Thinking & Reasoning*, 8(2), 135–51.

O'Brien, D. P., Braine, M. D., Connell, J. W., et al. (1989). Reasoning about conditional sentences: Development of understanding of cues to quantification. *Journal of Experimental Child Psychology*, 48(1), 90–113.

Onifer, W., & Swinney, D. A. (1981). Accessing lexical ambiguities during sentence comprehension: Effects of frequency of meaning and contextual bias. *Memory & Cognition*, 9(3), 225–36.

Ortony, A. (1993). *Metaphor and Thought*. Cambridge University Press, Cambridge, MA.

Ortony, A., Schallert, D. L., Reynolds, R. E., & Antos, S. J. (1978). Interpreting metaphors and idioms: Some effects of context on comprehension. *Journal of Verbal Learning and Verbal Behavior*, 17(4), 465–77.

Osterhout, L., Bersick, M., & McLaughlin, J. (1997). Brain potentials reflect violations of gender stereotypes. *Memory & Cognition*, 25(3), 273–85.

Osterhout, L., & Holcomb, P. J. (1992). Event-related brain potentials elicited by syntactic anomaly. *Journal of Memory and Language*, 31(6), 785–806.

Osterhout, L., Holcomb, P. J., & Swinney, D. A. (1994). Brain potentials elicited by garden-path sentences: Evidence of the application of verb information during parsing. *Journal of Experimental Psychology: Learning, Memory, and Cognition*, 20(4), 786.

Osterhout, L., & Mobley, L. A. (1995). Event-related brain potentials elicited by failure to agree. *Journal of Memory and Language*, 34(6), 739.

Paolacci, G., & Chandler, J. (2014). Inside the Turk: Understanding Mechanical Turk as a participant pool. *Current Directions in Psychological Science*, 23(3), 184–8.

Papafragou, A., & Musolino, J. (2003). Scalar implicatures: Experiments at the semantics–pragmatics interface. *Cognition*, 86(3), 253–82.

Paris, S. (1973). Comprehension of language connectives and propositional logical relationships. *Journal of Experimental Child Psychology*, 16, 278–91.

Peleg, O., Giora, R., & Fein, O. (2001). Salience and context effects: Two are better than one. *Metaphor and Symbol*, 16(3–4), 173–92.

(2004). Contextual strength: The whens and hows of context effects. In *Experimental Pragmatics* (pp. 172–86). Palgrave Macmillan, UK.

Pexman, P. M. (2008). It's fascinating research: The cognition of verbal irony. *Current Directions in Psychological Science*, 17(4), 286–90.

Pierce K., Conant, D., Hazin, R., Stoner, R., & Desmond, J. (2011). Preference for geometric patterns early in life as a risk factor for autism. *Archives of General Psychiatry*, 68, 101–9.

Pickering, M. J., & Traxler, M. J. (1998). Plausibility and recovery from garden paths: An eye-tracking study. *Journal of Experimental Psychology: Learning, Memory, and Cognition*, 24(4), 940.

Pijnacker, J., Geurts, B., Van Lambalgen, M., et al. (2009a). Defeasible reasoning in high-functioning adults with autism: Evidence for impaired exception-handling. *Neuropsychologia*, 47(3), 644–51.

Pijnacker, J., Hagoort, P., Buitelaar, J., Teunisse, J. P., & Geurts, B. (2009b). Pragmatic inferences in high-functioning adults with autism and Asperger syndrome. *Journal of Autism and Developmental Disorders*, 39(4), 607–18.

Pinker, S. (1997). Words and rules in the human brain. *Nature*, 387(6633), 547.

(2015). *The Sense of Style: The Thinking Person's Guide to Writing in the 21st Century!* Penguin Books, New York, NY.

Politzer, G. (1986). Laws of language use and formal logic. *Journal of Psycholinguistic Research*, 15(1), 47–92.

(1993). *La psychologie du raisonnement : lois de la pragmatique et logique formelle.* Doctorat d'Etat, Paris 8.

(2016). The class inclusion question: A case study in applying pragmatics to the experimental study of cognition. *SpringerPlus*, 5(1), 1133.

Politzer, G., & Noveck, I. A. (1991). Are conjunction rule violations the result of conversational rule violations? *Journal of Psycholinguistic Research*, 20(2), 83–103.

Politzer-Ahles, S., & Gwilliams, L. (2015). Involvement of prefrontal cortex in scalar implicatures: Evidence from magnetoencephalography. *Language, Cognition and Neuroscience*, 30(7), 853–66.

Popper, K. R. (1959). *The Logic of Scientific Discovery.* Hutchinson, London.

Popper, K. (1963). *Conjectures and Refutations: The Growth of Scientific Knowledge.* Routledge & Kegan Paul, London.

Potts, C., Lassiter, D., Levy, R., & Frank, M. C. (2016). Embedded implicatures as pragmatic inferences under compositional lexical uncertainty. *Journal of Semantics*, 33(4), 755–802.

Pouscoulous, N., Noveck, I. A., Politzer, G., & Bastide, A. (2007). A developmental investigation of processing costs in implicature production. *Language Acquisition*, 14(4), 347–75.

Prado, J., & Noveck, I. A. (2006). How reaction time measures elucidate the matching bias and the way negations are processed. *Thinking & Reasoning*, 12(3), 309–28.

(2007). Overcoming perceptual features in logical reasoning: A parametric functional magnetic resonance imaging study. *Journal of Cognitive Neuroscience*, 19(4), 642–57.

Prado, J., Van Der Henst, J. B., & Noveck, I. A. (2010). Recomposing a fragmented literature: How conditional and relational arguments engage different neural systems for deductive reasoning. *Neuroimage*, 51(3), 1213–21.

Premack, D., & Woodruff, G. (1978). Does the chimpanzee have a theory of mind? *Behavioral and Brain Sciences*, 1(4), 515–26.

Pustejovsky, J. (1995). *The Generative Lexicon*. MIT Press, Cambridge, MA.

Pylkkänen, L. (2008). Mismatching meanings in brain and behavior. *Language and Linguistics Compass*, 2(4), 712–38.

Pylkkänen, L., & McElree, B. (2007). An MEG study of silent meaning. *Journal of Cognitive Neuroscience*, 19(11), 1905–21.

Pynte, J., Besson, M., Robichon, F. H., & Poli, J. (1996). The time-course of metaphor comprehension: An event-related potential study. *Brain and Language*, 55(3), 293–316.

Recanati, F. (1986). On defining communicative intentions. *Mind & Language*, 1(3), 213–41.

(2004). *Literal Meaning*. Cambridge University Press, Cambridge, MA.

Reverberi, C., Cherubini, P., Rapisarda, A., et al. (2007). Neural basis of generation of conclusions in elementary deduction. *Neuroimage*, 38(4), 752–62.

Reverberi, C., Shallice, T., D'Agostini, S., Skrap, M., & Bonatti, L. L. (2009). Cortical bases of elementary deductive reasoning: Inference, memory, and metadeduction. *Neuropsychologia*, 47(4), 1107–16.

Rieber, R. W. (1980). *Psychology of Language and Thought: Essays on the Theory and History of Psycholinguistics*. Plenum Press, New York, NY.

Rohrbacher, B. (2015). Jewish law and medieval logic: Why eating horse meat is a punishable offense. *The Journal of Law and Religion*, 30(2), 295.

Rosenwald, M. S. (2013, September 29). Washington Post Empty Stomach? Try filling up at a Gas Station. Retrieved from *Washington Post*.

Rubio-Fernandez, P. (2007). Suppression in metaphor interpretation: Differences between meaning selection and meaning construction. *Journal of Semantics*, 24(4), 345–71.

Rumain, B., Connell, J., & Braine, M. D. (1983). Conversational comprehension processes are responsible for reasoning fallacies in children as well as adults: If is not the biconditional. *Developmental Psychology*, 19(4), 471.

Rundblad, G., & Annaz, D. (2010). Development of metaphor and metonymy comprehension: Receptive vocabulary and conceptual knowledge. *British Journal of Developmental Psychology*, 28(3), 547–63.

Russell, B. (2006). Against grammatical computation of scalar implicatures. *Journal of Semantics*, 23(4), 361–82.

Russell, J. (2002). Cognitive theories of autism. In J. E. Harrison & A. M. Owen (eds.), *Cognitive Deficits in Brain Disorders* (pp. 295–323). Dunitz, London.

Rutherford, M. D., Baron-Cohen, S., & Wheelwright, S. (2002). Reading the mind in the voice: A study with normal adults and adults with Asperger syndrome and high functioning autism. *Journal of Autism and Developmental Disorders*, 32(3), 189–94.

Sauerland, U. (2004). Scalar implicatures in complex sentences. *Linguistics and Philosophy*, 27(3), 367–91.

Saussure, F. D. (1910). Third course of lectures on general linguistics. Retrieved 21 August 2015. www.marxists.org/reference/subject/philosophy/works/fr/saussure.htm

Saxe, R., & Kanwisher, N. (2003). People thinking about thinking people: The role of the temporo-parietal junction in "theory of mind". *Neuroimage*, 19(4), 1835–42.

Saxe, R., Xiao, D. K., Kovacs, G., Perrett, D. I., & Kanwisher, N. (2004). A region of right posterior superior temporal sulcus responds to observed intentional actions. *Neuropsychologia*, 42(11), 1435–46.

Schelling, T. C. (1960). *The Strategy of Conflict*. Harvard University Press, Cambridge, MA.

Schiffer, S. R. (1972). *Meaning*. Clarendon Press, Oxford.

Schultz, D. (1975) *A History of Modern Psychology*. Academic Press, New York, NY.

Schumacher, P. B. (2011). "The hepatitis called...: electrophysiological evidence for enriched composition," in *Experimental Pragmatics/Semantics*, eds J. Meibauer and M. Steinbach (Amsterdam: John Benjamins), 199–219.

  (2013). When combinatorial processing results in reconceptualization: toward a new approach of compositionality. Frontiers in psychology, 4, 677.

  (2014). Content and context in incremental processing: "The ham sandwich" revisited. *Philosophical Studies*, 168(1), 151–65.

Scott-Phillips, T. (2014). *Speaking our Minds: Why Human Communication is Different, and How Language Evolved to Make It Special*. Palgrave MacMillan, UK.

Schwarz, F. (2007). Processing presupposed content. *Journal of Semantics*, 24(4), 373–416.

Schwarz, F., & Tiemann, S. (2017). Presupposition projection in online processing. *Journal of Semantics*, 34(1), 61–106.

Schwitzgebel, E. (2004). Introspective training apprehensively defended: Reflections on Titchener's lab manual. *Journal of Consciousness Studies*, 11(7–8), 58–76.

  (2011). *Perplexities of Consciousness*. MIT Press, Cambridge, MA.

Schwoebel, J., Dews, S., Winner, E., & Srinivas, K. (2000). Obligatory processing of the literal meaning of ironic utterances: Further evidence. *Metaphor and Symbol*, 15(1–2), 47–61.

Searle, J. (1979). Expression and meaning. Cambridge: Cambridge University Press.

Searle, J. R. (1980). The background of meaning. In J. Searle, F. Keifer & M. Bierwisch (eds.) *Speech Act Theory and Pragmatics*, Reidel, Dordrecht pp. 221–32.

Sedivy, J. C. (2003). Pragmatic versus form-based accounts of referential contrast: Evidence for effects of informativity expectations. *Journal of Psycholinguistic Research*, 32, 3–23.

Sedivy, J. C., Tanenhaus, M. K., Chambers, C. G., & Carlson, G. N. (1999). Achieving incremental semantic interpretation through contextual representation. *Cognition*, 71(2), 109–47.

Senju, A., Csibra, G., & Johnson, M. H. (2008). Understanding the referential nature of looking: Infants' preference for object-directed gaze. *Cognition*, 108(2), 303–19.

Shannon, C. E., & Weaver, W. (1949). *The Mathematical Theory of Information*. University of Illinois Press, Urbana, IL.

Shetreet, E., Chierchia, G., & Gaab, N. (2014a). When some is not every: Dissociating scalar implicature generation and mismatch. *Human Brain Mapping*, 35(4), 1503–14.

(2014b). When three is not some: On the pragmatics of numerals. *Journal of Cognitive Neuroscience*, 26(4), 854–63.

(2014c). Linguistic inability or poor performance: Dissociating scalar implicature generation and mismatch in the developing brain. *Developmental Psychology*, 50(9), 2264.

Shipley, E. F., & Kuhn, I. F. (1983). A constraint on comparisons: Equally detailed alternatives. *Journal of Experimental Child Psychology*, 35(2), 195–222.

Simons, M. (2001). On the conversational basis of some presuppositions. In R. Hastings, B. Jackson, and Z. Zvolensky (eds.), in Proceedings of Semantics and Linguistic Theory 11, CLC Publications, Ithaca, NY.

Skinner, B. F. (1957). *Verbal Behavior*. Copley Publishing Group, Acton, MA.

(1986). The evolution of verbal behavior. *Journal of the Experimental Analysis of Behavior*, 45(1), 115–122.

Skordos, D., & Papafragou, A. (2016). Children's derivation of scalar implicatures: Alternatives and relevance. *Cognition*, 153, 6–18.

Smith, C. L. (1980). Quantifiers and question answering in young children. *Journal of Experimental Child Psychology*, 30, 191–205.

Solan, L. M. (1993). *The Language of Judges*. University of Chicago Press, Chicago, IL.

Spenader, J. (2002). Presuppositions in spoken discourse. PhD thesis, University of Stockholm. Computational Linguistics.

Sperber, D., Cara, F., & Girotto, V. (1995). Relevance theory explains the selection task. *Cognition*, 57(1), 31–95.

Sperber, D., Clément, F., Heintz, C., et al. (2010). Epistemic vigilance. *Mind & Language*, 25(4), 359–93.

Sperber, D., & Wilson, D. (1981). Irony and the use-mention distinction. In P. Cole (ed.), *Radical Pragmatics* (pp. 295–318). Academic Press, New York, NY.

(1986). *Relevance: Communication and Cognition* (Vol. 1). Harvard University Press, Cambridge, MA (2nd edn, 1995, Blackwell, Oxford).

(2008). A deflationary account of metaphors. In R.W. Gibbs (Ed.), *The Handbook of Metaphor and Thought*, (pp. 171–203), Cambridge University Press, Cambridge.

(2015). Beyond speaker's meaning. *Croatian Journal of Philosophy*, 15(2 (44)), 117–49.

Spivey, M. J., Grosjean, M., & Knoblich, G. (2005). Continuous attraction toward phonological competitors. *Proceedings of the National Academy of Sciences of the USA*, 102(29), 10393–8.

Spotorno, N., Koun, E., Prado, J., Van Der Henst, J. B., & Noveck, I. A. (2012). Neural evidence that utterance-processing entails mentalizing: The case of irony. *NeuroImage*, 63(1), 25–39.

Spotorno, N., Cheylus, A., Van Der Henst, J. B., & Noveck, I. A. (2013). What's behind a P600? Integration operations during irony processing. *PLoS One*, 8(6), e66839.

Spotorno, N., & Noveck, I. A. (2014). When is irony effortful? *Journal of Experimental Psychology: General*, 143(4), 1649.

Stalnaker, R. C. (1973), Presuppositions. *Journal of Philosophical Logic*, 2(4): 447–57.

Sternberg, R. J. (1979). Developmental patterns in the encoding and combination of logical connectives. *Journal of Experimental Child Psychology*, 28(3), 469–98.

Stiller, A. J., Goodman, N. D., & Frank, M. C. (2015). Ad-hoc implicature in preschool children. *Language Learning and Development*, 11(2), 176–90.

Stroop, J. R. (1935). Studies of interference in serial verbal reactions. *Journal of Experimental Psychology*, 18(6), 643.

Swinney, D. A. (1979). Lexical access during sentence comprehension: (Re) consideration of context effects. *Journal of Verbal Learning and Verbal Behavior*, 18(6), 645–59.

Tanenhaus, M. K., & Donnenwerth-Nolan, S. (1984). Syntactic context and lexical access. *The Quarterly Journal of Experimental Psychology*, 36(4), 649–61.

Taplin, J. E., Staudenmayer, H., & Taddonio, J. L. (1974). Developmental changes in conditional reasoning: Linguistic or logical? *Journal of Experimental Child Psychology*, 17(2), 360–73.

Tian, Y., Breheny, R., & Ferguson, H. J. (2010). Why we simulate negated information: A dynamic pragmatic account. *The Quarterly Journal of Experimental Psychology*, 63(12), 2305–12.

Tian, Y., Ferguson, H., & Breheny, R. (2016). Processing negation without context – Why and when we represent the positive argument. *Language, Cognition and Neuroscience*, 31(5), 683–98.

Tomasello, M., Carpenter, M., & Liszkowski, U. (2007). A new look at infant pointing. *Child Development*, 78(3), 705–22.

Tomasello, M. (2010). *Origins of Human Communication.* MIT Press, Cambridge, MA.

Tomlinson, J. M., Bailey, T. M., & Bott, L. (2013). Possibly all of that and then some: Scalar implicatures are understood in two steps. *Journal of Memory and Language*, 69(1), 18–35.

Topál, J., Gergely, G., Miklósi, Á., Erdőhegyi, Á., & Csibra, G. (2008). Infants' perseverative search errors are induced by pragmatic misinterpretation. *Science*, 321(5897), 1831–34

Tooby, J., & Cosmides, L. (1992). Tile psychological foundations of culture. In J. H. Barkow, L. Cosmides, & J. Tooby (eds.), *The Adapted Mind: Evolutionary Psychology and the Generation of Culture.* Oxford University Press, New York, NY.

Trabasso, T., Rollins, H., & Shaughnessy, E. (1971). Storage and verification stages in processing concepts. *Cognitive Psychology*, 2(3), 239–89.

Traxler, M. J., Pickering, M. J., & McElree, B. (2002). Coercion in sentence processing: Evidence from eye-movements and self-paced reading. *Journal of Memory and Language*, 47(4), 530–47.

Trouche, E., Johansson, P., Hall, L., & Mercier, H. (2016). The selective laziness of reasoning. *Cognitive Science*, 40(8), 2122–36.

Trueswell, J., & Tanenhaus, M. (1994). Toward a lexical framework of constraint-based syntactic ambiguity resolution. In C. Clifton, Jr., L. Frazier, & K. Rayner (eds.), *Perspectives on sentence processing*, (pp. 155–180). Erlbaum, Hillsdale, NJ.

Tummeltshammer, K. S., Wu, R., Sobel, D. M., & Kirkham, N. Z. (2014). Infants track the reliability of potential informants. *Psychological Science*, 25(9), 1730–8.

Tversky, A., & Kahneman, D. (1973). Availability: A heuristic for judging frequency and probability. *Cognitive Psychology*, 5(2), 207–32.

Tversky, A., & Kahneman, D. (1974). Judgment under uncertainty: Heuristics and biases. *Science*, 185(4157), 1124–1131.

Tversky, A., & Kahneman, D. (1983). Extensional versus intuitive reasoning: The conjunction fallacy in probability judgment. *Psychological Review*, 90(4), 293.

van der Auwera, J. (1997). Pragmatics in the last quarter century: The case of conditional perfection. *Journal of Pragmatics*, 27(3), 261–74.

van der Henst, J. B., Bujakowska, K., Ciceron, C., & Noveck, I. A. (2006). How to make a participant logical: The role of premise presentation in a conditional reasoning task. *Reasoning and Cognition*, 3, 7–18.

Van Herwegen, J., Dimitriou, D., & Rundblad, G. (2013). Development of novel metaphor and metonymy comprehension in typically developing children and Williams syndrome. *Research in Developmental Disabilities*, 34(4), 1300–11.

Van Overwalle, F. (2009). Social cognition and the brain: A meta-analysis. *Human Brain Mapping*, 30(3), 829–58.

Van Overwalle, F., & Baetens, K. (2009). Understanding others' actions and goals by mirror and mentalizing systems: A meta-analysis. *Neuroimage*, 48(3), 564–84.

Van Rooij, R., & Schulz, K. (2004). Exhaustive interpretation of complex sentences. *Journal of Logic, Language and Information*, 13(4), 491–519.

van Tiel, B. (2014). Embedded scalars and typicality. *Journal of Semantics*, 31(2), 147–77.

Vlach, F. (1981). Speaker's meaning. *Linguistics and Philosophy*, 4(3), 359–91.

Wang, A. T., Dapretto, M., Hariri, A., Sigman, M., & Bookheimer, S. Y. (2001). Processing affective and linguistic prosody in autism: An fMRI study. *Neuroimage*, 13(6), 621.

Wang, A. T., Lee, S. S., Sigman, M., & Dapretto, M. (2006). Neural basis of irony comprehension in children with autism: The role of prosody and context. *Brain*, 129(4), 932–43.

(2007). Reading affect in the face and voice: Neural correlates of interpreting communicative intent in children and adolescents with autism spectrum disorders. *Archives of General Psychiatry*, 64(6), 698–708.

Wang, Y., Wang, H., Cui, L., Tian, S., & Zhang, Y. (2002). The N270 component of the event-related potential reflects supramodal conflict processing in humans. *Neuroscience Letters*, 332(1), 25–8.

Wason, P. C. (1960). On the failure to eliminate hypotheses in a conceptual task. *Quarterly Journal of Experimental Psychology*, 12(3), 129–40.

(1961). Response to affirmative and negative binary statements. *British Journal of Psychology*, 52(2), 133–42.

(1965). The contexts of plausible denial. *Journal of Verbal Learning and Verbal Behavior*, 4(1), 7–11.

(1968). Reasoning about a rule. *The Quarterly Journal of Experimental Psychology*, 20(3), 273–81.

Wason, P. C., & Jones, S. (1963). Negatives: Denotation and connotation. *British Journal of Psychology*, 54(4), 299–307.

Watson, J. B. (1913). Psychology as the behaviorist views it. *Psychological Review*, 20(2), 158.

Weiland, H., Bambini, V., & Schumacher, P. B. (2014). The role of literal meaning in figurative language comprehension: Evidence from masked priming ERP. *Frontiers in Human Neuroscience*, 8, 583. doi:10.3389/fnhum.2014.00583.

Wharton, T. (2009). *Pragmatics and Non-Verbal Communication*. Cambridge University Press, Cambridge, MA.

Wilkes-Gibbs, D., & Clark, H. H. (1992). Coordinating beliefs in conversation. *Journal of Memory and Language*, 31(2), 183–94.

Wilson, D. (1973). Presuppositions and non-truth-conditional semantics (Doctoral dissertation, Massachusetts Institute of Technology).

(1975). Presupposition, assertion, and lexical items. *Linguistic Inquiry*, 6(1), 95–114.

(2006). The pragmatics of verbal irony: Echo or pretence? *Lingua*, 116(10), 1722–43.

(2009). Irony and metarepresentation. *UCLWPL*, 21, 183–226.

Wilson, D., & Carston, R. (2007) A unitary approach to lexical pragmatics: Relevance, inference and ad hoc concepts. In N. Burton-Roberts (ed.), *Advances in Pragmatics* (pp. 230–60). Palgrave Macmillan, Basingstoke.

(2008). Metaphor and the "emergent property" problem: A relevance-theoretic treatment. *The Baltic International Yearbook of Cognition, Logic and Communication*, 3(2007), 1 40.

Wilson, D., & Sperber, D. (1998). Pragmatics and time. In R. Carston & S. Uchida (eds.), *Relevance Theory: Applications and Implications* (pp. 1–22). John Benjamins, Amsterdam.

Wilson, D., & Wharton, T. (2006). Relevance and prosody. *Journal of Pragmatics*, 38(10), 1559–79.

Wilson, N. L. (1959). *The Concept of Language*. University of Toronto Press, Toronto.

Wimmer, H., & Perner, J. (1983). Beliefs about beliefs: Representation and constraining function of wrong beliefs in young children's understanding of deception. *Cognition*, 13(1), 103–28.

Winer, G. A., Cottrell, J. E., Mott, T., Cohen, M., & Fournier, J. (2001). Are children more accurate than adults? Spontaneous use of metaphor by children and adults. *Journal of Psycholinguistic Research*, 30(5), 485–96.

Wing, L. (1981). Asperger's syndrome: A clinical account. *Psychological Medicine*, 11(1), 115–29.

Wing, L., & Gould, J. (1979). Severe impairments of social interaction and associated abnormalities in children: Epidemiology and classification. *Journal of Autism and Developmental Disorders*, 9(1), 11–29.

Wright, R. (2014). The Wright show (with guest Leda Cosmides). Last retrieved August 23, 2017 from https://bloggingheads.tv/videos/25161

Wu, S., & Keysar, B. (2007). The effect of culture on perspective taking. *Psychological Science*, 18(7), 600–6.

Index